# CICERO'S USE OF JUDICIAL THEATER

T0355732

# CICERO'S USE OF JUDICIAL THEATER

*Jon Hall*

The University of Michigan Press

Ann Arbor

Published in the United States of America by
The University of Michigan Press
Printed and bound by CPI Group (UK) Ltd, Croydon, CR0 4YY


2017   2016   2015   2014      4   3   2   1

A CIP catalog record for this book is available from the British Library.

Library of Congress Cataloging-in-Publication Data

Hall, Jon (Jon C. R.), 1961–

Cicero's use of judicial theater / Jon Hall.
      pages      cm
      Includes bibliographical references and index.
      ISBN 978-0-472-07220-0 (hardback)—ISBN 978-0-472-05220-2 (paperback)—
ISBN 978-0-472-12036-9 (e-book)
      1. Cicero, Marcus Tullius. Speeches.    2. Speeches, addresses, etc., Latin—
History and criticism.    3. Oratory, Ancient.    4. Theater—Rome. I. Title.
PA6351.H35      2014
875'.01—dc23
                                                            2014007569

# Acknowledgments

Thanks are due to various colleagues and friends who have helped in the preparation of this book. Ellen Bauerle, Alexa Ducsay, and Mary Hashman at the University of Michigan Press shepherded the project from proposal to finished product with kindness and efficiency. Dean Alexander at the University of Otago provided invaluable help, both with research and preparing the indexes. His deep engagement with Late Republican history brought many useful comparanda and modern discussions to my attention. In the United States, Kathleen Coleman, Chris Craig, John Dugan, and Sander Goldberg have encouraged me in my work (likewise Luis Unceta Gómez in Spain). In the United Kingdom, Catherine Steel invited me to deliver a research paper on Ciceronian tears at the University of Glasgow, and Elsbeth Hymes, one at the University of St. Andrews. In Australia, Han Baltussen, Lea Beness, Eleanor Cowan, Tom Hillard, and Kathryn Welch have given advice on different aspects of the material. And in New Zealand, Alan Musgrave and David Ward have, on a weekly basis, provided informative illustrations of opposing philosophical approaches to misfortune. I owe most, however, to Jeff Tatum and Nicola Richmond, in part for their wisdom—but mostly for their wit.

Finally, thanks also to my parents for helping to keep things in perspective. (That copy of my first book is still not, I suspect, on a plinth in a glass case illuminated by a spotlight, but on the floor, in a corner, covered by scattered newspapers.)

# Contents

# *Abbreviations*

OLD  *Oxford Latin Dictionary* Ed. P. G. W. Glare (Oxford 1982).
RE  *Real-Encyclopädie der classischen Altertumswissenschaft*. Eds. A. von
  Pauly, G. Wissowa, and W. Kroll (Stuttgart 1893–1980).
TLL  *Thesaurus Linguae Latinae* (Leipzig 1900– ).

All references to ancient texts are to works by Cicero unless stated otherwise. Abbreviations for ancient authors and their works follow the conventions used in the *Oxford Classical Dictionary* (Fourth Edition), except
for: Quintus Cicero *Commentariolum Petitionis*, for which the abbreviation
Q. Cic. *Comm. Pet.* is used; pseudo-Caesarian *Bellum Alexandrinum*, abbreviated to [Caes.] *B Alex*; and Fronto's letters to M. Caesar, abbreviated to
Fronto *ad M. Caes.*

# Note on Texts and Translations

The texts of Cicero's works have been drawn from the Teubner editions (with minor changes for orthographical purposes), except for those listed below. (See bibliography for full details.) Any occasional divergences in the text used are identified in the footnotes. English translations are my own (although I have consulted available published translations). The references to Plutarch's *Parallel Lives* use the section numbers given in the Teubner texts edited by Ziegler (see bibliography), not those given in the Loeb series.

## TREATISES

| | |
|---|---|
| *Brutus* | Douglas (1966). |
| *De Officiis* | Winterbottom (1994). |

## LETTERS

| | |
|---|---|
| *Epistulae ad Atticum* | Shackleton Bailey (1999). |
| *Epistulae ad Familiares* | Shackleton Bailey (2001). |
| *Epistulae ad Q. Fratrem* | Shackleton Bailey (2002). |

## SPEECHES

| | |
|---|---|
| *In Pisonem* | Nisbet (1961). |
| *In Verrem* | Peterson (1917). |
| *Philippics* | Shackleton Bailey (2009). |
| *Pro Cluentio* | Boyancé (1953). |
| *Pro Flacco* | Clark (1909). |
| *Pro Fonteio* | Clark (1911). |

| | |
|---|---|
| *Pro Ligario, Pro Marcello, Pro Milone* | Clark (1918). |
| *Pro Quinctio* | Kinsey (1971). |
| *Pro Roscio Amerino* | Dyck (2010). |
| *Pro Sulla* | Berry (1996). |

# INTRODUCTION

In a rhetorical treatise written toward the end of his life, Cicero reveals that on at least two occasions as an advocate he had used small children as oratorical props (*Orat.* 131):[1]

> *qua nos ita dolenter uti solemus, ut puerum infantem in manibus perorantes tenuerimus, ut alia in causa excitato reo nobili, sublato etiam filio parvo, plangore et lamentatione compleremus forum.*

[I am in the habit of deploying this [type of appeal] with such high emotion that I have held an infant in my arms during a peroration. In another case, having urged the high-ranking defendant to stand, I lifted up his small son as well, and filled the forum with wailing and lamentation.]

These scenes depict a judicial world alien to most modern readers. We do not today expect to see lawyers parading around the court carrying children in their arms. The impartial administration of justice (we would like to think) has no business with this kind of manipulative showmanship.

Evidently, however, Roman expectations were rather different. Orators in the forum appear to have enjoyed considerable freedom to engage in lively theatrics. It is this aspect of Cicero's technique as an advocate that forms the subject of the following chapters. How often did he employ such stunts in the courts? What do the rhetorical handbooks have to say about their planning and execution? And what factors shaped his decision to use them in some situations but not in others? As I hope to show, a consideration of these issues will give us not only significant insights into Cicero's skill as a practising advocate but also a deeper appre-

---

1. Several scholars have identified the second incident with Cicero's defense of L. Flaccus; see Sandys (1885) 133; Kroll (1913) 117–18; Webster (1931) 108; and Hubbell (1939) 402, n. C. The extant text of *Pro Flacco*, however, makes no explicit reference to such action.

ciation of the links between judicial oratory and the social and political customs of the Late Republic. The devices that he deployed during these performances often had as much to do with Roman cultural practices as with Hellenistic precepts of rhetoric.

In many respects, then, this book is a study of showmanship—of the ways in which Cicero made his speeches in court lively and compelling. As my title suggests, I use the phrase "judicial theater" as a generic label for these aspects of his technique, and I include under the term all non-verbal devices employed by advocates in order to enhance the impact of their words and argument.[2] This definition thus encompasses a broad range of elements, from the orator's use of gestures, to his exploitation of costume and props. The phrase "judicial theater" also helps to stress (I hope) the close connection of these devices with live performance. Such theatrics were the stage business of the orator's art. To be sure, they were often tightly integrated with the text of a speech; but their success-ful execution required a set of skills quite separate from those involved in literary composition.[3] As the Romans themselves recognized, the ora-tor needed—in part at least—to be an actor too.[4]

For many years, this aspect of Cicero's pleading was largely over-looked by modern scholars. Academic interest tended to focus primarily on textual matters, such as the manuscript tradition, linguistic usage, and literary tropes. In recent decades, however, there has been grow-ing appreciation of the more practical side of Cicero's craft. One col-lection of essays, for example, has addressed the element of "spectacle" in Roman court proceedings ("lo spettacolo della giustizia"), with prof-

---

2. Note that I use "judicial theater" as the more conceptual, generalizing term (mod-elled on the phrase "political theater" now in common usage). On occasion I also use the phrase "judicial theatrics" when referring to specific examples of these techniques.

3. The commentary on *Pro Caelio* by Austin (1933), for example, has very little to say about matters of performance and delivery. This deficiency is remedied to an extent in the second edition with the addition of some extra commentary (Austin [1952] 141–43), and in the third edition with some further notes (Austin [1960] 173–75). But even then little attempt is made to consider how the text of *Pro Caelio* might have been brought to life in an actual performance. This tendency still persists. Cf. Usher (2008), where the terms "performance" and "in action" refer, not to the stagecraft of Cicero's speeches, but to the strategies deployed in his published orations as opposed to those recommended by rhetorical treatises.

4. The connection between acting and oratory will be explored in greater detail in the following chapters. For the application of stage metaphors to Roman oratory by mod-ern scholars, see, e.g., David (1992) 3 ("le théâtre et ses règles"); Moretti (2004) on "le scenografie dell' oratoria." Oratorical performance in ancient Athens likewise had many connections with the stage; see Hall (1995).

itable results.[5] Other studies have identified some of the specific ways in which Cicero used props, visual cues, and gesture in his orations.[6] Although the following chapters naturally build upon these insights, I have directed my attention principally to three main areas: Cicero's integration of physical action into his pleas and entreaties; his deployment of tears in perorations (a particularly challenging and potentially risky type of performance); and the curious practice of individuals donning *sordes* (dirtied clothes) for their appearances in court. As we shall see, all three topics involve Roman cultural practices that flourished outside the courts as well. Judicial oratory was thus much more than a self-contained rhetorical genre; in matters of performance, it drew a good deal on the everyday customs of Roman life.

And yet, although Cicero's use of judicial theater is closely tied to his own time and place, it has a contemporary resonance as well. Lawyers and politicians today still try to find ways to enliven their speeches in performance. On November 7, 2009, for example, in the U.S. House of Representatives, John Shadegg (a Republican congressman from Arizona) attempted to deploy a child prop during a debate on health-care reform.[7] Holding an infant called Maddie in one arm, he tried to link the basic principles of his argument with the aspirations of the younger generation, prefacing his assertions with phrases such as "Maddie believes . . ." and "Maddie wants. . . ." The stunt was effective up to a point (it certainly elicited applause from Shadegg's supporters). But it also exposed Shadegg to ridicule from his opponents, who made much of its likeness to a ventriloquist's act. Nevertheless, the attention garnered by his performance seems to have provoked Democratic congressman Pete Stark later in the day to try to outdo this attempt at showmanship. He arranged for *two* children to stand beside him as he made his own contribution to the debate.[8] Eventually the Speaker of the House was moved to assert: "Members on both sides of the aisle are reminded not to use guests of the house as props."[9]

---

5. See Petrone and Casamento (2006).

6. See, e.g., David (1980); Calboli (1983); Graf (1991); Vasaly (1993); Gotoff (1993b); Aldrete (1999); Dyck (2001); Moretti (2004); Steel (2010).

7. A video clip can be accessed at www.c-spanvideo.org/program/289864–1 (at time-point 6.40.47–6.42). Also available at www.youtube.com, using the keywords "Shadegg," "baby," and "prop."

8. See www.c-spanvideo.org/program/289864–1 (at time-point 7.27.33–7.29). Also available at www.youtube.com, keywords "Stark speaks out for Health Care reform."

9. See www.c-spanvideo.org/program/289864–1 (at time-point 7.30.08). Also available at www.youtube.com, keywords "Stark speaks out for Health Care reform."

It is tempting perhaps to dismiss this episode as simply an amusing diversion in the history of American political oratory. Yet matters would be rather different (one imagines) if Shadegg's performance had proved pivotal in the outcome of this nationally important debate. These devices stop being whimsical curiosities the moment they threaten to exert some meaningful influence on events. And, as we shall see, various Roman sources do indeed depict such showmanship as being crucial to the outcome of certain judicial and deliberative proceedings in the forum. Modern commentators (like ancient rhetoricians) may have the luxury of leaving such matters to one side in order to concentrate on more intellectual themes; but Cicero, as an ambitious advocate, had practical decisions to make regarding his technique. We should not be surprised if his desire for victory led him to exploit whatever devices gave him an advantage over his opponents.

Nevertheless, our engagement with aspects of performance poses some significant methodological challenges. Although the extant texts of Cicero's orations usually give us an accurate indication of what was *said* on a particular occasion, they give us only a few clues about the manner of their delivery, with just the occasional reference to a gesture here or a prop there. The rhetorical handbooks supplement this information to a degree; yet the picture is far from complete.[10] The precise extent of these limitations will become clearer as our investigations proceed; but before we embark upon our detailed analyses of these performances, we need to understand the oratorical tradition and judicial environment in which Cicero was operating. In my opening chapter, then, I address several related topics: the use of showmanship by Roman orators in the decades before Cicero; the cultural tendency in Rome toward theatricality in social and political life; the nature of the courts in which Cicero practiced his advocacy; and his general accomplishments as a performer. I conclude with two examples of judicial theater from early in Cicero's career in the courts, which help to illustrate his creativity in the use of showmanship, while also drawing attention to some specific issues of methodology.

---

10. As Laws (2004) 409 has eloquently noted: "In one sense advocacy is a melancholy art. Its brilliance fades as soon as the words are spoken. Its red blood is in the seduction of the tribunal, judge or jury, then and there."

# CHAPTER 1

# JUDICIAL THEATER IN ANCIENT ROME
## Some Basic Considerations

### PART 1: SHOWMANSHIP IN ROMAN ORATORY BEFORE CICERO

There is considerable evidence to suggest that a strong tradition of show-manship flourished in Roman oratory before Cicero's time. In 167 BCE, for example, the former consul, M. Servilius, delivered a speech in front of the people supporting the triumph proposed for Aemilius Paullus following his successful campaigns in Macedonia.[1] According to Livy, Servilius made the following proud claim near the end of his oration (Livy 45.39.16):

> *ego ter et viciens cum hoste provocato pugnavi; ex omnibus, cum quibus manum conserui, spolia rettuli; insigne corpus honestis cicatricibus, omnibus adverso corpore exceptis, habeo.*

> [As for myself, twenty three times have I challenged and fought hand-to-hand with an enemy. I have carried off spoils from all with whom I engaged. I have a body decorated with scars of honor, all of them received on the front.]

At this point, Servilius provided striking visual proof of this valor by stripping off his clothes and providing detailed commentary about each scar (Livy 45.39.17: *nudasse deinde se dicitur et quo quaeque bello vulnera accepta essent rettulisse*).

As we shall see, this trick of displaying battle-scars became something

---

1. Livy's account in Book 45 is paralleled in Plut. *Aem.* 30–32. On M. Servilius (Pulex Geminus) (cos. 202 BCE), see Broughton (1951) 315; (1952) 619. For discussions of this incident, see Hölkeskamp (1995) 43–44; Briscoe (2012) 730–47.

of a trope in Roman oratory.[2] Indeed, Livy incorporates similar scenes into episodes from the early period of Rome's history.[3] Although these instances almost certainly involve some historical fabrication, our anecdote featuring Servilius derives from more credible sources.[4] Moreover the detail that follows gives the episode a distinctive twist that moves it beyond a straightforward stock example (Livy 45.39.17–18):

> quae dum ostentat, adapertis forte quae velanda erant, tumor inguinum proximis risum movit. tum, "hoc quoque, quod ridetis," inquit, "in equo dies noctesque persedendo habeo, nec magis me eius quam cicatricum harum pudet paenitetque, quando numquam mihi impedimento ad rem publicam bene gerendam domi militiaeque fuit."

[While he was displaying these wounds, he accidentally uncovered areas that should have stayed concealed, and a growth on his groin provoked laughter amongst those nearby. At this he said: "This very thing too that you are mocking I acquired by sitting whole days and nights on my horse, and I am no more ashamed or distressed by it than I am about these scars, since it has never stopped me from serving the state well, both at home and on campaign."]

According to Plutarch (*Aem.* 32.1), this impassioned performance proved crucial to the course of the debate, and Paullus was awarded his triumph.[5]

The anecdote provides a memorable instance of oratorical theater at

---

2. See the detailed discussion in Leigh (1995), who associates the device with "popular" rhetoric. Cf. Quint. *Inst.* 6.3.75 for a clever remark by Caesar Strabo Vopiscus (aed. 90) intended to undercut an opponent's use of this trope. On the displaying of scars (for evidentiary purposes) in the Athenian courts, see Hall (1995) 52–53.

3. See Livy 6.14.6: *ipse tumultum augebat, cicatrices acceptas Veienti Gallico aliisque deinceps bellis ostentans*; and Livy 6.20.8: *nudasse pectus insigne cicatricibus bello acceptis.* Cf. Oakley (1997) 561.

4. On Livy's penchant for historical retrojection, especially in his early books, see, e.g., Ogilvie (1965) 10–12; Oakley (1997) 86–88; cf. Kaster (2006) 178. See also Leigh (1995) 204 on depictions of the much scarred L. Siccius Dentatus: "Licinius Macer makes of Dentatus a 5th century mouthpiece for a popular rhetoric with a decidedly contemporary ring." For the incident featuring Servilius, by contrast, Livy had at his disposal the works of Claudius Quadrigarius (see, e.g., Livy 44.15), Valerius Antias (Livy 42.11, 44.13) and Polybius (Livy 45.44). These sources were not immune to invention, but the episode is less likely to be the product of wholesale fabrication. See also Briscoe (2012) 730.

5. The manuscript of Livy breaks off briefly before the end of Servilius's speech; see Briscoe (2012) 747. Livy 45.40 resumes with a description of Paullus's triumphal procession.

Rome, over half a century before Cicero's birth. Servilius deploys his own body as a prop, both to provide proof of his assertions and to heighten their rhetorical impact. This kind of device required a certain skill in performance, and we may admire Servilius's poise as he turned to his advantage the chance mishap that threatened to ruin his whole stunt. This potential calamity, however, raises a broader issue that will be important throughout our discussion of judicial theater: the extent to which oratorical showmanship compromised the *dignitas* of the Roman aristocrat. In Servilius's case, it was specifically the glimpse of his groin that first provoked the sniggers of the crowd. Nevertheless, even the earlier action of baring his chest involved a departure from the usual norms of aristocratic comportment in public. Indeed, this was precisely what gave the device its initial dramatic power.

As J.-M. David has demonstrated, aristocratic comportment in general was shaped significantly by an ideology of restraint and self-control. By adopting a poised and reserved manner, members of the social elite could distinguish themselves from the teeming masses.[6] This distinction (David asserts) was evident in two opposing styles of oratory that arose in Rome: a traditionally aristocratic style, characterized by a certain hauteur and moderation, and a style that relied on a more forceful, hectoring tone, sometimes combined with overtly theatrical elements.[7] The latter he associates in particular with the political oratory deployed by populist agitators pushing for reform (labelled *eloquentia popularis*). According to this model, then, a "true" aristocrat would recoil from the idea of behaving in public in a way that compromised his image of poise, restraint, and *auctoritas*.

David's analysis identifies an important influence upon Roman oratory. As we shall see in chapter three, it is likely that several of Cicero's defendants refused to engage in public entreaty because they regarded such pleas as *infra dignitatem*. Not everyone, then, was willing to take part in the antics that oratorical showmanship sometimes required. And yet these norms of social comportment were only an ideal. It is also clear that many of the elite were happy enough to sacrifice these principles of decorum for the sake of political gain. As the example of Servilius shows,

---

6. On this model, see David (1980); (1992) 553–56; also Corbeill (2002) 186–88; (2004) 130–38. Cf. Narducci (2002) 407–8.

7. See David (1980) 183, with reference to "la bipolarité de l'éloquence" and "cette dualité de modèles oratoire"; cf. David (1992) 553–56. A link is then forged between this duality and the two poles of "le système politique et social romain"; see David (1980) 189. Cf. David (1992) 622–23.

in this high-stake, feud-driven environment, defeating an opponent often mattered more than social etiquette. It should be no surprise if there was frequently a gap between the ideology of aristocratic manners and how these ambitious men actually behaved.[8]

Indeed, Servilius's flair for showmanship was not unique. His contemporary, Cato the Elder, likewise used a prop to add punch to his anti-Carthaginian rhetoric (Plut. *Cat. Mai.* 27.1):[9]

φασὶ τὸν Κάτωνα καὶ σῦκα τῶν Λιβυκῶν ἐπίτηδες ἐκβαλεῖν ἐν τῇ βουλῇ, τὴν τήβεννον ἀναβαλόμενον, εἶτα θαυμασάντων τὸ μέγεθος καὶ τὸ κάλλος, εἰπεῖν, ὡς ἡ ταῦτα φέρουσα χώρα τριῶν ἡμερῶν πλοῦν ἀπέχει τῆς Ῥώμης.

[It is said that Cato even contrived to drop a Libyan fig in the senate, as he shook out the folds of his toga. As the senators admired its size and fine appearance, he noted that the land that produced it was only three days' sailing from Rome.]

This trick, although not as dramatic as that of Servilius, possessed an effective element of surprise (evidently the fig was small enough to be easily concealed prior to its sudden appearance); and the freshness of the fruit provided a tangible representation of the swiftness with which merchants—and so too the Carthaginian fleet—could sail to Rome. Clearly Cato understood that a good performance in the senate need not rely on words alone.[10]

Yet another contemporary provides an early precedent for Cicero's own use of children as oratorical props. In 149 BCE, Servius Sulpicius Galba was accused of misconduct while governor of Lusitania the previous year.[11] Several hearings seem to have been held in front of the people as the would-be prosecutors tried to get the case brought to tri-

---

8. David (1992) 623 also asserts, however, that only traces of this bipolarity remained in the courts of Cicero's time. On the complexities of Roman reactions to such aspects of delivery, see also Wisse (2013) 178–82.

9. For the text, see Ziegler (2000). Note that Cato had spoken on the same side as Servilius in the debate regarding the triumph of Aemilius Paullus. See Gell. *NA* 1.23.1; Astin (1978) 118–19; Malcovati (1976) 67 (fr. 172).

10. The same incident is reported by Pliny the Elder at *HN* 15.74–75. Cf. Aldrete (1999) 27.

11. See Alexander (1990) 3 (no. 1); cf. Broughton (1951) 456–57. It was alleged that Galba had treacherously slain a number of Lusitanians and sold others into slavery. App. *Hisp.* 59–60 provides the basic narrative. Val. Max. 9.6.2 puts the number of those slain at 8,000; Suet. *Galb.* 3.2 gives a figure of 30,000. On Galba's oratory in general, see *Brut.* 82; 88–94; Kennedy (1972) 72–73; Malcovati (1976) 109–15; David (1992) 619–20; 680–81; Clarke (1996) 42. Cf. Flaig (2003) 119–20; Moretti (2004) 65.

al.[12] According to our sources, Galba's arguments in his defense seemed bound for failure, until he delivered a highly emotional appeal based on several children whom he displayed in front of the audience. This appeal was so effective in winning the crowd's sympathy that the case against him was dropped.[13]

In such cases it is all too easy to fixate on the theatrical aspect of the performance and conclude that this was the *sole* factor in the orator's success. As we shall see, however, Cicero's showmanship regularly relied on the effective integration of action with words. It was not enough simply to parade a child before the audience. The orator also had to be able to supply appropriate sentiments in order get the most out of his emotional scene. From Cicero's account, we can see that Galba too knew well how to integrate his showmanship with verbal skill. He began, for example, by lifting up, not his own son, but the son of Sulpicius Galus, who had been entrusted into his care (*De or.* 1.228: *is C. Sulpici Gali, propinqui sui, Quintum pupillum filium ipse paene in umeros suos extulisset*). As he did so, he commemorated the life and achievements of the child's father (*De or.* 1.228: *patris clarissimi recordatione et memoria*). This move cannily broadened the audience's frame of reference beyond the alleged crimes, and portrayed Galba himself as a responsible and dutiful friend (an obvious contrast to the image of him as a scheming murderer).

Moreover, when he turned the attention to his own sons, he depicted himself as a soldier making his last will and testament before going into battle, entrusting his loved ones to the Roman people (*De or.* 1.228: *ac se tamquam in procinctu testamentum faceret sine libra atque tabulis populum Romanum tutorem instituere dixisset illorum orbitati*). By thus placing the spectators in a position of responsibility over his sons, Galba astutely appealed to their paternal sensibilities.[14] And by portraying himself as a soldier heading into war, he deftly reduced the submissive element of his appeal. He presented himself not as a man of abject desperation, but as a warrior taking the measures necessary for the safety of his family. Indeed,

---

12. On the legal procedure, see Richardson (1987) 2, n. 12, who notes that the occasion "was almost certainly the *contio* held by the tribune . . . in his attempt to pass a plebiscite to establish a *quaestio* in order to try Galba." Cf. the references to a *rogatio* at *Brut.* 89 and Livy *Per.* 49, and a *quaestio* at *De or.* 1.227. The reference of Livy at 39.40 to a *iudicium populi* seems to be a mistake; cf. Ferguson (1921) 94, n. 1; Douglas (1966) 77.

13. See Cato's observation in his *Origines* (reported at *De or.* 1.228): *quod item apud Catonem scriptum esse video: nisi pueris et lacrimis usus esset, poenas eum daturum fuisse.* Cf. Val. Max. 8.1. abs. 2, where Galba's tactics are presented as a dramatic measure of last resort. See also Livy *Per.* 49: *ipse quoque Galba cum se damnari videret*; Quint. *Inst.* 2.15.8. Rutilius Rufus also vehemently criticized Galba's actions (*De or.* 1.228). Cf. Dugan (2005) 143–45.

14. Cf. Cicero's remark at *Cat.* 4.23: *commendo vobis parvum meum filium.*

Cicero (followed by Valerius Maximus) notes specifically that Galba kept the emphasis away from his own plight.[15]

Galba's successful exploitation of theatrics, however, seems to have caused some consternation amongst his contemporaries. According to Fronto, Cato proposed that women, children, and other relatives should be excluded from taking part in these kinds of appeal.[16] Later practice indicates that this suggestion gained little traction. Yet many modern scholars do see a close connection between Galba's acquittal in 149 BCE and the establishment later in the year of the first standing court (*quaestio perpetua de repetundis*) under the *lex Calpurnia*. At first glance, Galba's mass slaying of Lusitanians seems perhaps to have little connection with the financial peculations commonly perpetrated by provincial governors;[17] but his apparent evasion of justice presumably highlighted the shortcomings in the mechanisms available for bringing provincial governors to trial. (If our reconstruction of the incident is correct, his opponents were unable even to get a court established to try his case.) The *lex Calpurnia* at least improved the chances of allegedly corrupt governors appearing before a jury.[18]

## ORATORICAL THEATER AND RHETORICAL THEORY

Where did this aristocratic facility with oratorical theatrics come from? We can be sure enough that it was not derived from books: the ancient

15. See *Brut.* 90: *tum igitur <nihil> recusans Galba pro se.* The word *nihil* seems to have fallen out of the Ciceronian manuscript tradition, but editors restore it on the basis of the parallel in Val. Max. 8.1 abs. 2: *reus pro se iam nihil recusans;* cf. Douglas (1966), *apparatus criticus* to *Brut.* 90.

16. Fronto *ad M. Caes.* 3.21.4: *Cato igitur dissuadet vel suos neve alienos quis liberos ad misericordiam conciliandam producat neve uxores neve adfines vel ullas omnino feminas.* For the text, see van den Hout (1988) 52. Cf. *Brut.* 90. Note, however, that Galba's defense did not rely solely on the exploitation of props. In his speech against Cornelius Cethegus, he seems to have argued that his attack on the Lusitanians was a preemptive strike taken in response to reports that these forces were planning their own treacherous assault. See Livy *Per.* 49. Cf. *Brut.* 89, where the phrase *ut existimebatur* suggests that the technicalities of the treaty were disputed at some point in the hearings. The accusation of treachery would have gained some credence given the Lusitanians' earlier actions against Atilius, the previous commander. See also the tendentious version of the trial presented at *Mur.* 59.

17. Cf. Richardson (1987) 2.

18. See, e.g., Cloud (1994) 507: "The [*Lex Calpurnia*] may have been a response, if a rather feeble one, to this situation as well as to complaints about extortion, for, however useless to provincials in the Lusitanians' situation, the legislation did at least serve as a warning to men like Galba that the Senate intended to keep a permanent watch on the conduct of governors." Cf. Ferguson (1921) 94; Gruen (1968) 12–15; Forsythe (1988) 116–19; Brennan (2000a) 235; Fantham (2004) 122.

rhetorical treatises had very little to say about such matters. The sophist Thrasymachus evidently appreciated the link between oratorical delivery and the ways in which pity could be generated, but whatever he wrote on the topic seems not to have made a significant impact on later writers.[19] Indeed, by the time of Aristotle, rhetorical theorists were rejecting practical matters of performance as a viable topic of study, on the grounds that it was a field unsuited to systematic analysis.[20] Social and intellectual biases also appear to have played a part in this rejection of the subject. The business of performance as a whole was regarded as rather vulgar (φορτικόν);[21] and, from an intellectual perspective, the power of delivery was treated with contempt because it relied not upon reason but on the weak or corrupt character of the audience that was influenced by it (Arist. *Rh.* 3.1: διὰ τὴν τοῦ ἀκροατοῦ μοχθηρίαν). Over the following centuries, then, it was the content of appeals to pity that came to dominate rhetorical study, rather than the ways in which (for example) relatives of an accused could be brought into court to aid such pleas. Thus, in *Rhetorica ad Herennium* (2.50) and Cicero's *De Inventione* (1.106–9), we find catalogues of the kinds of thing to *say* in a peroration, but not what to *do*.

Nevertheless, despite this significant divide between the intellectual and the practical, Hellenistic rhetoric did come to recognize "delivery" (*actio / pronuntiatio*) as the final, necessary task (*officium*) of the orator, and formulated some guidelines on the subject.[22] These guidelines, however, were relatively narrow in scope, restricted primarily to matters of voice and gesture, with some attention paid on occasion to facial expres-

---

19. See Arist. *Rh.* 3.1: ἐγκεχειρήκασιν δὲ ἐπ' ὀλίγον περὶ αὐτῆς [sc. τῆς ὑποκριτῆς] εἰπεῖν τινές, οἷον Θρασύμαχος ἐν τοῖς Ἐλέοις. Cf. Diels and Kranz (1952) 325 (no. 85, fr. B 5); Bers (2009) 81.

20. See Arist. *Rh.* 3.1 for the assertion that delivery (in this case, theatrical delivery) is not easily reduced to artistic rules (ἀτεχνότερον). Cf. *Rhet. Her.* 3.19; Calboli (1983) 32. Note that Quintilian's attribution of this view to Thrasymachus (*Inst.* 3.3.4) may be a misreading of this Aristotelian passage; see Freeman (1946) 378. Aristotle did, however, appreciate the role played by the orator's delivery, both in the overall persuasive effect of a speech and in its style (*Rh.* 2.8, 3.12). Cf. Wöhrle (1990) 33–34, who explores some of the discrepancies between Greek rhetorical discussions of delivery and its practice; also Bers (2009) 56–63.

21. See Arist. *Rh.* 3.1: καὶ δοκεῖ φορτικὸν εἶναι, καλῶς ὑπολαμβανόμενον. ("And it [sc. delivery] seems a vulgar matter when rightly understood.") Cf. Hall (1995) 41. This aversion to the academic discussion of topics such as gesture is not solely an ancient phenomenon. As Kendon (1981) notes at 129: "for much of [the twentieth] century, [the study of gesture] has been almost wholly disregarded, apparently because there was no way in which its study could be integrated with prevailing theoretical concerns." Cf. Quint. *Inst.* 3.3.4–5; Fantham (1982) 258.

22. See Quint. *Inst.* 3.3.3 and 7–9 for the development of different systems and divisions.

sion.[23] *Rhetorica ad Herennium* provides our best indication of the modest progress that had been made in this respect. Delivery is treated in nine sections (3.19–28), while *elocutio* ("oratorical style") receives a full sixty-nine (4.1–69).[24] Aspects such as the clothes of the defendant, the deployment of props, the use of supplication, and the introduction of relatives into court, remained outside the interests of the rhetoricians.

At the same time, however, whatever the interests of the rhetoricians, it is clear that theatrics did play a part in the Athenian courts. Aristophanes's *Wasps* brilliantly parodies the custom of bringing forward weeping family relatives during the course of a trial;[25] and Socrates in Plato's *Apology* refers scathingly to similar practices.[26] Yet actual examples of these techniques are difficult to find in the surviving speeches of the Greek orators. Speech 20 in the Lysianic corpus illustrates at least the basic framework. The speaker asserts that it is commonplace for a defendant in a lawsuit to bring forward his children and to engage in tears and laments (Lysias 20.34: ἐάν τις παῖδας αὑτοῦ ἀναβιβασάμενος κλαίῃ καὶ ὀλοφύρηται, τούς τε παῖδας δι᾽ αὑτὸν εἰ ἀτιμωθήσονται ἐλεοῦντας).[27] Today, however, he has done something different: he has brought his *father* into court (20.35: ἡμεῖς δὲ τὸν πατέρα τουτονὶ καὶ ἡμᾶς ἐξαιτούμεθα). He

23. Theophrastus's discussion of delivery, for example, pays some attention to facial expression; see Fortenbaugh (1985) 272–75.

24. Cicero is similarly brief in his discussion of gesture at *De or.* 3.220–27 and *Orat.* 55–60. Detailed study of gesture seems to have been undertaken by Plotius Gallus (Quint. *Inst.* 11.3.143), presumably after *Rhetorica ad Herennium* had been written in the 80s BCE (see *Rhet. Her.* 3.19), and by Nigidius Figulus (Quint. *Inst.* 11.3.143). These works have not survived, however, and it is difficult to know exactly what topics they addressed. On Plotius Gallus, see Suet. *Gram. et rhet.* 26; Kaster (1995) 291–97. On Nigidius Figulus, see Rawson (1985) 151.

25. See Ar. *Vesp.* 975–84, especially the exhortation for the defendant's puppies/children to cry (line 978): αἰτεῖτε κἀντιβολεῖτε καὶ δακρύετε. The play was first performed in 422 BCE. On the scene and Aristophanes's parody of oratorical pleading, see MacDowell (1971) 258–59; MacDowell (1995) 175. On tears in the Athenian courts, see Cronin (1939) 473–75; Arnould (1990) 68–70; 201–2; Johnstone (1999) 115. On the generally rowdy atmosphere of the Athenian courts, see Bers (1985); Johnstone (1999) 117.

26. Pl. *Ap.* 34c: ἐδεήθη τε καὶ ἱκέτευσε τοὺς δικαστὰς μετὰ πολλῶν δακρύων, παιδία τε αὑτοῦ ἀναβιβασάμενος ἵνα ὅτι μάλιστα ἐλεηθείη, καὶ ἄλλους τῶν οἰκείων καὶ φίλων πολλούς. Cf. Dem. 30.32: ἀναβὰς ἐπὶ τὸ δικαστήριον ἐδεῖθ᾽ ἱκετεύων ὑπὲρ αὑτοῦ καὶ ἀντιβολῶν καὶ δάκρυσι κλάων ταλάντου τιμῆσαι. In *Laws* Plato seeks to exclude emotional appeals from the courts of his ideal state (*Laws* 949b: μήτε ἱκετείαις χρώμενον ἀσχήμοσι μήτε οἴκτοις γυναικείοις).

27. See Carey (2007) 199–208; Bers (2009) 83. Other speeches confirm the deployment of relatives in such instances. See, e.g., Lys. 21.25: τοὺς παῖδας τούτους; Hyp. *Eux.* 41: λοιπὸν δ᾽ ἐστὶ δεῖσθαι τῶν δικαστῶν καὶ τοὺς φίλους παρακαλεῖν καὶ τὰ παιδία ἀναβιβάζεσθαι; Dem. 21.99: παιδία γὰρ παραστήσεται καὶ κλαήσει καὶ τούτοις αὐτὸν ἐξαιτήσεται;. Dem. 54.38: φασὶ γὰρ παραστησάμενον τοὺς παῖδας αὐτὸν κατὰ τούτων ὀμεῖσθαι. Cf. Dover (1974) 195–201; Hall (1995) 51; Berry (1996) 311; Johnstone (1999) 115; Roisman (2005) 149.

then proceeds to ask the jurors to show pity to the old man (20.35: ἀλλὰ ἐλεήσατε καὶ τὸν πατέρα γέροντα ὄντα καὶ ἡμᾶς), and finally they plead to-gether for acquittal (20.36: δεόμεθα οὖν . . . ἐλεήσαντας ἀποψηφίσασθαι). Here, then, are the essential elements of an emotional appeal deploying human props. Yet it is worth noting that the speaker makes no reference to his father's tears or his own. The scene is thus rather different from those mockingly described in various extant speeches.[28]

Now, it is not impossible that Romans such as Sulpicius Galba were fa-miliar with some of this Greek oratorical material. According to Cicero, a number of Romans were well versed in Greek literature by this time.[29] But we should hesitate before positing a direct connection between the practices that prevailed in the Athenian courts and those in the Roman forum. In the first place, defendants in Athens generally did not use advocates to plead on their behalf; speeches from such a context would thus have been of limited utility to the Roman *patronus*.[30] Second, as we have seen, the texts of such speeches still left a good deal of their theat-rics unclear. It would have been much simpler and more productive for Roman orators to study at first hand the speakers that they saw perform-ing in the forum.

Yet how frequently would the oratorical tiro in Rome have witnessed such theatrics? After all, the examples of showmanship discussed so far are not especially impressive in numerical terms. Can we reasonably view them as typical of general practice? This issue of typicality is one that will arise regularly in the course of this study. Unfortunately, it is one that cannot be settled decisively: our extant evidence regarding Roman ora-tory is simply too limited in scope to allow such conclusions. Neverthe-less, a consideration of the wider social context in which Roman orators operated suggests that showmanship was in fact an integral part of life for many aristocrats.

---

28. Our information about the high emotional tenor of such pleas derives primarily from hostile characterizations of them. See, e.g., Andoc. 4.39: ἔστι μὲν οὖν Ἀλκιβιάδου . . . αὐτὸν δὲ ἱκετεύειν καὶ δακρύειν οἰκτρῶς. Lycurg. *Leoc.* 150: οὐ πλέον ἰσχύει παρ᾽ ὑμῖν ἔλεος οὐδὲ δάκρυα. Dem. 38.27: οὐ τοίνυν θαυμάσαιμ᾽ ἄν, εἰ καὶ δακρύειν καὶ ἐλεινοὺς ἑαυτοὺς πειρῷντο ποιεῖν. Cf. Lys. 27.12: <οἱ> ἀδικούμενοι δακρύουσι καὶ ἐλεινοί εἰσιν. See also the contemptuous use of the verb ὀδύρομαι (probably implying a tearful performance) at Dem. 37.48; 38.19; 39.35. As Bers (2009) 85 notes, there was presumably a degree of truth be-hind these barbs, although he concludes overall (p. 93) that the desire to uphold ideals of manly restraint inhibited excessive displays of grief in these contexts.

29. See, e.g., *Brut.* 78 on C. Sulpicius Galus (*qui maxime omnium nobilium Graecis litteris studuit*); and *Brut.* 81 on A. Albinus (*qui Graece scripsit historiam . . . et litteratus et disertus fuit*).

30. See Kennedy (1968b); May (1981); (1988) 9–12.

## SOCIAL AND POLITICAL THEATER IN ROME

The Roman grandee lived much of his daily life in the public eye. As Cicero notes, the ambitious aristocrat was closely scrutinized by those around him from a young age (*Off.* 2.44):

> *in hunc oculi omnium coniciuntur, atque in eum quid agat, quemadmodum vivat inquiritur, et, tamquam in clarissima luce versetur, ita nullum obscurum potest nec dictum eius esse nec factum.*

[Upon this individual are turned the eyes of the world. What he does and how he behaves are closely scrutinized, and, as if he moved in the brightest of lights, nothing that he says or does can be concealed.]

This constant surveillance was in part a natural consequence of Rome's system of social patronage, in which crowds of clients clustered around powerful individuals and their families.[31] But success in Roman politics also depended upon the active projection of a memorable public image on the streets and in the forum. Quintus Cicero's advice to his brother during the latter's campaign for the consulship was to make his canvass full of display and ostentation.[32] This energetic self-fashioning through visual spectacle could be accomplished in various ways. Reception halls decorated with busts of prestigious ancestors and spoils from foreign wars proudly proclaimed a family's heritage and power; the sponsorship of public buildings and grand entertainments likewise demonstrated wealth and ambition; and aristocratic funerals regularly provided a vehicle for the promotion of family propaganda.[33] Roman grandees were thus well versed in striking poses calculated to elicit specific responses from onlookers. This was how they conducted much of their business. Daily life was in many respects a non-stop public relations exercise.[34]

---

31. Note in particular the crowded houses of the rich and powerful at the institutionalized morning reception or *salutatio*. See, e.g., *Att.* 1.18.1: *itaque cum bene completa domus est tempore matutino*; Q. Cic. *Comm. Pet.* 3; 34–38. Cf. Wiseman (1982) 28–31; Wallace-Hadrill (1989) 63–65; Morstein-Marx (1998) 270–71; Bell (2004) 214; Goldbeck (2010), esp. 235–46.

32. Q. Cic. *Comm. Pet.* 52: *postremo tota petitio cura ut pompae plena sit, ut illustris, ut splendida, ut popularis sit, ut habeat summam speciem ac dignitatem.* Cf. *Mur.* 44. See also Morstein-Marx (1998) 284: "a consular electoral campaign is to a significant extent treated as a public performance before the *populus*." Cf. O'Sullivan (2011) 54–76.

33. See, e.g., Flaig (2003); Bell (2004) 199–248; Flower (2004); Sumi (2005); Kaster (2009). Cf. also contributions on specific elements by (e.g.) Wiseman (1982); Marshall (1984); Gregory (1994); Flower (1996) 91–158; Braund (1998), Pierini (2006).

34. Cf. Morstein-Marx (1998) 270: "Visual spectacle is an aspect of politics never to

This tendency toward theatricality was reproduced also on the wider political stage. As Egon Flaig has recently discussed, conflicts between prominent individuals were often played out in the public eye, utilizing various forms of political theater, some long established, some improvised for the immediate purpose.[35] The bitter wrangling between Tiberius Gracchus and his opponents in 133 BCE provides an excellent example of these techniques. Although Flaig has discussed a few of these incidents briefly, it is worth reexamining them here in some detail so as to highlight an important point: many of the devices deployed by Tiberius and his enemies appear also in Cicero's later judicial theater.[36]

We may start with Tiberius's tribunician edict forbidding the transaction of public business, an action taken in response to stubborn opposition in the senate to his proposed laws regarding land redistribution.[37] Rome's prominent landowners—those who stood to lose most from the legislation—responded by staging a public protest. They dressed in dirtied clothes (*sordes*) and paraded through the forum.[38] This Roman tradition of wearing *sordes* as a form of protest will be discussed in greater detail in chapter two; for the present argument, we need note only its highly theatrical nature. The landowners expressed their sense of grievance not through speeches but through coordinated action in front of the Roman people. Moreover, the distinctive form of attire not only heightened the visual impact of their protest but also conveyed effectively their group solidarity. Indeed, the protest as a whole was probably intended in part as an intimidating show of strength.

Tiberius reacted with a similarly theatrical stunt (Plut. *Ti. Gracch.* 10.9): ὥστε κἀκεῖνον οὐδενὸς ἀγνοοῦντος ὑποζώννυσθαι ξιφίδιον λῃστρικόν. ("So Tiberius on his part—and everybody knew it—wore a concealed

---

be underestimated, least of all in Rome, a city whose life was a series of public events and rituals for the urban spectator to look upon: *contiones*, trials, *ludi* and *munera*, funerals, triumphs." See also Edmondson (2008) 29: "Rome was a culture of spectacle." Cf. Hölkeskamp (1995) 30–31; van der Blom (2010) 91–93.

35. See Flaig (2003). Throughout this work, Flaig invokes theatrical metaphors in his discussion of Roman political activities (e.g., p. 120: "In welchem Verhältnis stand die tadellose Performanz zur veilleicht unpassenden Dramaturgie und Choreographie?").

36. This is a connection that Flaig himself does not develop at any length; see Flaig (2003) 99–104. The characterization of some of these episodes by Bernstein (1978) 172 as "melodramatic and not altogether dignified" misses the point. For a summary of Tiberius' tactics, see Flower (2013) 88.

37. Gracchus's legislation had been blocked up to this point by the veto of another tribune, M. Octavius; see Plut. *Ti. Gracch.* 10.1–8.

38. See Plut. *Ti. Gracch.* 10.9: ἐντεῦθεν οἱ κτηματικοὶ τὰς μὲν ἐσθῆτας μετέβαλον, καὶ περιῄεσαν οἰκτροὶ καὶ ταπεινοὶ κατὰ τὴν ἀγοράν. ("Upon this, the men of property changed their attire and went about the forum dressed in a pitiful and impoverished fashion.") For the text and section numbering, see Ziegler (1996).

short-sword of the type that bandits use.") Plutarch's phrasing highlights the element of posturing in Tiberius's actions. Self-defense was not the only reason he carried the dagger; he also hoped to draw attention to the danger he was in, and thus stir up public indignation. No doubt he could have achieved something of the same effect by means of a speech; but this public pose possessed a directness and succinctness that an oration lacked. It could also broadcast his dilemma to a wider range of audiences as he went around the city.[39]

This conflict continued with several other highly public forms of confrontation and negotiation. As Tiberius attempted to pass his legislation through the popular assembly, two respected consulars (Manlius and Fulvius) engaged in an energetic public supplication, urging him to abandon the vote (Plut. *Ti. Gracch.* 11.2): Μάλλιος καὶ Φούλβιος, ἄνδρες ὑπατικοί, προσπεσόντες τῷ Τιβερίῳ καὶ χειρῶν ἁπτόμενοι καὶ δακρύοντες ἐδέοντο παύσασθαι. ("Manlius and Fulvius, men of consular rank, fell down in front of Tiberius, clasped his hands, and with tears begged him to desist.")[40] Supplication, as we shall see in chapter three, could smack of demeaning desperation for those who engaged in it; nevertheless, in this case, the highly public context endowed it with considerable persuasive leverage. Tiberius now had to make an open declaration of his character: was he a man of moderation who cared about the reputation of his elders, even if this meant yielding in the political dispute at hand? Or was he so ruthless that he was prepared to rebuff the earnest pleas of such men?[41] Such was the tense public drama that these maneuverings created.

Tiberius chose to relent—a decision that did little in fact to placate those opposing his policies. Indeed, as the conflict continued, he found himself engaging in similar tactics as he urged the tribune M. Octavius to abandon his veto against legislation being passed in the popular assembly (Plut. *Ti. Gracch.* 11.5): καὶ πρῶτον μὲν ἐδεῖτο φανερῶς αὐτοῦ, λόγους τε προσφέρων φιλανθρώπους καὶ χειρῶν ἁπτόμενος, ἐνδοῦναι καὶ χαρίσασθαι

---

39. Of course the threats of assassination to which Tiberius claimed to be reacting (Plut. *Ti. Gracch.* 10.9) may well have been real; his eventual demise demonstrates the ruthlessness of his opponents. The important point for our discussion is that Tiberius demonstrates a shrewd awareness of how to exploit the situation for his own political gain.

40. The identities of these individuals are not certain. Possibilities for Manlius include T. Manlius Torquatus (cos. 165), A. Manlius Torquatus (cos. 164) and M'. Manilius (cos. 149); for Fulvius, they include Ser. Fulvius Flaccus (cos. 135) and C. Fulvius Flaccus (cos. 134); see Stockton (1979) 28 (with n. 26).

41. On the dynamics of supplication, see Gould (1973) 81; Naiden (2006) 242. Cf. *Mur.* 9: *repudiatio supplicum superbiam, amicorum neglectio improbitatem coarguit.*

τῷ δήμῳ. ("First of all, however, he begged Octavius in public to relent and gratify the people, addressing him with conciliatory words and clasping his hands.") Tiberius evidently stopped short of full supplication, but by clasping Octavius's hands he endowed his request with a certain formality and intensity. Octavius, however, rebuffed the entreaty (*Ti. Gracch.* 11.6: διωθουμένου τοῦ Ὀκταβίου), thus forcing Tiberius to take the drastic step of having him voted out of office.

Even here, however, the political brinkmanship continued. When the vote to remove Octavius was on the verge of passing, Tiberius halted proceedings and once more appealed to him to withdraw his opposition voluntarily (Plut. *Ti. Gracch.* 12.2): αὖθις ἐδεῖτο τοῦ Ὀκταβίου καὶ περιέβαλλεν αὐτὸν ἐν ὄψει τοῦ δήμου καὶ κατησπάζετο, λιπαρῶν καὶ δεόμενος μήθ᾽ ἑαυτὸν ἄτιμον περιιδεῖν γενόμενον. . . . ("Tiberius again entreated Octavius, and embraced and kissed him in full view of the people, earnestly begging him not to allow himself to be dishonoured. . . .") Again, there was careful calculation behind the pose. Tiberius here was able to present himself as a man who retained a concern for his opponent's reputation even at a moment of bitter conflict. Moreover, Octavius's continued refusal to acquiesce could be characterized as "contumacy and obstinacy" (although he himself would presumably have represented his actions as staunch adherence to a matter of principle).[42]

These theatrics continued even after Tiberius's legislation had been passed. Suspecting that one of his friends had been killed by poison, he ostentatiously sought the protection of the people at a public assembly, utilizing various props as he did so: it was now his turn to dress *in sordibus* (μετέβαλε τὴν ἐσθῆτα); and, like Sulpicius Galba, he brought his children before the people (τοὺς παῖδας προαγαγὼν) and implored the crowd's protection for them and their mother (Plut. *Ti. Gracch.* 13.6: ἐδεῖτο τοῦ δήμου τούτων κήδεσθαι καὶ τῆς μητρός, ὡς αὐτὸς ἀπεγνωκὼς ἑαυτόν).[43]

These incidents are important at both a general and specific level. As we shall see in the following chapters, the specific devices deployed during this conflict appear also in judicial contexts during the Late Republic. The use, then, of *sordes* in Roman trials, along with supplications, entreaties, child props, and poses designed to convey a sense of fear,

---

42. For the phrase, see Astin (1967) 208. Cf. Steel (2010) 39–40. Plutarch's phrase ἐν ὄψει τοῦ δήμου draws attention to the knowing theatricality of Tiberius's actions. According to Plutarch, Octavius ended up being dragged through the streets by Tiberius's supporters (*Ti. Gracch.* 12.4–5); but contrast App. *B Civ.* 1.12.

43. See also App. *B Civ.* 1.14 and Astin (1967) 218. Cf. Tiberius's public supplication a little later at Plut. *Ti. Gracch.* 16.3: ἱκέτευε τοὺς ἀνθρώπους.

all have a heritage that stretches beyond the courts. Moreover, from the broader perspective, the very use of these devices attests to the Roman affinity for conducting public affairs in a distinctly theatrical way. This facility with showmanship was thus not something that grandees acquired through books; it was the product of observation and socialization. When we find these elements in the judicial arena, there is every reason to regard them as a natural extension of existing social practices, rather than specifically oratorical techniques.[44]

## M. ANTONIUS AND HIS DEFENSE OF M'. AQUILLIUS

In the fifty years or so between Tiberius Gracchus's demise and the rise of Sulla, several new standing courts (*quaestiones perpetuae*) were established in Rome, as the senate attempted to improve the mechanisms for bringing its members to justice.[45] Nevertheless, although these new courts reduced the influence of public assemblies on the administration of law, the potential for exploiting oratorical theatrics seems not to have been significantly diminished.[46] This point is crucial for our understanding of Cicero's techniques and is best illustrated by a well-known incident that took place in 98 (or perhaps 97) BCE during M. Antonius's defense of M'. Aquillius *de pecuniis repetundis*.[47]

Cicero (who seems to have been the main source for later accounts

---

44. Note that the events involving Tiberius Gracchus were not unusual. We find similar calculated posturing ten years later in his brother's conflict with the senate. See, for example, the consul Opimius's exploitation of an attendant's funeral to incite outrage (Plut. *C. Gracch.* 13–14). Plutarch's account again stresses the element of careful showmanship in Opimius's actions (Plut. *C. Gracch.* 14.1): γιγνώσκοντος μὲν τοῦ Ὀπιμίου τὰ πραττόμενα, προσποιουμένου δὲ θαυμάζειν, ὥστε καὶ τοὺς βουλευτὰς προελθεῖν. For another manipulation of a funeral from around this time (for political or perhaps economic ends), see Lucilius II.73–74 at Warmington (1967) 24 (= Lucilius 2.60–61 at Marx (1904) 7). The incident has been interpreted in contrasting ways; see Marx (1905) 30–31; Cichorius (1908) 243; Warmington (1967) 25, note (c); Gruen (1968) 115.

45. For convenient summaries of the development of the standing courts, see Greenidge (1901) 415–28; Balsdon (1938); Jones (1972) 45–90; Cloud (1994); Harries (2007) 59–83.

46. As Greenidge (1901) 417 notes, the move from *iudicia populi* to the standing courts was not a "sudden revolution." The latter supplanted the former only gradually. See also Jones (1972) 1–39; Cloud (1994) 501–3. For examples of *iudicia populi* in the decades after the Gracchi, see Alexander (1990) 25–35 (nos. 49, 59, 62, 63, 64, 66, 68). On special courts, see Jones (1972) 52–54; Alexander (1990) 21–22 (nos. 41, 42, 43, 44) and 26–29 on the *lex Mamilia* (nos. 52, 53, 54, 55, 56, 57).

47. Aquillius was prosecuted on charges of extortion committed while proconsul in Sicily in 100–99 BCE. See Alexander (1990) 44 (no. 84). For the charge *de pecuniis repetundis*, see Livy *Per.* 70, which assigns the trial to 98 BCE. On the arguments for assigning a date of 97, see Badian (1957) 330–31 and (1964) 45–46, and Gruen (1966) 39.

of the event) describes the memorable climax that Antonius contrived in the peroration of his speech (*Verr.* 2.5.3): *ipse arripuit M'. Aquillium constituitque in conspectu omnium tunicamque eius a pectore abscidit, ut cicatrices populus Romanus iudicesque aspicerent adverso corpore exceptas.* ("Antonius himself grabbed M'. Aquillius by the arm and placed him in full view of everyone. He then tore the tunic from the man's chest so that the Roman people and the jurors could see the wounds that he had received on the front of his body.")[48] As we have seen, this device of revealing scars as proof of an individual's martial valor had a tradition in Roman oratory going back at least several decades. The crucial point here, though, is that Antonius exploits it in the context of a *quaestio*, not a *contio*. Evidently these new courts granted advocates considerable latitude in how they presented their arguments.[49] Indeed, Antonius's emotional theatrics did not stop there, as Cicero's later account in *De Oratore* reveals (in this case the incident is put into the mouth of Antonius himself as an interlocutor in the dialogue) (*De or.* 2.196):

> *cum C. Marius maerorem orationis meae praesens ac sedens multum lacrimis suis adiuvaret cumque ego illum crebro appellans collegam ei suum commendarem atque ipsum advocatum ad communem imperatorum fortunam defendendam invocarem, non fuit haec sine meis lacrimis, non sine dolore magno miseratio omniumque deorum et hominum et civium et sociorum imploratio.*

> [C. Marius, who was present at the trial and sitting on the benches, contributed a great deal to the sorrowful tenor of my speech through his tears, and I repeatedly addressed him directly and entrusted to him the care of his former colleague in the consulship. I even urged him to speak himself in support of the common interests of military generals. This lamentation, together with my appeal to every god, man, citizen and ally, was combined with my own tears and my own sense of profound outrage.]

Antonius's theatrics, then, went beyond the defendant and his tunic. He integrated into his plea an additional prop from the defense benches, in the form of the great general, C. Marius. Indeed, both Marius and Anto-

---

48. For the claim that Cicero is the only source for the events of the trial, see Livy *Per.* 70: *Cicero eius rei solus auctor.*

49. Cf. Schottländer (1967) 140–41; see also Dugan (2005) 140–42. Note that Aquillius also had battle scars visible on his face, which Antonius spent some time discussing before he ripped the man's tunic (*Verr.* 2.5.3: *simul et de illo vulnere quod ille in capite ab hostium duce acceperat multa dixit*). The final flourish was thus hardly a necessary part of the argument; it was added solely for theatrical effect.

nius openly shed tears in the course of the emotional climax.[50] This was a grand performance that would have required careful orchestration.[51]

PART 2: THE ADMINISTRATION OF THE *Quaestiones Perpetuae*

Such antics may appear to us today obstructive to the impartial administration of the law, and we may well wonder why the Romans did not view matters in the same way. The officials who presided over these courts, for example, seem to have had little interest in placing restrictions on how advocates presented their cases.[52] We hardly ever hear of the *quaesitor* intervening in order to clarify points of law or procedure, or to challenge the arguments or methods of speakers.[53] Glabrio at the prosecution of Verres evidently adjourned one session early because of fears of popular unrest;[54] yet he seems not to have intervened—or been asked to offer a

---

50. On Antonius as a staunch Marian at this time, see Badian (1957) 331–33; Carney (1970) 47, n. 218. Cf. Gruen (1968) 194. The calculated nature of Marius's performance is consistent with his own exploitation of political theater in other contexts. See, for example, Plutarch's description of an exchange with Saturninus as he made a bid for the consulship (Plut. *Mar.* 14.12). The artifice involved in this piece of theater (according to Plutarch) was obvious (Plut. *Mar.* 14.14): καὶ φανερὸς μὲν ἦν ἀπιθάνως συνυποκρινόμενος τὸ προσποίημα τῷ Μαρίῳ. See also Plut. *Mar.* 9.2 on Marius's claim that the scars on his body were a better sign of his character than any family monuments; cf. Carney (1970) 40–44; 62.

51. Antonius employed his skill at generating pity in other judicial situations as well. See *Tusc.* 2.57 on a speech in his own defense: *genu mehercule M. Antonium vidi, cum contente pro se ipse lege Varia diceret, terram tangere;* and his defense of Norbanus (*De or.* 2.197–204; also 2.107; 2.124). Cf. Alexander (1990) 44–45 (no. 86). See also the remarks attributed to L. Crassus at *De or.* 2.125: *quid ego de Cn. Malli, quid de Q. Regis commiseratione dicam? quid de aliis innumerabilibus?* There is some debate, however, regarding the number of separate defenses alluded to in these remarks. See Alexander (1990) 33 (no. 64); cf. Malcovati (1976) 226 (frg. 17, *Pro Cn. Mallio Maximo*). Cf. also *Brut.* 142. On Antonius as orator, see Scholz (1962); Malcovati (1976) 221–37; Fantham (2004) 37–39; Walker (2011) 9–56.

52. In major trials, this official was usually a praetor, although on occasions he might appoint a representative in his place (usually termed a *quaesitor*). See Greenidge (1901) 428–33; 456–68; Frier (1985) 72–77; Brennan (2000a) 237–39; (2000b) 367–68; 416–24; Lintott (2004) 75–76.

53. Cf. Powell and Paterson (2004) 33: "There is no record of an advocate ever being interrupted for irrelevance." See also Frier (1985) 210, who refers to the "passivity" of the court president; Bablitz (2007) 89–90; Liva (2009). On the (often limited) legal expertise of the *praetor urbanus*, see Frier (1985) 47–48; Brennan (2000b) 451. On his selection by sortition, Brennan (2000a) 240–41; (2000b) 395; 450–51.

54. See *Verr.* 2.5.163. On another occasion (in 119 BCE), the presiding official evidently took it upon himself to adjourn a trial because of the young prosecutor's attack of nerves at the start of his speech; but this was evidently an act of generosity rather than one motivated by a concern with court protocol (*De or.* 1.121).

ruling—when Cicero departed significantly from the usual procedure of the courts by cutting short his opening speech during the first *actio* and introducing at this early stage a series of witnesses.[55]

Why this apparent passivity? As Bruce Frier has argued, in this openly adversarial system of justice, it was important that each side be given free rein to present its argument and evidence as it saw fit. To interfere in the course of these pleadings could readily be interpreted as a form of prejudice or favoritism.[56] From the Roman perspective, the praetor's main role was to get the case to trial in a fair and equitable fashion, a task whose trickiness should not be underestimated. Since motions for prosecution were often motivated by personal feuds between prominent politicians, arranging the schedule of trials to be held during the year, as well as supervising the registers of potential jurors, required considerable tact and integrity.[57] It was easy for the praetor to lay himself open to accusations of corruption.[58] Once a trial had begun, then, his lack of interference may well have been conceptualized more positively as proof of his impartiality.

It is worth noting too that, although the text of (what is probably) C. Gracchus's *lex repetendarum*, passed in 122 BCE, contains many detailed provisions regarding the selection of jurors, it has very little to say about the way in which advocates are to present their cases.[59] To the Roman mind, then, the prime threat to the integrity of the courts lay, not in the advocate's oratorical theatrics, but in the potential corruption of the jurors. The law thus attempts to control how the jurors are to be chosen, how votes are to be cast, and how suspicions of collusion are to be han-

---

55. See *Verr.* 1.55; 2.1.20; Alexander (1976); Vasaly (2009). Cicero gives a precedent for his procedure (*Verr.* 1.55), and asserts that the defense counsel will have the same opportunity for questions, arguments and comments as the prosecution (*Verr.* 1.55). These very remarks, however, alert us to the kind of objections that Hortensius (who was speaking for the defense) could have lodged. Yet there is no indication that he asked the praetor to intervene or called for a recess so that the procedural question could be resolved. (Any objections that he raised in the course of the trial seem to have been addressed to the jurors.) See Verr. 2.1.20–25.

56. Frier (1985) 246–50; cf. also Frier (2010) 77. The existence of "heavy procedural constraints" in such trials, as noted by Powell (2010) 36, need not contradict Frier's conclusions. *Rhet. Her.* 4.47 evidently expects the *quaesitor* to monitor the evidence presented by witnesses—but the tactics of the *accusator* (it seems) are not so closely constrained. (Note too the fictional context of these remarks.) See also Gell. *NA* 14.2.1–25.

57. See Brennan (2000a) 237–39; (2000b) 367–71; 416–24; 449–53.

58. For the involvement of praetors in possibly corrupt practices, see Asc. *Corn.* 59–60C; *Verr.* 1.41; 1.52; *Planc.* 43; *Q Fr.* 1.2.15. Cf. Brennan (2000b) 451 and 822 (notes 84 and 85).

59. See Lintott (1992); Crawford (1996) 39–112; Brennan (2000a) 237–39; Harries (2007) 63–64.

dled. No attempt, however, is made to restrict the activities of advocates during the actual trial.[60]

We must also resist the assumption that the Roman courts were characterized by the same rigid formality and deferential restraint that characterize many modern judicial proceedings. Although a degree of regulatory procedure existed, various factors combined to create a rather chaotic and unpredictable environment overall. The fact, for example, that most trials took place in the public space of the forum, open to the elements, made it difficult to impose the kind of control on events that we expect today.[61] Jurors also seem to have enjoyed considerable freedom as far as court protocol was concerned. Cicero vividly describes their typical listlessness during a less than compelling speech (*Brut.* 200): *videt oscitantem iudicem, loquentem cum altero, non numquam etiam circulantem, mittentem ad horas, quaesitorem ut dimittat rogantem.* ("[The passing critic] sees one of the jurors yawning, chatting to a juror beside him, occasionally even talking in a group, sending a slave to find out the time, asking the president of the court to adjourn the hearing.")[62] Evidently there was little sense of—or attempt to impose—"silence in court."[63] For jurors to chat together in a group while an advocate is speaking seems to us today rude enough; for one of them actually to be asking the *quaesitor* to adjourn the session borders on arrogance. (Perhaps we are to imagine here an especially prestigious juror with sufficient clout to be able to make such a request of the praetor.)

The physical layout of the court further contributed to the bustling and potentially unpredictable nature of proceedings. Events were typically organized around the raised tribunal of the presiding official, a temporary structure erected solely for the judicial business at hand.[64]

---

60. See Crawford (1996) 104 on line 39 and the implication that the juror may not engage in argument. "The rubric *ioudex nei quis disputet* perhaps refers to an obligation on a juror to accept the decision of the praetor on whether he is legitimately absent, rather than to an obligation on a juror to avoid disputation in general." Cf. Lintott (1992) 98 and 128. As Lintott (1992) 22 notes, however, some of the instructions for the trial itself may no longer be extant.

61. See Quint. *Inst.* 11.3.27 for the challenges presented by the heat, wind, and rain of the open forum. Cf. *Brut.* 317; Sen. *Controv.* 3, pref. 13; and 9, pref. 4; Bablitz (2007) 49.

62. On this meaning of *circulor*, see Douglas (1966) 144; cf. *OLD*, s.v. *circulo*, 2.

63. Cf. Kondratieff (2010) 109: "Romans clearly had a high level of tolerance for working in noisy and crowded conditions."

64. On the ancient tribunal, see Gabelmann (1984) plates 19 and 21.2; David (1992) 412–22 with figures 1–8; Bablitz (2008); Kondratieff (2010) 91–96. Cf. also Bablitz (2007) 29–31. The magistrate's lictors and other members of his entourage would have helped to transform into a temporary judicial arena a space in the forum that was usually accessible to the public. On this process and its conceptualization, see Blanshard (2004). The height of the tribunal further assisted in conveying the praetor's authority over the court.

Questions still remain regarding the exact location of these tribunals, but, wherever they were situated, it seems likely that the jurors sat just in front of them on rows of benches.[65] The number of jurors could vary between fifty and a hundred, according to the type of trial, and this created a context of performance very different from the modern courtroom.[66] As any modern-day teacher or lecturer will know, the size of an audience influences considerably the dynamics of a presentation. The larger the crowd, the more expansive and forceful the style of delivery typically needs to be. This principle would have been all the more relevant in an age lacking any technology for amplifying the voice.[67] Moreover, trials in Rome were usually attended by a crowd of onlookers from the general public (referred to as the *corona*), which further increased the scale of events.[68]

It is clear too that the physical layout of the Roman court provided ample space in which the enterprising orator could engage in theatrics. The jurors' benches seem to have formed one side of a roughly rectangular space in which the action of the court took place.[69] Two other sides were formed by two further sets of benches placed more or less at right angles to the benches of the jurors. On these sat the opposing litigants and their associates (who usually comprised advocates, friends, and relatives). The adversarial nature of the litigation was thus represented spatially, with the parties for prosecution and defense sitting opposite each other.[70] The advocates pleaded in the space between these three sets of benches, presumably facing the jurors most of the time, but able to turn

---

65. David (1992) 44–45 presents a plan of the forum with suggested sites of tribunals and courts, but, as Lintott (2004) 63, n. 8 observes, this is "highly conjectural and over-schematic." See also Coarelli (1985) 166–99, especially 180, who places the tribunals used in trials *de vi* and *de repetundis* in "un ristretto spazio compreso tra il Tempio di Vesta, la *Regia* e l'angolo sud-est della Basilica Emilia." Cf. Coarelli (2009) 6–8; Kondratieff (2010) 101–20.

66. Greenidge (1901) 441–56; McDermott (1977); Lintott (2004) 74–75. For the tentative suggestion that each bench seated ten individuals, see Bablitz (2007) 53, with n. 11.

67. As Aldrete (1999) 73–84 notes, even the best Roman speaker would have been unable to make himself heard clearly more than fifty or sixty meters away; cf. Calboli (1983).

68. The term *corona* suggests that this crowd usually encircled the main area of proceedings. See Scalais (1951) 192–95; Frier (1985) 235–36; David (1992) 471–74; Lintott (2004) 63; Bablitz (2007) 57–58. Cf. Atkinson (2004) 65–72.

69. See David (1992) 412–22 (with figures 1–8). A useful summary is provided by Lintott (2004) 62–64. There are good comments also in Bablitz (2007) 52–58, although her main concern is with the imperial period. See David (1992) 467 for the conjecture that the jurors' benches were slightly raised on "une sorte d'estrade peu élevée." There is, however, no real evidence to support the suggestion, which is based partly on practical concerns of visibility and partly on a putative symbolism of judicial hierarchy.

70. See David (1992) 464–74; Lintott (2004) 63–64; Bablitz (2007) 53–55; 59.

to left and right to refer to the various parties involved in the trial.[71] As we have seen, this space was large enough for M. Antonius to bring forward M'. Aquillius into the view of the whole crowd (*in conspectu omnium*) and rip open the man's tunic to such effect. Moreover, he was able to interact at the same time in a highly emotional way with Marius as he sat nearby on the defense benches.

Clearly, then, the Roman advocate faced various challenges—and enjoyed certain opportunities—that his modern counterpart does not. Most significantly, Cicero expects the orator to engage directly and energetically with the public audience and elicit audible responses from them. The truly eloquent speaker, he claims, is one who, when appropriate, can generate not just expressions of approval but also cheers, shouts, and applause (*Orat.* 236: *qui non approbationes solum sed admirationes clamores plausus, si liceat, movere debet*).[72] He himself was able to evoke such a response from onlookers during his defense of Roscius of Ameria (*Orat.* 107: *quantis illa clamoribus adulescentuli diximus [sc. de supplicio parricidarum]*). Hortensius likewise (in his younger years at least) regularly generated similar reactions.[73] The *corona* was thus fundamentally different in character from the "public gallery" in a modern westernized court. Indeed, Cicero even goes so far as to assert (through the character of Brutus) that a strong rapport with this public audience is absolutely essential for one's success (*Brut.* 192):[74]

> *ego vero, inquit ille, ut me tibi indicem, in eis etiam causis, in quibus omnis res nobis cum iudicibus est, non cum populo, tamen si a corona relictus sim, non queam dicere.*

71. See Lintott (2004) 63–64 on the relevance of *Clu.* 58–59 for our understanding of the orator's alignment and that of the benches.

72. See Aldrete (1999) 102–105 and Bablitz (2007) 133 and 188 on the kinds of remark shouted out by audiences at speeches. For their manipulation, see Morstein-Marx (2004) 136–43.

73. *Brut.* 326: *itaque Hortensius utroque genere florens clamores faciebat adulescens.* ("So Hortensius, skilled in both types of Asianism, stirred up shouts from the audience when a young man.") On the orator's exploitation of the *corona*, see also *Fin.* 4.74 (*aliquid etiam coronae datum*); *Flac.* 69 (*a iudicibus oratio avertitur, vox in coronam turbamque effunditur*). Cf. *Nat. Deor.* 2.1 (*corona tibi et iudices defuerunt*); also Catull. 53. Later in his career, when pleading on behalf of King Deiotarus in the unusual setting of Caesar's private house, Cicero complained that the confined venue cramped his oratorical style (*Deiot.* 7). Cf. Tac. *Dial.* 39.4.

74. On this passage, see Hölkeskamp (1995) 26–27; Iodice di Martino (1987). Cicero's emphasis (at both *Brut.* 192 and 290) on the importance of energetic interaction with the audience is to a degree self-interested: it validates his own style of oratory and undercuts the aesthetic of the Atticists. Cf. Schenkeveld (1988); Steel (2002–3) 202. But there is no reason to suppose that Cicero here is significantly misrepresenting an important ingredient of his success.

[Certainly, Brutus said, if I'm to disclose to you my own experience, even in those cases where the whole subject matter concerns the jurors, not the people, I am unable to speak if I am abandoned by the public audience.]

The astute advocate, then, played to the crowd and was able to compel its attention through the power of performance (*Brut.* 290):

> *volo hoc oratori contingat, ut cum auditum sit eum esse dicturum, locus in sub-selliis occupetur, compleatur tribunal, gratiosi scribae sint in dando et cedendo loco, corona multiplex, iudex erectus.*

[This is what I want my orator to experience: when word gets around that he is about to speak, every seat on the benches fills up, the tribunal gets crowded, the secretaries obligingly give up and share their seats, the *corona* stands several rows deep, and the jurors sit up straight and attentive.[75]]

There is perhaps no better description of the thrill of anticipation that oratorical performance could generate in Rome: onlookers from the elite scramble to find a free space on the tribunal or the benches, while those without such social connections join the public audience, forming a *corona* many rows deep (*multiplex*). Moreover, this eager crowd needs no close supervision from the praetor's lictors; it falls silent of its own accord as the great orator stands up to speak (*Brut.* 290: *cum surgat is qui dicturus sit, significetur a corona silentium*). And as the performance progresses, the star advocate is able to shape the audience's reactions, provoking tears and laughter at will (*Brut.* 290: *deinde crebrae adsensiones, multae admirationes; risus cum velit, cum velit fletus*).

We need then to discard our modern preconceptions regarding proper procedure and comportment in the courtroom; Roman trials differed significantly in the physical conditions in which they were conducted, in the role expected of the presiding official, in the behavior of the jurors, and the licence granted to advocates to engage interactively with the public audience. Oratorical theatrics were to an extent an understandable (if not inevitable) product of this environment. Let us turn now to examine what we know of Cicero's skill as a performer and his ability to exploit these conditions for best effect.

---

75. On the meaning of *iudex* here, see Douglas (1966) 214: "either collective for the jury, or the president of the court." In my view, the description is more complete and all-encompassing if *iudex* here refers to the jurors as a whole. Cf. *OLD*, s.v. *iudex*, 2a. For discussion of this passage, see also Vasaly (1985) 1–2; Fantham (1997) 125. On the orator's ability to hold an audience enraptured, see also *Brut.* 200 (*ut avem cantu aliquo . . . teneri*).

PART 3: CICERO AS PERFORMER

Cicero's account in *Brutus* of his early training as an orator gives us an important insight into his basic inclinations as a performer. As a young man (he states) he used to speak "without modulation or variation, with a very forceful vocal delivery and with tension throughout my whole body" (*Brut.* 313: *omnia sine remissione, sine varietate, vi summa vocis et totius corporis contentione dicebam*). As a tiro, then, his initial tendency was toward a vigorous and energetic manner; but since this style placed considerable strain on his body, he took steps to modify it through further study with leading professors in Asia (*Brut.* 314–16).

These remarks suggest that Cicero was temperamentally inclined toward a certain passion and grandeur in performance. Yet it is surprising how few details we possess regarding his qualities as a mature speaker. Plutarch, for example, claims that the orator's skill in delivery contributed greatly to his persuasive power (*Cic.* 5.6: οὐ μικρὰ δὴ πρὸς τὸ πείθειν ὑπῆρχεν ἐκ τοῦ ὑποκρίνεσθαι ῥοπὴ τῷ Κικέρωνι); but he provides no further information. Indeed, we are marginally better informed about the vocal styles of Julius Caesar and Licinius Calvus than we are about Cicero's.[76]

The situation is a little more promising with regard to Cicero's use of oratorical gesture.[77] As we shall see in chapter three, it is clear from the texts of certain speeches that on occasion he clasped a defendant to him in a dramatic embrace. In several trials too he affected to break down in tears at moments of high emotion (see discussion in chapter four). Such actions, according to our definition, qualify as forms of judicial theater: they provided nonverbal means of heightening the impact of his words. Yet Cicero probably employed many other gestures as well that go unmentioned in the extant texts of his orations. The rhetorical treatises, for example, refer to advocates striking their head or thigh at moments of high emotion, and, given the dramatic tenor of many of Cicero's perorations, it seems likely that he had recourse to such gestures.[78] His

---

76. In the case of Julius Caesar, we at least know that his voice was generally high pitched (see Suet. *Iul.* 55: *voce acuta*). Cf. *Brut.* 261. On the apparently vigorous style of Calvus's delivery, see Sen. *Controv.* 7.4.6–7; cf. Lebek (1970) 86–87; Calboli (1983) 44; Narducci (1997) 129–30. See also Gruen (1967); Fairweather (1981) 94–103.

77. The use of gesture in Roman oratory has received considerable attention in recent decades; see Fantham (1982); Maier-Eichhorn (1989); Wöhrle (1990); Graf (1991); Wülfing (1994); Aldrete (1999) 3–43; Blänsdorf (2001) 220–28; Fantham (2002); Hall (2004). For a discussion of Greek gesturing, see Boegehold (1999).

78. On striking the thigh and head, see *Rhet. Her.* 3.27; *Brut.* 278; Quint. *Inst.* 2.12.10;

published speeches, however, make few direct references to them. It is likely as well that Cicero made extensive use of the smaller hand gestures catalogued by Quintilian, thereby endowing his performances with an extra mode of expressiveness.[79] But again we have to rely a good deal on conjecture in order to reconstruct his usage in any detail. For the most part, then, this aspect of his judicial theater is unavailable for detailed analysis, and it thus receives little attention in the following chapters.[80]

Nevertheless, despite these difficulties in recovering the nuances of Cicero's performances, it seems clear enough that his style of delivery was influenced quite strongly by the Roman stage.

## ORATORY AND ACTING

As modern scholars have demonstrated, the generally low social status of actors, as well as their function as public entertainers, often engendered a condescending, dismissive attitude toward them among the Roman elite.[81] Cicero himself in *De Oratore* labels acting a trivial and inconsequential art (*De or.* 1.18: *histrionum levis ars*);[82] and its practitioners were often sneered at for adopting effeminate mannerisms on stage. When Cicero refers, for example, to the manly posture that the orator must adopt as he delivers a speech (*De or.* 3.220: *laterum inflexione hac forti ac virili*), he defines it in opposition to the way that actors typically presented themselves in their performances (*non ab scaena et histrionibus*).[83]

---

11.3.123. These were not in fact exclusively oratorical gestures; they were used in everyday life as well. Cicero, for example, refers to Clodius Pulcher using them in a nonoratorical context and interprets them (probably tendentiously) as indications of the man's impulsive behavior. See Stangl (1912) 172, line 21: *qui multis inspectantibus kaput feriebas, femina plangebas* (= Cic. *De Aere Alieno Milonis* frag. 14); Crawford (1994) 274 and 282. Cf. Hom. *Ody.* 13.198–99 for striking the head in a nonoratorical context; also *Att.* 1.1.1 (*ut frontem ferias*). Note, however, that by Quintilian's time, striking the head in the course of a speech could seem *too* theatrical (Quint. *Inst.* 11.3.123).

79. See Hall (2004) for the argument that Cicero used the same smaller hand gestures that Quintilian describes in *Inst.* 11.3, even though he never refers to them explicitly.

80. Quintilian offers some suggestions on how specific Ciceronian passages can be scored with appropriate gestures or vocal phrasing; see, e.g., *Inst.* 11.3.166–67 on *Lig.* 6–7 and *Arch.* 19; and *Inst.* 11.3.47–51 on the opening sentences of *Pro Milone*. Yet, since some of the passages were never actually delivered by Cicero himself, these reconstructions must be little more than Quintilian's own speculation, presented for pedagogical purposes. See, e.g., his comments on the *Second Philippic* at *Inst.* 11.3.39; 11.3.167.

81. See, e.g., Wright (1931) 23–30; Laidlaw (1960); Wistrand (1992) 30–40; Edwards (1997); Ridgway Jones (2001); Fantham (2002).

82. Cf. *De or.* 1.129: *in artificio perquam tenui et levi.*

83. On these issues of masculinity, see Gleason (1995); Corbeill (1996) 128–73;

This prejudice finds a yet more extreme form of expression in the taunt launched at Hortensius by an opposing advocate: his highly mannered style of delivery resembled not even that of a (male) actor, but of a female mime-artist and dancing girl.[84]

Yet this was only half the story. Cicero in fact appreciated that acting and oratorical performance had much in common. From a technical perspective, there was a good deal to be learned by observing how the best actors of the day manipulated their audience.[85] Cicero evidently discussed such matters at length with the actor Roscius, who wrote a work comparing oratorical eloquence with the art of the actor (Macrob. *Sat.* 3.14.12: *ut librum conscriberet quo eloquentiam cum histrionia compararet*).[86] And in the first book of *De Oratore* (1.128) Cicero states explicitly that the orator needs the vocal power of tragic performers (*vox tragoedorum*) and gestures similar to those of the best actors (*gestus paene summorum actorum*).[87] Cicero thus clearly conceives of some sort of productive interplay between the two arts, although again precise details are lacking.[88] Nevertheless, his description of the style of delivery pursued by P. Sulpicius Rufus (tribune in 88 BCE) points generally to the way in which oratorical performance could be influenced positively by the stage (*Brut.* 203):

> *fuit enim Sulpicius vel maxime omnium, quos quidem ego audiverim, grandis et, ut ita dicam, tragicus orator. vox cum magna tum suavis et splendida; gestus*

---

Enders (1997); Richlin (1997); Gunderson (2000); Dugan (2005) 104–37; Connolly (2007).

84. Gell. *NA* 1.5.3: *non iam histrionem eum esse diceret, sed gesticulariam Dionysiamque eum notissimae saltatriculae nomine appellaret.* Cf. *Div. Caec.* 46; *Brut.* 303. See also Graf (1991) 44–47; Gunderson (2000) 128–30; Wisse (2013) 175–76.

85. See, e.g., Laidlaw (1960) 58: "Cicero never ceases to think of the pleader as some kind of an actor." Cf. Pöschl (1975) 206; Vasaly (1985) 2; Axer (1989) 299–300; Aldrete (1999) 67–84; Fantham (2002); Moretti (2004); Petrone (2004) 40–48; Dugan (2005) 133–37.

86. See also Plut. *Cic.* 5.4: λέγεται . . . τοῦτο μὲν Ῥωσκίῳ τῷ κωμῳδῷ, τοῦτο δ' Αἰσώπῳ τῷ τραγῳδῷ προσέχειν ἐπιμελῶς. ("Cicero is said . . . to have devoted conscientious attention to Roscius, the comic actor, on the one hand, and Aesop, the tragic actor, on the other.") On Roscius, see Fantham (2002), in particular 365: "it is not unlikely that some of Cicero's knowledge comes from private study of elocution with [Roscius] as a boy." Cf. Wright (1931) 16–20; Winniczuk (1961) 218–21; Dumont (2004).

87. Note that even here the qualification implicit in *paene* attests to Cicero's concern to maintain some distinction between the orator and the actor. Cf. the comments at Quint. *Inst.* 10.1.119 and 12.5.5; and Sen. *Controv.* 3, pref. 3 [on Cassius Severus]: *pronuntiatio quae histrionem posset producere, <nec> tamen quae histrionis posset videri.*

88. On the interplay between acting and oratory, see further Wright (1931) 10–22; Laidlaw (1960) 56–60; Fantham (2002) 367–69; Petrone (2004) 125–31.

*et motus corporis ita venustus ut tamen ad forum, non ad scaenam institutus videretur.*

[For, of all the orators whom I personally heard speak, Sulpicius was the most elevated in style and the most grandly theatrical (so to speak). His voice was powerful, but it also possessed charm and clarity. His gestures and comportment were graceful, yet appeared to be designed for the forum rather than the stage.]

Sulpicius, it seems, was able to strike the best possible balance between the artistry of the stage and the dignified comportment required of a speaker in the forum.[89] He succeeded in introducing a certain grand theatricality into his performances without compromising his masculinity. Cicero, we may suppose, aimed for a similarly judicious combination of qualities. As a youth, he avidly studied Sulpicius's performances in the forum,[90] and his inclusion of the man as an interlocutor in *De Oratore* further attests to his admiration for this style of oratory.

Thus, even though we lack detailed accounts of Cicero's skills as a performer, we can gain a decent enough general sense of how he went about the business of delivery. He seems to have been temperamentally inclined toward a vigorous and forceful manner, although he had learned as a mature speaker to temper this with a measured charm in voice and gesture, one informed by the style of those he saw on the stage. Presumably too he accompanied the high emotion evident in the perorations of his speeches with the calculated theatrics he had observed in the performances of mentors such as M. Antonius and Sulpicius Rufus. Such theatrics would have relied heavily upon a direct and active engagement with both the public audience and the jurors (such as he describes in his depiction of the star advocate at *Brut.* 290 quoted above). As we shall see in chapter four, at times this overt emotionality led him even to break down in tears.

Cicero's oratorical delivery, then, relied on a good deal more than the careful exploitation of voice and gesture. Indeed, it is revealing that he concludes his description of the star advocate with a further reference to the actor Roscius (*Brut.* 290): *ut qui haec procul videat, etiam si*

---

89. See Desmouliez (1976) 160; Krostenko (2001) 99; Steel (2002–3) 205. Several other orators did not strike this balance so well. Cf. Ridgway Jones (2001) 134 and 138.

90. On Cicero's close study of the style of Sulpicius, see *Brut.* 306: *tum P. Sulpici in tribunatu cotidie contionantis totum genus dicendi penitus cognovimus.* Cf. his description of the man's delivery at *De or.* 1.132, 2.88 and 3.31; also Malcovati (1976) 278–82; Leeman and Pinkster (1981) 89–90; 94–95; Fantham (2004) 99.

*quid agatur nesciat, at placere tamen et in scaena esse Roscium intellegat.* ("If someone were to watch these events at a distance, even if he did not know what was going on, he would nevertheless realize that the speaker was succeeding and that a Roscius was on stage.") One aim of the comparison is to portray this orator as a master of his craft, just as Roscius stood as the preeminent actor of his day.[91] But it also highlights the charismatic power of the skilled speaker. Amidst the often chaotic conditions of judicial hearings, the truly great orator was the one who could compel the audience's attention and keep them hanging on his every word. This skill was not one confined to the emotional peroration of a speech: Roscius in fact was as renowned for his comic performances as for his tragic ones.[92] Rather, it was the speaker's ability to charm and engage that was crucial. Cicero's accomplishments in this respect are now impossible to recreate; it remains significant, however, that he describes these more complex and elusive dynamics of performance by reference, not to rational precepts, but to the art of the actor.[93]

## CICERO AND THE *Genus Populare Dicendi*

Yet it is striking that Cicero does not approve of every form of oratorical theater. In *Brutus* in particular, he adopts a generally disparaging view of the showmanship deployed by orators pursuing a populist political agenda. (Cicero refers to this type of oratory as the *genus populare dicendi*.)[94] His assessment of L. Saturninus, for example, treats the man's style of delivery with disdain (*Brut.* 224):

> *seditiosorum omnium post Gracchos L. Appuleius Saturninus eloquentissimus visus est; magis specie tamen et motu atque ipso amictu capiebat homines quam aut dicendi copia aut mediocritate prudentiae.*

[Of all the politically disruptive speakers who followed the Gracchi, L. Appuleius Saturninus seemed the most eloquent. Yet he won men over

---

91. Cf. *De or.* 1.129–30; Douglas (1966) 214.

92. See Quint. *Inst.* 11.3.111; cf. *Q Rosc.* 20; *De or.* 2.242. For Roscius's performance of tragedy, see *De or.* 3.102.

93. On the Roman actor's energetic engagement with his audience, see *Att.* 2.19.3; 14.2.1; 16.2.3; *Sest.* 115–16. Cf. Wright (1931) 5–9; Leach (2000); Kaster (2009).

94. See, e.g., *Brut.* 247: *duo etiam Metelli, Celer et Nepos, nihil in causis versati, nec sine ingenio nec indocti, hoc erant populare dicendi genus adsecuti.* Cf. David (1980), who prefers the term *eloquentia popularis.*

more by his appearance, comportment and even his clothing, than by the fluency of his speech or the mediocre quality of his judgement.]

Evidently Saturninus used various nonverbal elements (*specie* / *motu* / *amictu*) to enhance the impact of his oratory; but Cicero brushes these devices aside with contempt. They are an unsatisfactory substitute (he suggests) for the more reputable qualities of *prudentia* and *copia dicendi*.[95] And yet it seems clear enough that such theatrical elements proved highly effective in certain oratorical contexts, and their use continued in the following decades. L. Quinctius, for example, the tribune of 74 BCE, apparently conducted his business wearing a long purple robe that extended to his ankles.[96] Julius Caesar too may have dabbled with this kind of showmanship.[97] There is then a certain inconsistency in Cicero's attitude: he himself energetically deploys theatrics in the courts, but he disapproves of their use by others in the political sphere. Presumably this double standard derives from his antipathy toward the radical populist goals of these orators. (Note, for example, his characterization of Saturninus as one of the *seditiosi*.)[98] When oratorical theatrics are used in the service of such disreputable ends, they deserve (in Cicero's view) little respect—and hence are not worthy of careful analysis.[99]

When it came to the courts, however, he felt fewer scruples. The point is best illustrated by a passage in *De Oratore*, in which the character of M. Antonius expresses disdain for those who eschew the use of theatrical

---

95. Cf. *Sest.* 105; Corbeill (1996) 165–67; Steel (2002–3) 204; Morstein-Marx (2004) 273. Cicero was too young to be able to base this portrait of Saturninus upon his own observations of the man. (Saturninus was killed when Cicero was only some six years old.) Cf. Broughton (1951) 576.

96. On Quinctius, see *Clu.* 111: *facite enim ut . . . vultum atque amictum atque etiam illam usque ad talos demissam purpuram recordemini.* Cf. *Brut.* 223; *Clu.* 74; 77; 90–91; 103; 108. Quinctius also engaged in judicial oratory, in one civil case speaking against Cicero; see Malcovati (1976) 349–54; Crawford (1984) 47–50; Alexander (1990) 86 (no. 173); David (1992) 772–73. See also David (1980) 184; Pina Polo (1996) 113–19.

97. See Morstein-Marx (2004) 273, who suggests that Julius Caesar's donning of a long-sleeved tunic may have had populist connotations.

98. On this *genus seditiosorum*, see Douglas (1966) 165–66; Rathofer (1986) 220–21.

99. Note that Cicero's disparagement of populist orators who enjoyed success among the mob raises an inconsistency with his claim elsewhere that the public audience is the best judge of a speaker's ability; see *Brut.* 183–200; Douglas (1966) xvi and 142. In general, Cicero undercuts the achievements of populist orators either by describing them in morally loaded terms (see, e.g., the terms *fervido . . . et petulanti et furioso* at *Brut.* 241 in connection with C. Staienus); or by depicting them as technically limited and therefore far short of the oratorical ideal. See, e.g., Atticus's comments at *Brut.* 244. Cf. Schenkeveld (1988); Dugan (2005) 204. On the association of *furor* with populist orators, see *Sest.* 99; Seager (1972) 328; Achard (1981) 242–47. Cf. Morstein-Marx (2004) 237–39; 271–72.

appeals. To prove his point, Antonius invokes the notorious example of P. Rutilius Rufus, who was convicted (probably in 94 BCE) when put on trial for corruption. Rutilius, he claims, actually contributed to the guilty verdict against him by refusing to allow emotional theatrics to be used in his defense (*De or.* 1.230):[100]

> *nemo ingemuit, nemo inclamavit patronorum, nihil cuiquam doluit, nemo est questus, nemo rem publicam imploravit, nemo supplicavit. quid multa? pedem nemo in illo iudicio supplosit, credo, ne Stoicis renuntiaretur.*

> [Not one of his advocates uttered a groan or protested, no one expressed distress, no one lamented, no one invoked the republic, no one engaged in entreaty. In short, no one in that trial even stamped his foot, scared stiff (I suppose) that he might be reported to the Stoics.]

Rather than admire Rutilius's adherence to ethical principle, Antonius presents him as hopelessly out of touch with the realities of the Roman courts. This style of pleading (he notes) might have been appropriate for the ideal world of Plato's *Republic* (*De or.* 1.230: *ut si illa commenticia Platonis civitate res ageretur*); but given the grubby realities of the Roman judicial system—where the jurors were themselves not immune to prejudice and vindictiveness—the astute advocate should feel no scruples about adopting a more vigorous and emotional manner.[101] Indeed, such techniques could even prevent injustice. Rutilius's unrealistic attitude (he claims) led to an innocent man (*De or.* 1.229: *ille vir exemplum, ut scitis, innocentiae*) being convicted (*De or.* 1.230: *nunc talis vir amissus est*).

Behind this argument we can perhaps discern a justification for Cicero's own use of theatrics. It is clear that he was well aware of the

---

100. See Alexander (1990) 49–50 (no. 94); Kallet-Marx (1990). According to Cicero, Rutilius declined offers of oratorical assistance from L. Crassus and M. Antonius, preferring to pursue instead a style of defense that concentrated upon sober argument rather than emotion (*De or.* 1.229; *Brut.* 115). Cotta and Mucius Scaevola spoke in his defense but did so in a restrained manner. Kallet-Marx (1990) 135–36 seems to me mistaken in rejecting Cicero's assertions that Crassus and Antonius offered their assistance to Rutilius; cf. Fantham (2004) 43–44. In my view, it is unlikely that Cicero would introduce such a fiction into his dialogue; moreover, it is risky to try to reconstruct the shifting political alliances of a period for which we possess very little evidence. The better documented later decades suggest that associations in the matter of lawsuits could be very fluid.

101. On the bias of the jurors in this particular trial, see *De or.* 1.230: *quamvis scelerati illi fuissent, sicuti fuerunt, pestiferi cives, supplicioque digni*. Elsewhere, in a criticism of Cato the Younger's similarly misplaced idealism, Cicero contrasts the man's high-minded principles with the cesspool of Roman politics (*Att.* 2.1.8: *in Romuli faece*). Cf. the general principle set out at Quint. *Inst.* 2.17.27.

long-standing academic arguments against such manipulation of the emotions.[102] Indeed, as we shall see, some of his contemporaries also probably criticized his exploitation of such techniques. But, for the hard-headed advocate, it was the final result that mattered.

Rutilius's trial also highlights the variety that existed in the styles of delivery practiced by Roman orators. Not every speaker relied on grand gestures and dramatic showmanship. C. Piso, for example, consul in 67 BCE, appears to have pursued a purposefully conversational mode of delivery (*Brut.* 239: *sermonis plenus*), with minimal movement of the body (*statarius*). We may suspect that this restrained style of performance did not prove especially successful at *contiones*, but evidently it was effective enough to enable him to secure elevation to the highest political office.[103]

Exactly how many of Cicero's contemporaries regularly exploited theatrics in their speeches is a question that I attempt to answer in chapter five. For the present discussion, it is enough simply to note that not everyone aimed to achieve the grand manner that seems to typify many of his own performances. Cicero himself, however, as we have seen, seems to have possessed both the talent and the inclination to engage in a highly dramatic mode of delivery. So let us turn now to examine two instances from early in his career as an advocate that illustrate more directly his keen eye for a theatrical opportunity. As we shall see, these examples also raise several methodological issues that need to be addressed before we can undertake our more detailed studies.

## PART 4: TWO EARLY EXAMPLES OF JUDICIAL THEATER

### PRO ROSCIO AMERINO

From a brief remark toward the beginning of Cicero's speech on behalf of Roscius Amerinus, we learn that the defendant arrived at the trial surrounded by a bodyguard (*praesidium*) (*Rosc. Am.* 13):

> *accusant ii qui hunc ipsum iugulare summe cupierunt, causam dicit is qui etiam ad hoc ipsum iudicium cum praesidio venit ne hic ibidem ante oculos vestros trucidetur.*

---

102. See Vickers (1988), both on the Platonic background and Cicero's response to it.

103. On C. Calpurnius Piso, see Broughton (1952) 142–43; Malcovati (1976) 354–55; Douglas (1966) 175–76. Cicero defended Piso in 63 *de repetundis*. See Alexander (1990) 112 (no. 225). On actors described as *statarii*, see also *Brut.* 116.

[The very men who desperately wished to murder my client are here in the role of accusers. This man is the defendant—he who came even to this present trial accompanied by a bodyguard, so that he wouldn't be slaughtered on this very spot in front of your eyes.]

The detail well demonstrates Cicero's highly developed sense of theater. Through this deftly orchestrated entrance into the forum, he could portray Roscius—who had been accused of murdering his father—as the target of violence rather than its perpetrator. This first impression was important. Cicero could anticipate that the opposing advocate would try to depict Roscius as a scheming assassin;[104] he therefore attempts to shape the jurors' view of the man before the prosecutor has even stood up to speak. Indeed, the scene provided an effective visual representation of the menacing *potentia* that, according to Cicero, Chrysogonus and his cronies were exerting on the case.[105] Roscius appears as a vulnerable victim, physically intimidated by these powerful opponents.

The bodyguard—which presumably consisted of various friends, freedmen, and slaves, some perhaps supplied by Caecilia Metella— served a further function as well.[106] As far as we can tell, Roscius seems to have been in the unfortunate position of having few family relatives available to accompany him to court. By the time of the trial, his sole brother was dead, and his mother (for some reason, not necessarily suspicious) receives little mention in the proceedings.[107] Worse, there is no sign of a wife or children standing loyally at his side.[108] Cicero was thus unable to present the defendant sympathetically as one who belonged to a loving but distressed family that deserved the jurors' pity. (See further discus-

---

104. From Cicero's speech, we can infer that Erucius the prosecutor depicted Roscius as a brooding and aggrieved son, banished to the family's country estates by his father. See, e.g., *Rosc. Am.* 40; 52; 75; cf. Vasaly (1985) 4–10; Dyck (2010) 121; 139; 199.

105. For references to the abuse of *potentia*, see *Rosc. Am.* 35; 60; 122. Cf. Dyck (2010) 66. Kinsey (1980) 184 offers a reverse reading of Cicero's claims: "Chrysogonus' *potentia*, then, was much inferior to that supporting Roscius." Cf. Kinsey (1985) 189.

106. Cf. Dyck (2010) 77. On the use of bodyguards and *praesidia* in politics, see Lintott (1999) 83–85; 90–92. See also the bodyguard provided for jurors during the Bona Dea trial (*Att.* 1.16.5; Plut. *Cic.* 29.6); but there is a difference between the use of a *praesidium* to make sure that a trial runs without disruption, and the use to protect the accused from his private enemies. Cf. Asc. *Corn.* 60C: *praesidebant ei iudicio.*

107. Kinsey (1985) 194 regards the apparent absence of Roscius's mother from his side as suspicious; cf. Dyck (2003) 236. Note, however, the observation by Seager (2007) 900: "The absence of distraught and weeping relatives, in particular Roscius' mother, is indeed noteworthy. But explanations are possible." The woman is mentioned directly only at *Rosc. Am.* 96, a reference that suggests she was still alive when her husband was murdered.

108. Cf. Kinsey (1985) 192; Dyck (2010) 198.

sion in chapter three.) His orchestration of the bodyguard, then, at least allowed him to generate some sort of emotional response to Roscius's entrance into the forum; it cleverly repackaged the man's *lack* of relatives as something pitiable, with Roscius arriving in court bereft of loved ones and fearful for his life.[109]

Cicero did not need to draw upon the rhetorical handbooks for this strategy; as we have seen, such stunts were common currency among Roman aristocrats. Roscius's bodyguard reminds us in some respects of Tiberius Gracchus's ostentatiously concealed dagger: both were designed to draw attention to the supposed threats and intimidation against them. Indeed, Cicero himself deployed a similar device during his consulship in 63, when, following an aggressive speech by Catiline in the senate, he appeared in the Campus Martius with a breastplate clearly visible beneath his tunic (*Mur.* 52):

> *descendi in campum cum firmissimo praesidio fortissimorum virorum et cum illa lata insignique lorica, non quae me tegeret . . . verum ut omnes boni animadverterent et, cum in metu et periculo consulem viderent, id quod est factum, ad opem praesidiumque concurrerent.*

> [I went down to the Campus Martius with a very strong bodyguard of the bravest men and that broad and conspicuous breastplate of mine, not with the idea that it would protect me . . . but so that all respectable men would take notice, and when they saw the consul in fear and danger would rush together to provide help and protection—which is exactly what happened.][110]

Cicero here acknowledges quite openly the theatrical nature of the stunt: it was deliberately contrived to stir up indignation at Catiline's supposed threats against the state. Such political savoir faire is not remarkable perhaps in a consul; but Cicero's use of such a device in his first major criminal defense points to a remarkable poise and astuteness in the young advocate.

---

109. Evidently Roscius was able to muster a few family acquaintances (*Rosc. Am.* 49: *ex his propinquis eius*); but Cicero's lack of specificity in this description suggests that he felt unable to generate much sympathy from them. Likewise, several prominent individuals attended court to support Roscius (*Rosc. Am.* 1: *homines nobilissimi*); but, although their presence lent his cause some much-needed *auctoritas*, their emotive potential appears to have been limited.

110. See also Plut. *Cic.* 14.7–8; Dio Cass. 37.29.3–4.

## CICERO AND THE YOUNGER JUNIUS

Our second example comes from Cicero's prosecution of Verres in 70 BCE. One of the many accusations laid against Verres was that he had swindled money from the inheritance of a young boy named Junius following the death of his father. During the first hearing, Junius's uncle gave evidence in support of this allegation; as he did so, Cicero arranged for Junius to stand nearby (*Verr.* 2.1.151):

> *hic etiam priore actione Q. Hortensius pupillum Iunium praetextatum venisse in vestrum conspectum et stetisse cum patruo testimonium dicente questus est, et me populariter agere atque invidiam commovere, quod puerum producerem, clamitavit.*

[I might add that, at this point in the course of the first hearing, Q. Hortensius complained about the fact that young Junius came before you dressed in the *toga praetexta* and stood with his uncle while the latter was giving evidence, and loudly protested that, by bringing the boy into court, I was conducting the case in a demagogic fashion and arousing hostility against his client.]

Hortensius's objections suggest that this stagecraft was unusual. As we shall see, Cicero uses children as oratorical props in several of his perorations; but this is our only example of the device being deployed during the presentation of evidence by witnesses. There was perhaps good reason then for Hortensius's consternation. Moreover, his barb about Cicero's demagoguery (*me populariter agere*) may have had a more specific reference. A few years earlier, another Junius (C. Junius, aedile in 75), when put on trial at a *iudicium populi*, had brought in front of the crowd his weeping son.[111] It may well have been this event that enabled Hortensius to brand Cicero's stunt a cheap trick typical of those who stirred up the mob.[112] Whatever the case, there is an irony in Hortensius's claim that Cicero was pleading *populariter*. As we have seen, Cicero later in his career expresses disdain for such techniques. It is clear, however, that in

---

111. See *Clu.* 137: *idem [sc. populus] C. Iuni fili, pueri parvuli, lacrimis commotus maximo clamore et concursu totam illam legem et quaestionem repudiavit.* For the trial (in 74 BCE), see Alexander (1990) 77 (no. 153). In the end, Junius was convicted and fined (*Clu.* 91: *his de causis C. Iunius condemnatus est*).

112. Cf. Dyck (2008) 152: "[Hortensius] wanted to suggest to the senatorial jury that his opponent was engaged in demagoguery that could pose a danger to ordered society." Cf. David (1980) 185; Chinnici (2006) 222.

the prosecution of Verres, he was willing to experiment with new and different forms of judicial theater.

Cicero's published account of this incident raises an important methodological issue. If we can take his words at face value, evidently he also arranged for the young Junius to attend the trial without a *bulla* around his neck. Traditionally the *bulla* (a kind of amulet) provided an assertion of a boy's free-born status, and was laid aside only when he assumed the *toga virilis*.[113] Such an item often possessed a strong sentimental value within the family—a token bestowed by a proud Roman father upon his beloved son. Cicero, it appears, cleverly exploited these emotional connotations in his presentation of Junius at the trial (*Verr.* 2.1.152):

> *neque te tam commovebat quod ille cum toga praetexta, quam quod sine bulla venerat. vestitus enim neminem commovebat is quem illi mos et ius ingenuitatis dabat; quod ornamentum pueritiae pater dederat, indicium atque insigne fortunae, hoc ab isto praedone ereptum esse graviter tum et acerbe homines ferebant.*

[Nor was it the fact that [Junius] came in the *toga praetexta* that disturbed you [Hortensius], so much as the fact that he came without his *bulla*. For the clothing [i.e. the *toga praetexta*] that convention and the privileges of free birth entitled him to wear bothered no one, but people were seriously and indeed bitterly upset that the childhood ornament his father had given him, as a sign and symbol of good fortune, had been snatched from him by this plundering thief.]

By claiming that Verres had stripped the boy even of this precious trinket, Cicero neatly transforms the alleged fraud into dastardly rapacity.

Yet can we really believe this detail? Since the speeches in the second *actio* of the *Verrines* were never actually delivered, it is possible that the published text here incorporates a good deal of literary fiction. Indeed, this issue applies more generally to Cicero's orations as a whole. How closely do our surviving texts of the speeches reflect what Cicero actually said (and did) on the day of their performance?

This question is a familiar one to Ciceronian scholars, and in recent decades a generally optimistic consensus seems to have emerged. Most agree that, although the extant texts on occasion contain deliberate omissions and additions that cause them to diverge from what Cicero actually said, for the most part they provide a fair representation of the

---

113. See Saglio (1877) 755. Cf. Sebesta (1994) 47; Dolansky (2008).

main arguments and events of the trial.[114] This conclusion is in a sense double-edged. The acknowledgment that *some* passages are indeed inventions or additions opens the door for critics to challenge the authenticity of any specific detail in particular. On the other hand, the assertion that the published texts are *generally* accurate imposes limits on the degree to which such skepticism can be taken.

Overall, this general accuracy places the burden of proof squarely upon those who wish to assert the existence of an invention in any given passage. If no specific evidence can be adduced for supposing a fabrication, the text ought to be taken as a reliable guide to the action that took place in court. Thus, in the following chapters, when Cicero in a text represents himself as (for example) embracing the defendant during a peroration, I have assumed—unless there is some specific reason for doubt—that this action did indeed take place.[115]

In fact, a more significant obstacle to our understanding of Cicero's judicial theater is that his speeches tend to provide *only an outline* of the physical actions that must have taken place. Our texts generally abbreviate events to just one or two dramatic moments—an embrace, perhaps, or the shedding of a tear. Intervening actions are often omitted. This compression is not in itself surprising. During the actual speech, there was no need for Cicero to give a running commentary on the actions that jurors could see in front of them; nor, when writing up the text for publication, would he have felt obliged to provide minutely detailed stage directions for Roman readers familiar with the practices of the courts. And yet, for the present study, the absence of such details is frustrating. At the end of *Pro Caelio*, for example, we may suspect that Caelius and his father engaged in some sort of physical action as Cicero concluded his speech (see discussion in chapter three); but such details are not stated explicitly. In such cases, my method has been to start from examples where the evidence is more secure, and to base conjectures regarding other instances on these, noting clearly at what point firm evidence fails us.

---

114. The important but often overstated observations of Humbert (1925) have been challenged and modified by various scholars; see e.g. Laurand (1938) 1–23; Settle (1962) 60–67; Stroh (1975) 31–54; Riggsby (1999) 178–84; Alexander (2002) 15–26; Powell and Paterson (2004) 52–57; Manuwald (2007) 54–90; Lintott (2008) 19–32; Gildenhard (2011) 14.

115. Cf. Powell and Paterson (2004) 57: "Treated (as was the practice of antiquity) as scripts for performance, [the published speeches] would provide a plausible reconstruction of Cicero's pleading on each particular occasion, and there is certainly no reason why we cannot take them generically as evidence for the kinds of strategies, arguments and rhetorical techniques that Cicero would have employed in an actual court."

There are other methodological limitations as well. Since most of Cicero's judicial speeches were delivered on behalf of the defense, our information on his technique is biased toward this perspective. (His prosecution of Verres naturally redresses the balance a little, but the general problem remains.) As we shall see in chapter five, it is also difficult to compare Cicero's practices with those of his contemporaries. Because only a few fragments remain from the speeches of other advocates, it is all too easy to view Cicero as Rome's main exponent of judicial theatrics. A few isolated incidents, however, suggest that the situation was rather more complex. Nevertheless, as I hope to show, the texts of Cicero's speeches, when combined with other assorted testimonia, allow us to draw some worthwhile conclusions about his use of judicial theatrics, in particular his exploitation of dirtied clothes (*sordes*), gestures of entreaty, and tears.

CHAPTER 2

A SORDID BUSINESS

The Use of "Mourning Clothes"
in the Courts

At modern trials, we often see defendants dressing up smartly for their
appearances in court. This formal attire usually aims to convey an image of the accused as one who respects the authority of the judge and
jurors, and who adheres to society's rules. At times, this mask may slip a
little, especially if the defendant seems entirely ill at ease with this type
of dress. Yet the practice persists, presumably because lawyers believe it
is effective in shaping the attitudes of the jury.[1] But if the modern defendant's attire aims at an impression of safe conformity, Roman practices
suggest a starkly different mentality. Aristocrats on trial in ancient Rome
usually appeared in court dressed in filthy clothes (*sordes*), with beard
and hair untrimmed.[2] Evidently the goal was not to blend in but to stand
out. There is an obvious theatricality to this garb that calls for close ex-
amination.[3]

It is easy perhaps to assume that the main purpose of the defendant's

---

1. Cf. Mortimer (1983) 258; Hall (1995) 52; Bers (2009) 70–71. On Quintilian's advice regarding the neatness of dress required of the Roman advocate (rather than defendant), see *Inst.* 11.3.137–49; 156; 160–61.

2. This was the typical form of dress at trials when the charges were particularly serious. See, e.g., Kaster (2009) 312: "It had become customary, for example, for a defendant
in a 'capital' trial, where his 'life as a citizen' (*caput*) was at stake, to 'change garments'
(*vestem mutare*)." It is not clear, however, how far the practice extended to other proceedings in court. The phrase *ne . . . quidem* at Suet. *Tib.* 2.4 may suggest that such attire was
appropriate in cases where the charges were less serious (*ne capitis quidem quisquam reus*).
Cf. Greenidge (1901) 472.

3. This aspect of Roman trials is treated only briefly in traditional commentaries; see,
e.g., Austin (1960) 49; Nisbet (1961) 159. It has received greater attention, however, in
recent decades. See, e.g., Heskel (1994) 141–45; Flaig (2003) 101–2; Kaster (2006) 111;
177–78; 181–82; Edmondson (2008) 30–31; Blonski (2008). Blonski's assertion (see pages 53–55) that *sordes* paradoxically ended up being the normal attire of the Roman aristocrat seems to me more piquant than plausible.

dress was to assist with appeals to pity made during the trial.[4] But in fact, as we shall see, Cicero draws relatively little attention to such attire during his perorations. To this extent, then, it was not usually integrated with the text of the advocate's speech. Rather, it contributed to the visual theatrics that took place during the trial *as a whole*—and indeed to the social and political dramas in which individuals engaged even before the proceedings in court began.

## A HISTORY OF *Sordes*

The custom of donning *sordes* had a long tradition in Roman culture prior to its association with courts of law. Its origins lie in the context of (literal) bereavement. Upon hearing the news of an acquaintance's death, Roman men regularly donned darkened clothes and refrained from trimming their hair and beard.[5] The Latin terms *squalor* and *sordes* attest to the soiled and disshevelled state that the mourner achieved, as do the associated adjectives *sordidatus, squalidus,* and *obsoletus*.[6] It is not entirely clear how this soiled appearance was produced. It may be that the clothes were deliberately smeared with dirt, but given the squalid conditions of ancient Rome, their unkempt condition may have followed readily enough if the bereaved did not change into clean garments for several days.[7] Wealthy men typically possessed a specially darkened toga (the *toga pulla*) for use on specific ceremonial occasions;[8] but donning

---

4. See, e.g., Dyck (2012) 161: "in order to appeal to the jurors' pity in the peroration"; and 164: "a routine appeal to pity in the peroration." Cf. Blonski (2008) 50.

5. See Kübler (1927); Herzog-Hauser (1937); Blonski (2008) 44. This rejection of cosmetic concerns probably reflects the psychological rupture regularly experienced by the bereaved. The distress caused by death often leads to the neglect of routine matters, such as the daily attention given to dress. Cf. Olson (2007) 100: "The essence of mourning, then, was ideally to demonstrate grief by a lack of interest in personal appearance."

6. Cf. *OLD*, s.v. *sordes*, 1a; *squalor*, 2a; *obsoletus*, 1b. See also Herzog-Hauser (1937) cols. 2229–31; Heskel (1994) 141–45; Kaster (2006) 111; Blonski (2008) 46–47. Freyburger-Galland (1993) discusses the Greek terms used by Dio Cassius.

7. The term *sordida veste* is on occasion associated with the grimy work clothes of the lower classes; see, e.g., Calp. *Ecl.* 7.26–27: *venimus ad sedes ubi pulla sordida veste / inter femineas spectabat turba cathedras*; cf. Sen. *De Ira* 3.35.5: *maiorem partem occurrentium squalidam*; Edmondson (2008) 33.

8. See Dessau (1954) 37 (no. 139, line 18) for an inscription from Pisa concerning the rites to be carried out in recognition of the death of L. Caesar in 2 CE (*togis pullis amictos*). This ceremonial context may not be quite the same as that of public mourning involving all citizens, as mentioned in Dessau (1954) 38 (no. 140, line 23) with the phrase *cunctos veste mutata*. Cf. Edmondson (2008) 30. For the phrase *toga pulla*, see also *Vat.* 30

such a toga for a single formal event was a practice distinct from adopting *sordes* for an extended period of time.[9] Since the mourning period could continue for several weeks, these dirtied clothes would have included the tunic as well as the toga.

This garb also came to be used to signal a person's distress at misfortunes other than actual death. Livy, for example, depicts the bereft parents of the kidnapped Sabine women as dressing *in sordibus* and making an appeal to their king, Titus Tatius.[10] This attire presumably helped to convey the extent of their distress and so added urgency to their request. Although we may doubt the historical veracity of Livy's account, it is plausible enough that the association of this attire with appeals, requests, and supplication had existed for several centuries before the Late Republic.[11] This association was certainly strong in Cicero's time and provides the most straightforward justification for the use of this attire in the courts: the defendant demonstrates his distress at the present accusation and seeks assistance from the jury.[12]

It remains to be seen, however, how far Cicero actually exploits this convention in his defense speeches. Moreover, at times the act of donning *sordes* could have a more provocative and aggressive dimension to it. This aspect is well illustrated by an episode involving M. Livius Salinator, consul in 219 BCE. Having celebrated a triumph for his victories over the Illyrians, Salinator was later prosecuted for keeping too large a share of the campaign spoils for himself.[13] His conviction was secured in part

and 31. The precise color of this garment may have ranged from black to dark grey or brown. See Olson (2007) 100–6; also Herzog-Hauser (1937) cols. 2229–31.

9. See Heskel (1994) 141: "It has often been assumed that the word *sordes* was simply another term for the *toga pulla*, but scrutiny of the contexts in which the two terms appear suggests that Cicero did not use them interchangeably."

10. See Livy 1.10.1: *at raptarum parentes tum maxime sordida veste lacrimisque et querellis civitates concitabant.*

11. For other examples (possibly historical retrojections as well), see, e.g., Livy 3.47.1 (where Verginius in 449 BCE is *sordidatus* in order to protest against the actions of Appius Claudius with regard to his daughter Verginia); and 3.58.1 (where C. Claudius is *sordidatus*). On Livy and historical retrojection, see n. 4 in chapter one. The example at Sen. *Controv.* 10.1 suggests the continuation of this basic social practice through the centuries.

12. On the use of mourning clothes in conjunction with the courts and supplication, see [Caes.] *B. Alex.* 67.1: *reorum habitu supplex ad Caesarem venit.* Cf. Naiden (2006) 58–59. See also *Sest.* 27, where Cicero alludes to conventional uses of *sordes* in connection with *deprecatio* ("a plea for mercy") and *luctus* ("grief"). Kaster (2006) 182 sees in these two terms an antithesis between "formality and passion." It is possible, however, that Cicero is more concerned in this passage to play down the submissive element that *deprecatio* could involve, and to stress instead the connection with grief.

13. See Livy 27.34.4 and 29.37.4. On Salinator's career, see Münzer (1927); Brough-

through the testimony given against him by C. Claudius Nero.[14] The incident provoked a bitter enmity between the two men, and, following his payment of a fine, Salinator sullenly withdrew from politics to live a life of solitude in the country (Livy 27.34.4: *quam ignominiam adeo aegre tulerat ut rus migrarit et per multos annos et urbe et omni coetu careret hominum*).[15] When, some seven years later, he was eventually persuaded to reenter the political arena, his resentment still simmered. In a curmudgeonly piece of political theater, he went about his business in Rome dressed in dirtied clothes, and with beard and hair uncut (Livy 27.34.5: *veste obsoleta capilloque et barba promissa*). As Livy notes, there was a deliberately provocative intent to this gesture: Salinator wanted to advertise his continued sense of grievance at the disgrace inflicted upon him (Livy 27.34.5: *prae se ferens in vultu habituque insignem memoriam ignominiae acceptae*).[16] Indeed, the censors regarded this behavior as so disruptive that they eventually forced him to desist (Livy 27.34.6: *censores eum tonderi et squalorem deponere coegerunt*).[17]

As Andrew Lintott has noted, this use of *sordes* as an assertive form of protest functioned in effect as a visual version of *quiritatio*—the process by which an individual on the streets of Rome verbally invoked protection against the unjust actions of another.[18] Going around the community dressed *in sordibus* thus not only helped to advertise an individual's distress but also was meant to provoke indignation at his (or her) plight. Indeed, the later restrictions on this kind of behavior noted in the *Digest* make explicit reference to its ability to stir up *invidia* against an opponent.[19] This aggressive element takes on particular significance in the

---

ton (1951) 236. On Livy's likely sources for this period, see Campbell (1926) xvi–xxi; Walsh (1973) 38–42.

14. See Livy 29.37.10: *quod falsum adversus se testimonium dixisset*; Val. Max. 4.2.2: *testimonio eius praecipue adflictus*. Cf. Epstein (1987) 13.

15. Cf. Val. Max. 4.2.2: *Neronis odio ardens in exsilium profectus fuerat*.

16. Salinator was also bitterly critical of the Roman people's collaboration in this supposed injustice; see Livy 27.34.12 (*levitatem civitatis accusans*); cf. 29.37.13–16.

17. Salinator and Claudius Nero were in fact pressured into an uneasy alliance as consuls for 207 BCE. See Livy 27.34.15: *adnisi omnes cum C. Claudio M. Livium consulem fecerunt*. Cf. Val. Max. 4.2.2; 7.2.6a; Broughton (1951) 294. Their joint censorship in 204 BCE, however, saw a reemergence of their earlier acrimony (Livy 29.37.8–17).

18. See Lintott (1999) 20, and wider discussion at 11–21. Cf. the interesting observations of Wray (2001) 129–43.

19. See *Dig.* 47.10.15.27: *haec autem fere sunt quae ad infamiam alicuius fiunt: ut puta ad invidiam alicuius veste lugubri utitur, aut squalida, aut si barbam demittat, vel capillos submittat, aut si carmen conscribat, vel proponat, vel cantet aliquod quod pudorem alicuius laedat*. Cf. Sen. *Controv.* 10.1; Blonski (2008) 42–43.

feud-driven conflicts of Roman politics. As we saw in chapter one, by the time of Tiberius Gracchus, the use of *sordes* as an expression of political grievance had grown in scale: his opponents donned this attire en masse and then processed through the forum. Such a display could perhaps have been depicted as a humble petition of the people; but in this fraught conflict, it would also have served to inflame passions and present an intimidating show of force. Tiberius's own use of *sordes* in front of the assembly a short while later served precisely the same function. The use of this attire thus became closely associated with the advertisement of political grievances and the rallying of personal support.[20]

By Cicero's time, such posturing was a familiar part of the agonistic political landscape. In early 62 BCE, for example, Q. Metellus Celer adopted *sordes* to protest against the treatment of his close relative, Metellus Nepos, who had just been stripped of his tribunician powers by the senate. (Presumably Nepos himself had donned such garb as well.)[21] In 59 BCE, Vatinius in his role as tribune of the people seems to have donned *sordes* in protest against the *supplicatio* awarded to Pomptinus, governor of Gallia Narbonensis, since this honor threatened to eclipse the achievements in Gaul of Caesar (Vatinius's ally).[22] And in 56 BCE, Lentulus Spinther the Younger dressed in this fashion in reaction to the attempts of the tribune C. Cato to deprive his father of the Cilician provincial command.[23]

---

20. For other uses in the following decades, see Diod. Sic. 36.15 (on Saturninus); and App. *B Civ.* 1.67 on Marius in 87 BCE; cf. Gran. Lic. 35.8 in Criniti (1981) 13.

21. *Fam.* 5.1.2: *itaque in luctu et squalore sum.* As Shackleton Bailey (1977) 276 notes, earlier commentators preferred to interpret this remark as metaphoric exaggeration rather than a literal statement regarding Celer's dress. On the dress of the senate during this period, see discussion below.

22. See *Vat.* 30–31, with the comments of the Scholia Bobiensia at Stangl (1912) 149 (line 26)—150 (line 5); cf. Pocock (1926) 118. In this instance we catch a glimpse of Vatinius's political imperative clashing with the day-to-day expectations of social protocol. Cicero at *Vat.* 30–31 mocks Vatinius for attending a post-funeral banquet in a *toga pulla*, when the custom seems to have been for guests at this point in proceedings to lay aside their mourning garb. Vatinius, however, evidently preferred political consistency over ceremonial etiquette; cf. Heskel (1994) 141.

23. *Q Fr.* 2.3.1: *C. Cato legem promulgavit de imperio Lentuli abrogando. vestitum filius mutavit.* Over time, the practice of donning *sordes* became familiar enough that it could be described using this more general phrase *vestem mutare*. Cf. McGushin (1992) 212 on Sall. *Hist.* 2.44, who refers to *vestem mutare* as the "technical term." Occasionally this phrase's lack of specificity creates the potential for confusion. At times of military emergency, for example, the Roman people sometimes collectively donned military cloaks in preparation for battle, a practice occasionally referred to simply as changing garb. See, e.g., *Phil.* 14.2: *vestitus mutetur*; Sen. *Ep.* 18.2: *in tumultu et tristi tempore civitatis . . . vestem mutavimus.* The more usual phrases, however, are *saga sumere* and *ad saga iretur*. See, e.g., *Phil.* 5.31; 6.2; 8.6; Livy *Per.* 72; Vell. Pat. 2.16.4. Cf. Marshall (1984). See the useful summary in Edmondson (2008) 26–32.

CICERO, *Sordes*, AND POLITICAL THEATER

Cicero himself was an ambitious exponent of this form of political theater during his conflict with Clodius during the first months of 58 BCE.[24]
As Clodius's attempts to drive him into exile gained momentum, Cicero's
allies rallied in a massed display of support.[25] A large number of equestrians donned *sordes*, paraded through the streets of Rome, and petitioned
the consul Gabinius prior to a meeting of the senate in the Temple of
Concord.[26] Our view of events is distorted by Cicero's rhetoric: in one
speech he refers to a crowd of remarkable size drawn from the entire city
and the whole of Italy (*Sest.* 26: *incredibilis in Capitolium multitudo ex tota
urbe cunctaque Italia*); in another he puts the number at twenty thousand
strong (*Red. pop.* 8: *praeterea viginti milia vestem mutaverunt*).[27] Whatever
the exact number, the protest seems to have constituted an impressive
mobilization of forces, although, as we have seen, such massed demon-
strations were nothing new in Rome.

More innovative in fact was the coordination of this stunt with a motion initiated in the senate that all its members should likewise adopt *sordes* (*Sest.* 26):. . . *L. Ninnius ad senatum de re publica rettulit, senatusque fre-
quens vestem pro mea salute mutandam censuit.* (". . . Lucius Ninnius brought
the issue before the senate as a matter pertaining to the public interest,
and a packed meeting of the senate voted to don *sordes* for the sake of
my well-being.")[28] There was a recent precedent for this proposal. Dio

---

24. On events leading up to Cicero's exile, see most conveniently Tatum (1999) 151–
56; Kelly (2006) 110–25.

25. Dio Cass. 38.16.2–3 reports that Hortensius and Curio were leading figures in
the organization of this stunt, although whether he refers here to the elder consulars or
their respective sons is debated. See Tatum (1999) 154–55 and 299, n. 22; Morstein-Marx
(2004) 166, n. 23.

26. See *Sest.* 26; *Red. pop.* 8; Dio Cass. 38.16.4. Cf. *Red. sen.* 12; 31. Dio states that
Gabinius did not allow the equestrian deputation to enter the temple. If this was the case,
presumably there was an encounter on the steps of the temple, after which Gabinius refused the equestrians entry to the debate. Cf. Kaster (2006) 179.

27. Lintott (2008) 177 suggests that the figure "presumably represents Cicero's esti-
mate of the total number of senators and *equites* combined." Cf. Plut. *Cic.* 31.1. See also
*Red. sen.* 12: *cunctique mutassetis*. Cicero states explicitly that this change of attire consisted
of *sordes* (*Red. sen.* 12): *multitudo . . . sordidata venisset*. Berry (2003) has plausibly explained
why Cicero was able to gather support from the equestrian class; its full extent on this occasion, however, must remain a matter of speculation.

28. Plut. *Cic.* 31.1 depicts Clodius as surrounding this senate-meeting with armed men
(Κλωδίου δὲ σιδηροφορουμένου περὶ τὸ βουλευτήριον); but as Moles (1988) 177 notes, we
have no other authority for this. It may be that Clodius took no direct part in the meeting
(and hence did not veto the motion) because he preferred to fight his battles in front of
the people. Indeed, he convened a *contio* shortly after, which some of Cicero's supporters
attended. See *Sest.* 27; Dio Cass. 38.16.5; Kaster (2006) 183.

reports that in January 62 BCE the senate collectively dressed in mourning in order to signal their disapproval of the violence recently provoked by the tribune Metellus Nepos; they also voted to give emergency powers to the consuls.[29] The situation, then, was framed as a matter of national crisis, and this too may have been how Ninnius attempted to depict the situation in 58 BCE (note the phrase *de re publica rettulit*).

In this case, however, even though the proposal secured enough votes to pass, it did not gain the approval of the consuls. Indeed, Gabinius attended the next meeting of the senate in his usual magistrate's attire (the *toga praetexta*) and issued a consular edict requiring senators to put aside their *sordes*.[30] This response can be attributed in large part to the consuls' general support for Clodius and antipathy toward Cicero.[31] Yet there was also a principle at stake that would have furnished a plausible pretext for their objections (one that Cicero naturally chooses not to mention): Ninnius's proposal and its implementation of collective *sordes* threatened to turn meetings of the senate into a venue for the assertion of factional interests. The line between national emergency and partisan policy was at risk of becoming ever more blurred.[32]

These stunts, when considered together, form an ambitious piece of political theater. By combining a massed street protest *in sordibus* with an attempted public supplication of the consul and a provocative senatorial decree, Cicero and his allies extended and enlivened familiar forms of showmanship. Indeed, their focus on the equestrian and senatorial echelons was a shrewd strategy given Clodius's manipulation of the popular assembly. Unfortunately for Cicero, however, these actions did little to disrupt the progress of Clodius's legislation, and he was soon forced to engage in more extreme measures. If we can trust the details in our later sources, he seems first to have made individual petitions to prominent aristocrats (τούς τι δυναμένους), probably at their

29. Dio Cass. 37.43.3: οἱ βουλευταὶ συνῆλθον . . . καὶ τά τε ἱμάτια ἠλλάξαντο καὶ τοῖς ὑπάτοις τὴν φυλακὴν τῆς πόλεως . . . ἐπέτρεψαν. Cf. Plut. *Cat. Min.* 26.2–29.2. In 56 BCE the senate deployed a similar technique to try to intimidate the tribune C. Cato (Livy *Per.* 105): *cum C. Catonis tribuni plebis intercessionibus comitia tollerentur, senatus vestem mutavit.* Cf. Dio Cass. 39.27–28.

30. See *Sest.* 32: *cum subito edicunt duo consules ut ad suum vestitum senatores redirent*; cf. *Red. sen.* 12.

31. On Clodius's relationship with Piso and Gabinius, see Tatum (1999) 152–53.

32. Cicero himself acknowledged as much several years later after his return from exile. At *Planc.* 87 he boasts that this was the only occasion on which the senate changed its garb for the sake of a single individual (*pro me uno*). For another curious—and evidently unsuccessful—attempt to exploit *sordes* in the senate, see the incident involving Pompey and Crassus when consuls in 55 BCE, reported at Dio Cass. 39.39.2–3.

private houses on occasions such as the morning reception (Dio Cass. 38.14.7):[33]

καὶ τὴν βουλευτικὴν ἐσθῆτα ἀπορρίψας ἐν τῇ ἱππάδι περιενόστει, πάντας τε τούς τι δυναμένους, οὐχ ὅπως τῶν ἐπιτηδείων ἀλλὰ καὶ τῶν ἀντιστασιωτῶν, καὶ μάλιστα τόν τε Πομπήιον καὶ τὸν Καίσαρα . . . ἐθεράπευε.

[In particular, Cicero discarded his senatorial garb and went about in equestrian dress, trying to solicit support from all those who had any influence, not only among his friends but also among his opponents, and most of all . . . Pompey and Caesar.]

According to this account, then, Cicero did not adopt *sordes* for these petitions but chose instead a less extreme form of self-degradation that involved setting aside his senatorial insignia (a practice sometimes followed in other contexts of mourning).[34] These attempts to mobilize support, however, seem to have achieved little, and he went on to essay a yet more drastic strategy: public appeal on the streets of Rome dressed *in sordibus*.

It was a decision that Cicero came to regret, and he appears to have carefully omitted all references to these events in his later published accounts of the period. An anguished comment in a private letter to Atticus, however, hints at the disastrous consequences (*Att.* 3.15.5): *caeci, caeci inquam, fuimus in vestitu mutando, in populo rogando.* ("We were blind, blind, I say, in changing our dress and making appeal to the people.") Fortunately for us, Plutarch fills in some of the details (Plut. *Cic.* 30.6–7):[35]

κινδυνεύων οὖν καὶ διωκόμενος ἐσθῆτά τε μετήλλαξε καὶ κόμης ἀνάπλεως περιιὼν ἱκέτευε τὸν δῆμον. πανταχοῦ δ᾽ ὁ Κλώδιος ἀπήντα κατὰ τοὺς στενωπούς, ἀνθρώπους ἔχων ὑβριστὰς περὶ αὐτὸν καὶ θρασεῖς, οἳ πολλὰ μὲν

---

33. For the text, see Lachenaud and Coudry (2011). Whether these supplications took place before or after the parade of equestrians and Ninnius's decree is not clear. *Att.* 3.15.5 may just imply that Cicero adopted *sordes* soon after Clodius's initial promulgation of his bill (*ut est promulgata*); cf. Kaster (2006) 177.

34. See, e.g., *Planc.* 98; Val. Max. 6.4.4; Dio Cass. 40.46.1; 56.31.2; Livy 9.7.8; Suet. *Aug.* 100.2. Cf. Freyburger-Galland (1993) 121–26; Heskel (1994) 142; Edmondson (2008) 29–30.

35. Given what we know of Clodius's use of gangs and Cicero's regrets regarding his tactics, there is no reason to doubt the basic elements of the account. App. *B Civ.* 2.15 records similar details. For the text and section numbering, see Ziegler (1994).

χλευάζοντες ἀκολάστως εἰς τὴν μεταβολὴν καὶ τὸ σχῆμα τοῦ Κικέρωνος, πολλαχοῦ δὲ πηλῷ καὶ λίθοις βάλλοντες, ἐνίσταντο ταῖς ἱκεσίαις.

[And so, being threatened with prosecution, Cicero changed his attire, and with his hair untrimmed went about supplicating the people. But Clodius met him everywhere in the streets, accompanied by violent and aggressive men, who made many abusive taunts about his change of clothes and appearance, and often pelted him with mud and stones, and so interfered with his supplications to the people.]

The use of supplication in political contexts will be examined in greater detail in chapter three. For the present discussion, Cicero's unpleasant experience provides an important example of political theatrics that failed. It is a stark reminder that striking a distinctive public pose in Rome was an inherently risky business. Although the aristocrat had much to gain from these attempts at self-fashioning, such theatricality also exposed him to ridicule and abuse from opponents. It was this unpredictability that prevented such tactics from becoming stale and clichéd. As we have seen, politicians in Rome for over a century had donned *sordes* in their attempts to shape public opinion in their favor; to this extent, the strategy was a familiar, even conventionalized one. It would be wrong, however, to assume that this conventionalization necessarily emptied it of all power and impact (a mistaken assumption that, for the sake of convenience, I shall refer to as the "fallacy of conventionalization"). The public and highly interactive nature of the device meant that its effectiveness could not be guaranteed. The Roman aristocrat hoped his audience would accept and support the public pose that he adopted; but Cicero's experience in the face of Clodian opposition shows how badly wrong these stunts could go.[36]

Indeed, Cicero himself on occasion attempted to sabotage—or at least undermine—the use of *sordes* by other politicians. In the course of his invective against Piso, for example, he mocks the man's reaction to his early recall from the post of governor of Macedonia (*Pis.* 89): *quid quod tu totiens diffidens ac desperans rebus tuis in sordibus lamentis luctuque iacuisti . . . ?* ("What about all those occasions on which you despaired and lost confidence in your affairs and lay prostrate dressed in mourning, with lamentations and sobbing?") According to Nisbet, the account

---

36. Cf. Appian's observation (*B Civ.* 2.15) that Cicero's attempts to elicit pity ended up provoking ridicule (τὸ ἔργον διὰ τὴν ἀπρέπειαν ἀπὸ οἴκτου μεταπίπτειν ἐς γέλωτα).

here "has all the appearance of fiction."[37] But the detail of Piso's attire is plausible enough. As our other examples show, it is reasonable to suppose that he had donned *sordes* in order to display his distress and indignation at this blow to his political career. What Cicero presents, then, is not an extravagant fiction but satirical distortion. Piso's assertive advertisement of his grievance becomes in Cicero's account a ridiculous show of excessive and undignified grief. The verb *iacuisti* in particular portrays Piso as a defeated individual, grovelling miserably on the ground.

We find a similar device in the second speech *De Lege Agraria* as Cicero mocks the tribune Rullus and his controversial land legislation (*Leg. Agr.* 2.13):

> *iam designatus alio vultu, alio vocis sono, alio incessu esse meditabatur, vestitu obsoletiore, corpore inculto et horrido, capillatior quam ante barbaque maiore, ut oculis et aspectu denuntiare omnibus vim tribuniciam et minitari rei publicae videretur.*

> [As soon as he was elected, he practiced putting on a different expression, a different tone of voice, and a different gait; his clothing was rather ragged, his body uncared for and unkempt, his hair longer than before, and his beard thicker, so that eyes and appearance seemed to proclaim to the world the power of the tribuneship and to threaten the republic.]

This depiction has recently been interpreted as an attempt to portray Rullus as a Cynic philosopher of questionable character.[38] But this view probably expects from Cicero's audience too subtle a knowledge of Greek philosophy. It seems simpler to suppose that here too Cicero is using satirical distortion to ridicule the tribune's use of *sordes*. He does this not (as in the previous example) by depicting his target as weak and feeble but by dwelling on the outlandish aspects of his appearance. Cicero encourages his audience to view the tribune not as a popular hero burning with a sense of injustice but as a repulsive weirdo.[39] Moreover, Cicero slyly suggests a degree of calculation and opportunism in the tribune's actions. It is *all* theater. The pose of wild-eyed, hairy agitator has been carefully rehearsed.

We should hesitate, then, before assuming that donning *sordes* was

---

37. Nisbet (1961) 159.

38. See Hopwood (2007) 82; contrast Lintott (1999) 19.

39. Cf. Corbeill (2002) 203–4; (2004) 132–33; Bell (2004) 225–26; Toner (2009) 146.

a straightforward and rather passive convention. This was perhaps the case in situations of literal bereavement; but its various other uses all involved a degree of theatrical assertiveness. An appeal for help against a perceived injustice could easily turn into a provocative challenge of the alleged wrongdoer. In the Roman political context, such poses were often contentious and could elicit ridicule from opponents. It is against this social and political background that we need to set the use of *sordes* in judicial contexts.

## *Sordes* IN JUDICIAL CONTEXTS

It is difficult to identify when *sordes* first began to be connected closely with judicial proceedings. An anecdote preserved by Aulus Gellius suggests that the association was already firmly established around 140 BCE (Gell. *NA* 3.4.1):[40]

> *scriptum esse animadvertimus P. Scipioni, Paulli filio, postquam de Poenis triumphaverat censorque fuerat, diem dictum esse ad populum a Claudio Asello tribuno plebis, cui equum in censura ademerat, eumque, cum esset reus, neque barbam desisse radi neque candida veste uti neque fuisse cultu solito reorum.*

[I have noticed it recorded that Publius Scipio, the son of Paullus, after the triumph awarded for his victory over the Carthaginians and following his time as censor, was brought to trial before the people by Claudius Asellus, tribune of the plebs, whom Scipio had demoted from equestrian rank during his censorship. Yet Scipio, even though he was facing prosecution, did not stop shaving his beard or wearing white clothes, and did not adopt the usual attire of defendant.]

Presumably Scipio's ostentatious rejection of *sordes* would only have produced the desired rhetorical effect if it diverged sharply from customary practice. Indeed, there is evidence that Scipio knew well how to exploit the emotional potential of dark attire when it suited him. According to Plutarch, on being appointed commander of the army at Numantia in 134 BCE, Scipio was so distressed at its ill-discipline that he went around

---

40. Alexander (1990) 5 (no. 6) gives a date of early 140 BCE for the trial. Scipio delivered at least five orations against Claudius Asellus (Gell. *NA* 2.20.6). Note that there is no comment in our extant sources as to whether Sulpicius Galba did, or did not, wear *sordes* during the notorious events of 149 BCE (see chapter one).

camp wearing a black military cloak.[41] (In a military context, this dark cloak was presumably the closest available equivalent to *sordes* or the *toga pulla*.)[42]

Gellius's anecdote, however, appears to contradict a comment made by Cicero in one of his speeches (*Red. sen.* 31): *nostra memoria senatores ne in suis quidem periculis mutare vestem solebant; in meo periculo senatus veste mutata fuit.* ("Within my [our?] recollection, senators were not accustomed to changing their garments even at a time of danger to themselves; and yet at a time when I was in danger, the whole senate changed their garments.") If we take this remark at face value, Cicero seems to be claiming that the use of *sordes* in court (*senatores ne in suis quidem periculis*) was still not firmly established by 100 BCE or so (depending on how narrowly we interpret the phrase *nostra memoria*). But Cicero's argument here is tendentious. His aim is to sharpen a rhetorical antithesis, not to provide a precise chronology of judicial attire. By understating the frequency of *sordes* in earlier trials, he can magnify the significance of the senate's adoption of this garb on his behalf in 58 BCE (discussed above). We should not, then, place too much weight on Cicero's remark. Nevertheless, it does seem reasonable to assume that the increase in the number of *quaestiones perpetuae* over the decades led to a growing number of aristocrats donning *sordes*, and so strengthened the association of this form of attire with the courts.[43]

By the time of Cicero, however, it is clear that donning *sordes* involved an extended social performance, rather than a simple costume change on the day of the court appearance. The accused aristocrat adopted a

---

41. Plut. *Mor.* 201c: αὐτὸς δὲ σάγον ἐμπεπορπημένος μέλανα περιήει, πενθεῖν τὴν τοῦ στρατεύματος αἰσχύνην λέγων. For Scipio's disapproval of the prevailing state of discipline among these troops, see also App. *Hisp.* 14.85, Livy *Per.* 57 and Val. Max. 2.7.1, although no mention is made of the dark cloak.

42. Military commanders also used the beard of mourning to parade a sense of distress or political dismay in front of their troops. See Suet. *Iul.* 67.2 on Caesar's refusal to shave until he had avenged the massacre of 15 cohorts in 54–53 BCE; Plut. *Cat. Min.* 53.1 on Cato in 49 BCE after Caesar's crossing of the Rubicon and taking of Ariminum; and Plut. *Ant.* 18.2 on Mark Antony in the aftermath of his defeat at Mutina in 43 BCE. Antony may also have maintained a pose of mourning following Caesar's death for far longer than regular social custom dictated, thus turning his grief as a friend of Caesar into something with wider political significance. At least the pose seems to have been important enough for Antony to depict it on his coins; see Crawford (1983) plate LVII (480/22); cf. Pelling (1988) 163. See also Plut. *Ant.* 44.3 on Antony's actions during his Parthian campaign (37 BCE).

43. Kaster (2006) 111 seems willing to accept Cicero's version of events at *Red. sen.* 31. Note that Cicero's own account of the trial of M'. Aquillius (98 / 97 BCE) depicts the defendant as dressed *sordidatum* (*De or.* 2.195). See also Blonski (2008) 53, who assumes that the elder Cato donned *sordes* whenever he was involved in litigation.

pose of distress and indignation that he had to maintain throughout the whole judicial process. This period could run to months, even years. Early in 56 BCE, for example, Clodius brought a charge against Milo *de vi*, probably within the framework of a *iudicium populi*.[44] Milo first appeared at a *contio* on 2nd February, and again on 7th February (*Q Fr.* 2.3.1–2). Another hearing was scheduled for 17th February (*Q Fr.* 2.3.2: *Clodius in Quirinalia prodixit diem*), with the matter dragging on through March and to early April, when we hear that the matter was further postponed to May (*Q Fr.* 2.6.4). Eventually, the whole affair seems to have been dropped. It is likely that Milo conducted his public business throughout this period dressed *sordidatus* in protest at the prosecution. Certainly in March he attended the trial of P. Sestius dressed in this fashion (*Sest.* 144). Although this attire coincidentally helped to convey a sense of solidarity with the accused, Cicero emphasized the fact that Milo himself was currently engaged in legal proceedings, describing him as *sordidatum et reum* ("dressed *in sordibus* and a defendant [sc. in another case]"). Presumably then Milo maintained this pose for the entire four months or so of his judicial wrangling with Clodius.[45]

In such instances, the line between political theater and judicial theater becomes hard to draw. Milo's garb is prompted in the first place by threats of prosecution; but its purpose and effect spill over into his daily social and political life. Indeed, as the actions of Verres's Sicilian victims illustrate, this kind of social posturing could become yet more complex and elaborate. When, for example, Heraclius of Syracuse and Epicrates of Bidis fled to Rome after Verres tried to extort money left to them in legacies (see *Verr.* 2.2.35–50 and 2.2.53–61 respectively), they stayed in the capital for almost two years, dressed *in sordibus* and with beard and hair untrimmed (*Verr.* 2.2.62: *sordidati, maxima barba et capillo, Romae biennium prope fuerunt*). Diodorus of Melita likewise fled Sicily upon being threatened with prosecution and petitioned for assistance in Rome while dressed *sordidatus* (*Verr.* 2.4.41): *Diodorus Romae sordidatus circum patronos atque hospites cursare, rem omnibus narrare.* ("At Rome Diodorus, dressed in mourning, rushed around visiting patrons and former guests, relating the affair to everyone.")

---

44. See Alexander (1990) 129 (no. 266). The procedure of the prosecution has been debated; Gruen (1974) 298, n. 139 argues that the charge was pressed in the courts established according to the *lex Plautia de vi*; other scholars interpret the trial as a *iudicium populi*; see Alexander (1990) 129, n. 2; Kaster (2006) 110. Ancient sources: *Q Fr.* 2.3.1–2; Dio Cass. 39.18; *Fam.* 1.5b; cf. *Vat.* 40.

45. Cf. the remarks of Cicero at *Att.* 1.16.2 on Clodius in 61 BCE: *non vidit illud, satius esse illum in infamia relinqui ac sordibus quam infirmo iudicio committi.*

At first sight, it is tempting to dismiss these accounts as exaggerated. Two years seems a long time to maintain such an inconvenient pose. Yet these were rich men with much at stake, and it is likely that this conflict dragged on longer than they expected, as Verres's governorship was extended beyond its original term.[46] Moreover, the example of Livius Salinator provides a powerful reminder of the bitter feeling and bloody-mindedness that these disputes could provoke. Once such a pose had been initiated, it could become a point of honor to play it out to the end.[47]

These conflicts involving Verres demonstrate well the varied functions that donning *sordes* could serve. This attire was prompted in the first place by Verres's judicial attacks on the Sicilians. Yet these individuals seem not to have actually attended any trials in their homeland. The main purpose of their dress, then, was to aid their appeals for help in the houses of the rich and powerful in Rome.[48] Indeed, these petitions appear to have achieved a measure of success. Heraclius and Epicrates gained the support—at least initially—of L. Metellus, who replaced Verres as governor.[49] And Diodorus was able to generate such outrage in Rome at his situation that the elder Verres wrote a letter to his son warning of the growing animosity against him (*Verr.* 2.4.41: *rem claram esse et invidiosam*). As a consequence, the governor removed Diodorus from the list of those committed for trial in Sicily (*Verr.* 2.4.41: *de reis eximit*).

Another influential Sicilian, Sthenius of Thermae, likewise fled the province in the face of malicious prosecution and was able to enlist the support of powerful men in Rome (*Verr.* 2.2.90–94).[50] Again the political wrangling was intense. When Verres made moves to try Sthenius *in absentia* on capital charges, the senate in Rome passed a motion express-

---

46. Q. Arrius was expected to succeed Verres as governor after the first year of his term, and Heraclius is said explicitly to have been eagerly awaiting this change (*Verr.* 2.2.37; cf. 2.4.42). Instead, Arrius was assigned to the campaign against Spartacus, causing Verres's appointment to be extended to three years. See Broughton (1952) 117.

47. The phrasing of Diodorus Siculus (36.16) suggests that Metellus Pius likewise wore *sordes* for a couple of years (c. 100–98 BCE) in protest at the exile of his father. Cf. Val. Max. 5.2.7.

48. As Brunt (1980) notes, the Sicilians' ties of patronage at Rome evidently did little to protect them from Verres's initial depredations; but their personal petitions successfully generated a measure of *post factum* protection and redress. For more general considerations, see Prag (2013) 278–79.

49. See *Verr.* 2.2.62: *cum L. Metellus in provinciam profectus est, tum isti bene commendati cum Metello una proficiscuntur. Metellus, simul ac venit Syracusas, utrumque rescidit, et de Epicrate et de Heraclio.*

50. On Sthenius's high status and social connections in Rome, see *Verr.* 2.2.110; 112; 117. Cf. Münzer (1929); Badian (1958b) 282; David (1992) 70.

ing disapproval of the procedure (*Verr.* 2.2.95).[51] Verres's father again conveyed his misgivings to his son about these developments, but Verres went ahead with the trial and convicted Sthenius (*Verr.* 2.2.92–99). This development required further intervention from Sthenius's allies in Rome. Cicero himself successfully argued before the college of tribunes that Sthenius was legally entitled to take up residency in Rome because his conviction *in absentia* was unjust (*Verr.* 2.2.100).[52] To this move, Verres reacted (Cicero claims) by clumsily falsifying the records in Sicily to make them show that Sthenius was in fact present at the trial (*Verr.* 2.2.101). In such cases, then, it is clear that *sordes* contributed as much to the social and political posturings involved in these conflicts as they did to the actual legal proceedings and accompanying pleading in court.[53]

Matters were very different, however, when Verres eventually returned to Rome and faced prosecution for his crimes. These long-standing poses of distress and indignation now finally made their way into a judicial context—although this showdown in the courts led *both* sides to try to exploit the occasion's theatrical potential. A passing quip from the second *actio* of Cicero's *Verrines* confirms that Verres himself attempted to claim the role of aggrieved victim and thus appeared in court *sordidatus*. In his discussion of the mistreatment of young Junius (discussed in chapter one) Cicero remarks (*Verr.* 2.1.152):

> *hic istius scelerato nefarioque latrocinio bonis patriis fortunisque omnibus spoliatus venit in iudicium, si nihil aliud, saltem ut eum cuius opera ipse multos annos esset in sordibus paulo tamen obsoletius vestitum videret.*

[This boy, who had been robbed of all his father's property and wealth by Verres' wicked and abominable pillagings, came into court, if for no other reason, then at least so that he might see the man, whose actions had kept him for many years in shabby poverty, dressed in clothes that are a bit shabbier still.[54]]

---

51. Sthenius had already been convicted and fined *in absentia* on lesser charges; see *Verr.* 2.2.93–94.

52. See Crawford (1984) 44–46; Marinone (2004) 63; Dyck (2008) 150.

53. It is not stated explicitly that Sthenius went around *sordidatus* during the course of these various negotiations; but his presence at Verres's actual trial in such garb (*Verr.* 2.5.128), together with the practices of his fellow provincials Heraclius, Epicrates, and Diodorus, strongly suggest that he did.

54. There is room for disagreement regarding the precise meaning of the phrase *in sordibus* in this passage. Mitchell (1986) 151 translates it "the shabby garb of mourning," with the idea that Verres had reduced young Junius to a state of mourning and protest for some years. But, by extension, *in sordibus* can also refer to a generally impoverished state;

Indeed, Verres's advocate, Hortensius, developed this stagecraft yet further, arranging for a deputation from the Sicilian city of Messana to attend the trial in support of the defendant (see *Verr.* 2.2.13; 2.4.3; 2.4.150–51). Although it is not stated explicitly that these men were dressed *in squalore*, it is quite possible that they were: in a later trial, Cicero organized a crowd of supporters from Cn. Plancius's hometown of Atina to attend the man's trial dressed in this fashion.[55] In addition to this deputation from Messana, Hortensius also ensured that Verres was accompanied to the trial by men of high political prestige.[56]

But Cicero was determined not to let Verres seize any visual advantage and arranged for many of his own witnesses to attend court dressed *sordidati*.[57] The days of the actual trial thus became a venue for competing displays of distress and indignation.[58] As we saw in chapter one, Cicero knew well the importance of a good entrance into the forum. The appearance, then, of the prosecution witnesses as they made their way to the court was presumably no less carefully orchestrated than Roscius's bodyguard almost a decade earlier.[59]

It is difficult, however, to know how innovative Cicero's tactics were in this instance. Diplomats from Sicily many years earlier had worn *sordes* as they undertook negotiations with the senate.[60] Jugurtha too had donned

---

see *OLD*, s. v. *sordes*, 3a and 3b. Cf. the translation of Greenwood (1928) 285 ("the man who had made him go threadbare these many years"). The latter interpretation allows for a deft wordplay in Cicero's remark (a shift from the metaphorical *in sordibus* to the more literal *obsoletius*).

55. See *Planc.* 21: *huius praefectura plena virorum fortissimorum, sic ut nulla tota Italia frequentior dici possit. quam quidem nunc multitudinem videtis, iudices, in squalore et luctu supplicem vobis*. Cf. similar deputations at the trials of Murena (*Mur.* 90) and Cluentius (*Clu.* 196–97).

56. See, e.g., *Verr.* 1.26–28 on Q. Metellus, who had been elected to the consulship for the following year and was certainly in court sitting close to Verres, although whether he himself was dressed *sordidatus* is not stated. See also *Verr.* 1.26 on M. Metellus, who had been assigned the praetorship *de pecuniis repetundis*. Cf. Gruen (1971) 9.

57. See *Verr.* 2.5.126 (discussed further below). The exploitation of *sordes* by both sides in the trial confirms that their use was not governed by strict regulation. As we saw in chapter one, court officials were not interested in monitoring such things. An individual's attire was thus more a matter of social convention, shaped by the astute advocate's eye for theatrical opportunity.

58. Cf. Blonski (2008) 50: "c'est, pour ainsi dire, *squalor* contre *squalor*."

59. For another likely form of theatricality at the trial, see Butler (2002) 63–64.

60. See Livy 26.29.3, where he reports that Sicilian representatives in 210 BCE went around the city *cum veste sordida* in order to protest against the appointment of Marcellus as governor. Cf. the Rhodian embassy (dated by Livy to 167 BCE) that initially arrived in Rome *in veste candida*, but soon adopted *sordes*; see Livy 45.22–24; Briscoe (2012) 668–72; Pina Polo (2013) 260–61. Cf. Polybius 30.4–5 and the reference to donning dark clothes (φαιὰ λαβεῖν ἱμάτια).

*sordes* for his trip to Rome in 111 BCE (Sall. *Iug.* 33.1: *igitur Iugurtha contra decus regium cultu quam maxume miserabili cum Cassio Romam venit*). Cicero's presentation of provincials in this garb, then, was not an entirely new phenomenon but rather a development on a larger scale of existing practices.[61]

At least one other prosecution, however, seems to have followed a rather different approach when it came to presenting aggrieved Roman subjects in court. Cicero in his defense of Fonteius (probably in 69 BCE) refers disparagingly to the native dress of the Gallic provincials lined up to give evidence for the prosecution and tries to interpret this garb as a sign of their arrogant disposition (*Font.* 33):

> *sic existimatis eos hic sagatos bracatosque versari, animo demisso atque humili, ut solent ei, qui adfecti iniuriis ad opem iudicum supplices inferioresque confugiunt? nihil vero minus.*

> [Do you suppose that the men who are here dressed in cloaks and trousers carry themselves with an unassuming and modest air, like those who take refuge humbly and submissively in the protection of a jury when they have suffered wrongs? Nothing could be further from the truth.[62]]

Cicero here slyly emphasizes the supplicatory element of conventional *sordes* in order to denigrate the provincials, and he develops his characterization yet further by depicting them as swaggering haughtily through the city (*Font.* 33): *hi contra vagantur laeti atque erecti passim toto foro cum quibusdam minis et barbaro atque immani terrore verborum.* ("On the contrary, these men strut everywhere throughout the forum proud and confident, with various threats and wild, dreadful words of terror on their lips.") The scene is certainly colored, perhaps even fabricated wholesale. Yet the concerted nature of Cicero's attack suggests there was a problem that he needed to address. We may conjecture then that the prosecution had in fact successfully engaged in its own form of political theater in

---

61. Powell (2010) argues that Roman advocates regularly distanced themselves from witnesses in order to avoid suspicion of collusion (a view based primarily on *Flac.* 21–22). But Cicero's argument in that passage is obviously self-interested and a standard way of undermining the credibility of an opponent's witnesses. The Roman jury would have understood that a prosecutor, who had been allotted a specific period of time in a province to assemble evidence, would need to marshall his witnesses at the time of the trial.

62. For the trial, see Alexander (1990) 94 (no. 186); Marinone (2004) 68; Dyck (2012) 12.

the days preceding the trial, parading the Gauls through the city in their native dress and generating a degree of sympathy for their grievances.

If this was the case, it would seem that Roman prosecutors had a range of strategies at their disposal when it came to theatrics. *Sordes* were not the only form of attire that could capture the public's attention (and consequent goodwill). The unfamiliar and eye-catching garb of the Gauls served this purpose no less effectively perhaps—even though, as we have seen, it offered opponents the chance to depict them as disrespectful and barbaric.

In his prosecution of Verres, however, Cicero goes beyond the simple visual spectacle of assembling numerous victims and witnesses *in sordibus*. In the second *actio*, he takes the further step—an unusual one, as we shall see—of basing an appeal to pity around their distressed physical appearance. He begins with a series of rhetorical questions drawing attention to the misfortunes of Rome's provincial allies (see, e.g., *Verr.* 2.5.126: *quo confugient socii? quem implorabunt?*). These men are not greedy litigants, he claims, but individuals desperately seeking protection (*Verr.* 2.5.127). At this point, he refers explicitly to the pitiful sight of the witnesses in court (*Verr.* 2.5.127–28): *hoc iam ornatu ad vos confugiunt. aspicite, aspicite, iudices, squalorem sordesque sociorum.* ("In this present dress these men seek refuge with you. Look, gentlemen, look at the dirty and unkempt condition of our allies.") He then moves from the group to the individual (*Verr.* 2.5.128): *Sthenius hic Thermitanus cum hoc capillo atque veste, domo sua tota expilata, mentionem tuorum furtorum non facit; sese ipsum abs te repetit, nihil amplius.* ("Sthenius of Thermae here, despite the unkempt hair and garments that you see, even with his entire home ransacked, makes no mention of your thefts. He only asks you for the return of his own self. Nothing more.")[63]

These appeals ask the jurors to interpret literally the conventional garb of those in front of them. The *sordes* usually adopted as a metaphorical expression of an individual's distress now represent quite directly (Cicero claims) the actual poverty and destitution that the Sicilians have suffered at Verres's hands. The claim works in part because it comes at the end of an exhaustive catalogue of the governor's thefts. Cicero has diligently cultivated the impression of a province picked bare by Verres's

---

63. Presumably the other men that Cicero mentions in the following sentences (*Dexo hic . . . hic tam grandis natu Eubulida*) were dressed in similar fashion, although the detail is not mentioned specifically. Given the earlier reference to Sthenius's garb, repetition of the detail in these other cases would be redundant.

rapaciousness. The cohesiveness of the witnesses as a group may also have facilitated the device: comprising at least thirty individuals, their metonymy with Sicily as a whole possessed a certain surface plausibility.[64] It was easy to forget the fact that these were rich, influential Sicilians who had donned *sordes* as part of a calculated social (and political) pose.

And yet, of course, since this appeal appears in the second *actio* of the *Verrines*, we know that Cicero never actually had the chance to deliver it. Perhaps the text presents a scene that he was *planning* to stage, if the trial had run its full course; but it is important to note that Cicero does not invoke *sordes* so extensively in any other speech. This difference in approach may derive in part from the fact that, in other instances, he is speaking on behalf of the defense rather than the prosecution. Yet it is possible too that he was well aware of the limitations inherent in this kind of appeal in an actual trial (as opposed to the fictionalized setting of the *Verrines'* second *actio*).

In his peroration in defense of Murena, for example, Cicero's reference to the defendant's attire appears as only one element within a list (*Mur.* 86: *nunc idem <in> squalore et sordibus, confectus morbo, lacrimis ac maerore perditus vester est supplex, iudices*).[65] Likewise, Cicero in *Pro Scauro* admits to his own distress at the sight of the defendant *in squalore* and invites the jurors to imagine how Scaurus's deceased father—the venerable M. Aemilius Scaurus (cos. 115 BCE)—would feel if he were looking down upon the present scene (*Scaur.* 49):

> te vero, M. Scaure, equidem video, video, inquam, non cogito solum, nec vero sine magno animi maerore ac dolore, cum tui fili squalorem aspexi, de te recordor.

> [As for you, M. Scaurus, I do not see you just in my imagination, but in front of my very eyes, and when I look upon the wretched state of your son, it is with great sorrow and sadness that I think of you.]

But he stops short of suggesting that *the jurors themselves* should find the attire pitiful. The remark thus relies as much on the trope of paternal distress at a son's plight, as it does on the jurors' direct reaction to Scaurus's *sordes*. Even in *Pro Ligario*, where Cicero draws attention to the number of close allies present who are dressed *in sordibus*, the focus of his appeal rests upon the noble virtues that this attire represents (*Lig.* 33: *pietas*

---

64. See Alexander (1990) 88–89 and (2002) 255–62.
65. For this textual reading, see, e.g., Berry (2000) xxxv; 105.

and *germanitas*), rather than the pity for the accused it might inspire.[66] His references to *squalor* in *Pro Caelio* and *Pro Sestio* are similarly brief.[67]

Cicero's general reticence in this regard can be discerned most clearly perhaps in his extended peroration on behalf of Roscius of Ameria. In theory, just as he portrayed the *sordes* of Sthenius and other Sicilians as evidence of the cruel rapaciousness of Verres, so he could have depicted Roscius's pitiful attire as evidence of Chrysogonus's merciless greed. And yet this connection is left implicit when he tries to generate pity for Roscius's state of financial ruin (*Rosc. Am.* 147):

> *et tamen oppugnas eum quem neque metuere potes neque odisse debes nec quicquam iam habere reliqui vides quod ei detrahere possis? nisi hoc indignum putas, quod vestitum sedere in iudicio vides quem tu e patrimonio tamquam e naufragio nudum expulisti.*

> [And yet do you [sc. Chrysogonus] attack a man whom you cannot fear and should not hate, and whom you see no longer possesses anything that you can steal? Unless you think it outrageous to see dressed and sitting in this court a man whom you drove from his patrimony as naked as if he had suffered a shipwreck.]

In formal terms, the repeated verb *vides* here is addressed to the absent Chrysogonus, as if he were present in court;[68] nevertheless its appeal to the visual appearance of Roscius naturally invites the jurors likewise to turn their eyes upon the accused. Presumably what they saw was Roscius dressed *sordidatus*—a sight that allowed Cicero to claim that the defendant had nothing left worth plundering (*nec quicquam iam habere reliqui vides, quod ei detrahere possis*). Moreover this attire would have added extra bite to his sarcastic suggestion that the jurors might feel outrage at seeing Roscius now sitting in court *vestitum*. Roscius is indeed now clothed, after having been driven naked from his estates; but even these

---

66. For the *sordes* of Ligarius's allies, see *Lig.* 32: *huius T. Brocchi, de quo non dubito quid existimes lacrimas squaloremque ipsius et fili vides. quid de fratribus dicam?* Since T. Brocchus and his son were dressed *in squalore*, we can assume that Ligarius's brothers were too. For the attire of other individuals supporting Ligarius, see *Lig.* 33 (*qui adsunt veste mutata*).

67. See the brief phrase *squalor patris* at *Cael.* 4, and the passing reference to Milo and Lentulus Spinther at *Sest.* 144. Cf. the even more oblique reference at *Sull.* 88: *ipse ornatum ac vestitum pristinum recuperabit.*

68. Cicero's comments at *Rosc. Am.* 60 indicate that Chrysogonus was absent when he began his speech, and there is no compelling reason to suppose that he had joined the proceedings in the meantime; cf. Dyck (2010) 199; 202.

garments are soiled and ragged. Roscius's *sordes*, then, help to depict visually the parlous state to which he has been reduced; yet Cicero does not integrate them explicity into his verbal appeals.[69]

Overall, then, a defendant's *sordes* played only a minor role in Cicero's efforts to stir pity in his audience *during his speeches*. For the most part, he relied on other oratorical tropes to achieve this end. Occasionally he made passing reference to what the jurors could see before them, but usually he let this visual element do its work unaided. Behind this approach lies perhaps an implicit acknowledgement that donning *sordes* was in fact a matter of deliberate choice on the part of the aristocrat, rather than the actual product of some grave misfortune.

Nevertheless, Milo's decision *not* to don *sordes* when brought to trial for the murder of Clodius in 52 BCE set Cicero a difficult challenge.[70] As we have seen, Milo did not object in principle to judicial theatrics; he was willing enough to wear *sordes* during his legal wranglings with Clodius in 56 BCE.[71] His decision not to do so in 52 BCE, then, presumably derived from strategic considerations rather than a general disapproval of the practice. The most likely explanation lies in the political events that took place in the immediate aftermath of Clodius's murder. According to Asconius, many Romans assumed that Milo would depart directly into voluntary exile: his involvement in the man's death was patent, and any chance of winning the upcoming election therefore lost (Asc. *Mil.* 33C: *Milo, quem opinio fuerat ivisse in voluntarium exsilium*).[72] Yet Milo adopted an unexpectedly defiant stance. At a public assembly he declared that the killing of Clodius was not a matter of murder but of self-defense, and that he still intended to run for the consulship.[73]

---

69. Cicero also refers to Roscius's *luctum* (grief) and *egestatem* (poverty) in section 13. Presumably these remarks were likewise reinforced by the sight of Roscius sitting there *sordidatus*. For the metaphor *nudus*, used in regard to Roscius's initial state after being driven from his estates, see *Rosc. Am.* 23 and 144.

70. Plutarch asserts that this decision contributed significantly to the guilty verdict passed against Milo (*Cic.* 35.5): καὶ κόμην θρέψαι καὶ μεταβαλεῖν ἐσθῆτα φαιὰν ἀπαξιώσαντος· ὅπερ οὐχ ἥκιστα δοκεῖ συναίτιον αὐτῷ γενέσθαι τῆς καταδίκης. This claim, however, oversimplifies matters. For Milo's rejection of a plea based around pity, see also *Mil.* 92 (*si in nostro omnium fletu nullam lacrimam aspexistis Milonis*) and *Mil.* 105 (*hic se lacrimis defendi vetat*). Valerius Maximus (6.4.4) asserts that Rutilius Rufus likewise refused to wear *sordes* for his trial on charges of provincial corruption (see chapter one). Cf. David (1980) 186.

71. In 54 BCE too he had appeared as a suppliant on behalf of Scaurus (see Asc. *Scaur.* 28C). It is likely, although not stated explicitly, that Milo and his fellow suppliants were *sordidati*. This supplication is discussed in greater detail in chapters three and five. Cf. David (1992) 630.

72. Cf. also *Mil.* 63: *negabant eum Romam esse rediturum.*

73. Asc. *Mil.* 33C: *petebatque nihil deterritus consulatum . . . contionem ei post aliquot dies*

This unapologetic pose had important consequences for the tactics that he and Cicero adopted from this point on. Having openly acknowledged his role in Clodius's death, Milo could not now with any plausibility assert his outrage and indignation when threatened with prosecution by members of the deceased's family. We may wonder too whether any such display of distress would have looked rather hollow when set beside the literal state of mourning adopted by Clodius's widow, Fulvia, who attended the trial and delivered her own tearful testimony (Asc. *Mil.* 40C). For Milo, far better the virtue of consistency in maintaining a stance of staunch forebearance. Nevertheless, as we shall see in chapter three, this stance posed problems for Cicero as he tried to construct an emotional appeal on Milo's behalf.

CONCLUSIONS

This chapter has attempted to place the deployment of *sordes* in the courts within the wider context of Roman social and political theater. As we have seen, aristocrats in Rome were used to striking poses of distress and indignation in their political business. Donning *sordes* in response to a perceived injustice was a familiar part of the jockeying for public and private support that characterized conflicts between grandees. There was thus a natural cross-fertilization between the judicial and political spheres. When Cicero and his allies organized the mass protest of equestrians *veste mutata* in 58 BCE they presumably drew on their experience in orchestrating similar displays in the courts. These in turn were themselves no doubt influenced by earlier social and political practices that extended back beyond the establishment of the standing courts. It is no surprise, then, to find this aspect of the advocate's technique entirely absent from the rhetorical handbooks prior to Quintilian.[74] This was a matter of Roman cultural theatrics, not verbal persuasion.

Indeed, it is worth stressing that parallels in Greek culture are dif-

---

dedit M. *Caelius tribunus plebis ac Cicero ipse etiam causam egit ad populum. dicebant uterque Miloni a Clodio factas esse insidias.* It seems unlikely, however, that Cicero had any direct input into Milo's course of action at this time. The active participation of Cicero depends on a contested reading (*ac Cicero*) printed by Clark (1907). Since the text of Cicero at *Mil.* 91 makes no reference to his presence at the *contio*, the deletion of the phrase seems preferable; cf. Lintott (1974) 70, n. 101; Ruebel (1979) 236; Lewis (2006) 239. Asconius (*Mil.* 41C) confirms that the fatal encounter between Clodius and Milo was not in fact planned by either side.

74. On the mention of *sordes* in Quintilian (*Inst.* 6.1.33), see chapter five.

ficult to find. Following the Athenian defeat at Arginusae in 405 BCE, Theramenes is said to have arranged for a group of people to attend a meeting of the assembly dressed in mourning clothes (μέλανα ἱμάτια ἔχοντας), pretending to be grieving relatives of those who had died in the battle.[75] But this cynical piece of political theater exploited mourning clothes in a context of literal bereavement; public posturing *in sordibus* as a means of self-help does not seem to have featured prominently in the Greek world. Likewise, litigants in Athenian courts sometimes appeared shabbily dressed, but the intent here was to plead literal poverty.[76] As our examples have shown, this was not usually the message conveyed by the rich Roman aristocrat's adoption of *sordes*.

Within Cicero's orations, then, *sordes* contributed very little to his arguments invoking pity for a defendant. During the days of a trial itself, their impact depended more on visual spectacle than on the advocate's verbal pleading—a factor that is, of course, difficult for us now to reconstruct and assess. It seems reasonable, however, to suppose that the presence of several individuals dressed in this fashion at a trial conveyed a welcome image of group cohesion that aided the aristocrat's cause. In a trial like that of Verres, such theatrics could reach a grand scale that required careful coordination by the opposing advocates as each sought to gain a visual advantage.

But in fact, as we have seen, the prime purpose of *sordes* had in many cases been accomplished *before* a trial actually began. By adopting this public pose in the days and weeks prior to a hearing, the aggrieved grandee was able to elicit support for his cause, both with regard to enlisting specific *patroni* to speak in his defense and more generally by mobilizing delegations from his hometown and elsewhere.[77] This assertive advertisement of distress and indignation thus shaped the legal proceedings quite significantly, even if they were not exploited to any great degree in the actual speeches. Nevertheless, this theatrical form of display also involved considerable inconvenience. The need to maintain this pose in public over several months (or even years) must have caused considerable irritation. Indeed, a remark by Suetonius suggests

---

75. See Xen. *Hell.* 1.7.8; cf. Diod. Sic. 13.101.6–7.

76. See Hall (1995) 52: "Litigants should not look too shabby, unless, like Cephisodotus (Isac. 5.11), or Lysias' invalid (24), poverty was an essential part of their case." Cf. Ar. *Vesp.* 564–65; *Ran.* 1065–66.

77. On the solicitation of *patroni*, see David (1992) 76–83. For the power of *sordes* to signify group solidarity and even intimidate a prosecutor, see App. *B Civ.* 2.24; cf. Val. Max. 9.5.3; David (1992) 242–44.

that, on occasions, a prosecution might be laid precisely to cause such inconvenience.[78]

Finally, these inconveniences, as well as Cicero's own disastrous exploitation of such garb in 58 BCE, remind us of the risks inherent in undertaking this practice. As I have suggested, we must be wary of the fallacy of conventionalization. To don *sordes* outside the context of bereavement was an act of self-assertion open to challenge and ridicule from onlookers. Such public theatricality thus always ran the risk of failure. The frequent deployment of *sordes* during the troubled decades of the Late Republic indicates not the emptiness of the convention but the fierce commitment with which Roman aristocrats engaged in their feuds—judicial or otherwise.

78. Suet. *Aug.* 32.2: *diuturnorum reorum et ex quorum sordibus nihil aliud quam voluptas inimicis quaereretur nomina abolevit condicione proposita.* Cf. Bablitz (2007) 85.

# CHAPTER 3

# TOO PROUD TO BEG

## Appeals and Supplications in the Courts

From Livy's *Periochae*, we learn that M. Antonius encountered a signifi-cant obstacle as he planned his emotional appeal on behalf of M'. Aquil-lius: the battle-hardened general evidently refused to address any direct pleas for acquittal to the jury (Livy *Per.* 70: *ipse iudices rogare noluit*). For an advocate who placed great importance on such appeals, Aquillius's reluctance posed quite a problem.[1] Antonius's solution was a deft one in two respects. By focusing on Aquillius's battle scars, he reduced the submissive element in the commander's position. (That is, Antonius presented him as a brave warrior who deserved respect for his valor.) Second, Antonius shifted the onus of generating tears and high emotion onto himself and Marius.[2] He thus secured the theatrical flourish that he wanted, while catering to the fastidiousness of his defendant.

In the present chapter, I examine the challenges that Cicero likewise faced in constructing his emotional appeals and combining with them elements of judicial theater.[3] Aquillius's reluctance to entreat the jurors was not an idiosyncratic exception. As W. J. Tatum has noted, many Ro-man aristocrats felt a similar squeamishness when it came to canvassing for votes among the populace in the annual elections.[4] The main stum-bling block was the grandee's hauteur: publicly requesting a favor from

---

1. Note that Aquillius did in fact don *sordes* for the trial (*De or.* 2.195). This fact shows again that wearing *sordes* was often an act of protest as much as a plea for sympathy.

2. For the tears of Antonius and Marius, see chapters one and four.

3. Modern discussions of Cicero's appeals have tended to focus on the orator's use of literary tropes; see, e.g., Rohde (1903) and Lussky (1928). For analyses from a wider perspective, see David (1992) 626–40; Flaig (2003) 100–102; Winterbottom (2004). On occasion a certain disdain for Cicero's techniques can be discerned. See, e.g., Powell and Paterson (2004) 33: "Nor was there any limit on barefaced appeals to sympathy." As we shall see, the adjective "barefaced" here obscures the numerous factors that shaped how Cicero formulated his appeals. Cf. also Todd (1990) 147 on the reluctance of modern bar-risters to recognize the "non-legal factors" that play a part in their pleading.

4. Tatum (2007) 111–15.

those regarded as social inferiors often proved too demeaning a task for the privileged aristocrat.[5] A similar dynamic could prevail in the courts as well. As *Rhetorica ad Herennium* notes, the defendant who entreats jurors demonstrates in effect his submission to their *potestas* (*Rhet. Her.* 2.50: *si . . . nos sub eorum quorum misericordiam captabimus potestatem subiciemus*). This was a pose that the prouder members of the elite were unwilling to adopt.[6]

At the same time, as Tatum observes, there were ambitious politicians aplenty in Rome who were prepared to undergo these perceived indignities in order to win the prizes they sought. Thus, in Cicero's day, election-time supplications of the people were a familiar feature of the canvassing process.[7] For those who engaged in such practices, the practical gains outweighed any temporary loss of prestige. The same principle seems to have applied for those involved in criminal trials. The need to save their political careers was simply more important than their *dignitas*. For these men, tearful pleas and even supplication constituted a viable tool in their quest for acquittal.

It is not always easy, however, to reconstruct the precise role that supplication played in these theatrics. Although Latin authors regularly use supplicatory terminology when describing the appeals used in court, sometimes it is difficult to tell whether we should interpret this language literally or figuratively. In *Rhetorica ad Herennium*, for example, the author makes the following remark about the tropes to be employed in the context of *deprecatio* (a plea for mercy) (*Rhet. Her.* 2.25):

> *hic ignoscendi ratio quaeritur ex his locis: . . . si qua virtus aut nobilitas erit in eo qui supplicabit . . . si ipse ille supplex mansuetus et misericors in potestatibus ostendetur fuisse.*

---

5. See, e.g., the potential criticisms faced by Metellus Pius when supplicating the people in support of the candidature of Q. Calidius (Val. Max. 5.2.7). Cf. *De or.* 1.112; *Planc.* 50; and the remarks in chapter one regarding aristocratic principles of comportment.

6. Cf. David (1992) 622: "la supériorité aristocratique s'inscrivait aussi dans un éthos de la hauteur et de l'affirmation sentencieuse du pouvoir. Il n'était pas question d'y déroger." See also the remark attributed to Cato the Younger at Plut. *Cat. Min.* 64.7: κεκρατημένων γὰρ εἶναι δέησιν, καὶ ἀδικούντων παραίτησιν; and [Sallust] *Invectiva in Ciceronem* 5, where the assertion that Cicero is suppliant to his enemies (*supplex inimicis*) is intended as a humiliating insult. (For the text, see Shackleton Bailey (2002) 366.) Cf. Epstein (1987) 22 and Johnstone (1999) 123 on similar attitudes in Greek society.

7. Tatum (2007) 109–11. Cf. Morstein-Marx (1998) 267–70; Naiden (2006) 231–33. Sall. *Iug.* 85.1 makes Marius observe cynically that this submissive pose with regard to the *populus Romanus* was swiftly forgotten once the grandee gained office; cf. Q. Cic. *Comm. Pet.* 16.

[In this case, the basis for seeking pardon is to be found in the following topics: . . . if there exists some impressiveness of character or high birth in the individual who will make the appeal . . . or if the individual making the appeal can be shown to have himself been compassionate and merciful when in a position of authority.]

As my translation suggests, the main purpose of the terms *supplicabit* and *supplex* in this passage is to identify the individual who takes on the role of petitioner in a court case.[8] There is no apparent suggestion that this individual is engaged in a literal supplication complete with prostration and outstretched arms. This kind of metaphorical usage often makes it difficult for us to assess precisely the degree of physical action that was involved in Cicero's appeals.[9]

Another problem hampers this kind of investigation: our own unfamiliarity with supplication as a cultural practice. Most readers of this book, I expect, will not need to engage in such an act in their lifetime. It takes an effort of the imagination, then, to appreciate the social dynamics that supplication involved, and the role that it played in the negotiation of conflict. Indeed, like the donning of *sordes*, the practice of supplication was not restricted to the courts; it featured in many different spheres of Roman activity. It is important to understand this social background, if we wish to gain an accurate perspective upon its use in judicial contexts.

---

8. Cf. *OLD*, s. v. *supplico*, 1a, "sue for mercy or forgiveness," with reference to *Rhet. Her.* 2.50; also *OLD*, s. v. *supplex*, 1, "making humble entreaty, suppliant." Cf. Unceta Gomez (2009) 171–78. For a Ciceronian example of the verb *supplico* and its cognates used in a metaphorical sense, see *Font.* 35: *cumque inimici M. Fontei vobis ac populo Romano minentur, amici ac propinqui supplicent vobis. . . .* ("And since the enemies of Fonteius threaten you and the Roman people, while his friends and relatives are suppliants. . . ."); cf. Winterbottom (2004) 222: "At another passage of the same speech (*Font.* 41) [the usage of the verb] is purely metaphorical."

9. The study of Naiden (2006) does not clarify this issue. It is asserted, for example, that "Wherever courts met, defendants must have supplicated them. So must have those who aided defendants, notably advocates. Cicero, for example, supplicated in his own person" (pp. 33–34). But this apparently concrete reconstruction is undercut by the accompanying footnote, which observes that some of the instances used to support it might be regarded as "instances of supplicatory language, not supplication"; see Naiden (2006) 34, n. 25. The table on pages 342–43 ("Acts of Supplication by Defendants, Supporters, and Advocates in Cicero") likewise does not attempt to distinguish figurative from literal supplication. On this problem of interpretation in Greek contexts, see Gould (1973) 77; Johnstone (1999) 116; Naiden (2006) 19; 62, n. 180.

APPEALS AND SUPPLICATION IN ROMAN SOCIETY

Two factors help to explain the prevalence of supplication in the Roman world: the vast inequalities in power and wealth that existed in society;[10] and the highly personalized nature of political and social influence. In even the lower social echelons, for example, the Roman *paterfamilias* possessed the power of life and death over his slaves.[11] How he treated these unfortunates thus depended largely upon whim. In most cases, direct personal appeal constituted the only viable means of trying to influence his actions.[12] A similar power differential—although in legal terms not so decisively defined—was replicated across the economic and social spheres of Rome as a whole. Rich patrons controlled immense resources that they could choose to distribute according to personal inclination. Fateful decisions therefore regularly depended upon individual favor.[13] Cicero, for example, records visits from desperate provincials seeking his aid via tearful appeals.[14] In the previous chapter, too, we saw Sicilians such as Diodorus of Melita appealing for help at the morning receptions of powerful Romans.

In modern westernized societies, such conflicts tend to be mediated through bureaucratic mechanisms designed precisely to administer policy according to "impersonal" principles. In ancient Rome, however, even within the elite classes, political influence and activity depended on the flow of services across highly personalized social networks. Cicero's letters are full of requests for assistance and support, ranging from the mutual exchange of small services (*mandata*) to more formal appeals for help in weighty affairs.[15] Indeed, as we saw in the previous chapter, in

---

10. Cf. Roisman (2005) 150.

11. See Gai. *Inst.* 1.52 on the *ius vitae ac necis*; cf. Crook (1967) 55–57. For the punishments that could be inflicted upon slaves, see Gardner and Wiedemann (1991) 18–24.

12. See Plin. *Ep.* 9.21.1–2 for the tears and supplication of a freedman in a similar position. In this case, his pleas attempt to solicit Pliny's intervention in the dispute as a third party.

13. See, e.g., Wallace-Hadrill (1989) 73: "The ruling nobility, priests, magistrates, judges, legal counsel, and generals rolled into one, stood astride all the major lines of communication with the centre of state power and the resources it had to distribute. Their success in control lay as much in their power to refuse as in their readiness to deliver the goods."

14. See *Att.* 6.2.9: *nam ad me Ephesum usque venerunt flentesque equitum scelera et miserias suas detulerunt.* Cf. *Fam.* 15.2.6.

15. See in general Saller (1982) 7–39; Verboven (2002) 35–48; 287–329. On the letters of recommendation in *Ad Familiares* Book 13, see Cotton (1985) and (1986); Deniaux (1993) 17–44.

the desperate days prior to his exile, Cicero himself supplicated power-ful individuals in an attempt to persuade them to exert influence on his behalf.

Naturally there were social costs involved in invoking these mecha-nisms of support, and one did not do so lightly. Yet at times the judicial and political stakes were high enough to warrant such measures. At a meeting of the senate in 61 BCE, for example, Clodius himself resorted to supplication, as a proposal was passed setting up a special tribunal to try him for sacrilege following the Bona Dea scandal (*Att.* 1.14.5): *cum decerneretur frequenti senatu, contra pugnante Pisone, ad pedes omnium singil-latim accidente Clodio, ut consules populum cohortarentur ad rogationem ac-cipiendam.* ("A full house voted a decree instructing the consuls to urge the people to accept the bill. Piso fought against it, and Clodius went on his knees to every member individually.") We glimpse a similar scene five years later, as a member of the equestrian class faced ejection from two *collegia* (*Q Fr.* 2.6.2): *non praetermittam ne illud quidem: M. Furium Flac-cum, equitem Romanum, hominem nequam, Capitolini et Mercuriales de colle-gio eiecerunt praesentem ad pedes unius cuiusque iacentem.* ("I shall not pass over even this event: M. Furius Flaccus, a Roman knight and thoroughly worthless individual, was expelled from the Capitoline College and the Guild of Mercury, he himself being present at the meeting and throwing himself at the feet of every member in turn.")

It is not clear how literally we should interpret the phrases *unius cui-usque* and *omnes singillatim* in these examples. Robert Kaster has recently suggested that Cicero is describing here a formulaic ritual in which the petitioner did indeed supplicate each member of the house individu-ally, a process that would have taken quite some time.[16] But in my view it is just as likely that the phrases function as sardonic exaggeration. By depicting Clodius and Flaccus as frantically supplicating each and every senator, Cicero succeeds in portraying them as especially desperate and humiliated.[17]

Whatever the case, the form of the supplication itself was certainly ur-gent and dramatic: the phrases *ad pedes accidente* and *ad pedes iacentem* in-

---

16. Kaster (2009) 314: "In fact, the practice appears to have been so common as to have had a highly formalized, quasi-scripted character." On Clodius's supplication, Kaster observes that "even granting no more than a rather feverish five seconds per senator [the process] would have taken over half an hour."

17. This seems to be the aim too in Cicero's description of Verres's father at *Verr.* 2.2.95 (*unum quemque senatorum rogabat*). Cicero's purpose is not to identify the man's use of a formal procedure but to create a snigger at the desperation of his actions.

dicate that the petitioners did literally throw themselves on the ground.[18] We may note too that the contexts in which they do so are similar to that of a Roman court: an individual's conduct is assessed by a body of powerful individuals whose function is to pass a kind of verdict. As part of this process, the "defendant" attempts to influence the outcome through a dramatic personal appeal.

A third example, however, from 57 BCE, following Cicero's return from exile, presents a rather different scenario. When the tribune Sex. Atilius Serranus Gavianus interposed his veto in order to obstruct proposals for the restoration of Cicero's house, various senators uttered threats against him, and Gnaeus Oppius Cornicinus, his father-in-law, threw himself at his feet in supplication (*Red. pop.* 12: *et Cn. Oppius socer, optimus vir, ad pedes flens iaceret*).[19] The phrase *optimus vir* here confirms that Cornicinus was acting in support of Cicero, attempting to persuade his son-in-law to abandon the veto. Yet Cicero's private account to Atticus presents the event rather more cynically (*Att.* 4.2.4): *Serranus pertimuit et Cornicinus ad suam veterem fabulam rediit; abiecta toga se ad generi pedes abiecit.* ("Serranus took fright, and Cornicinus repeated his old charade—flinging off his toga and throwing himself at the feet of his son-in-law.") The phrase *veterem fabulam* portrays Cornicinus's unrobing and supplication as a kind of tired and cynical stunt for which the man was notorious. This sarcastic tone in the context of a supplication in Cicero's own interests suggests perhaps that Cornicinus's previous uses of this device had not been in causes so close to Cicero's heart, or at least that Cicero wants to affect a certain disdain for the man's tricks when writing to Atticus.

Supplication, then, like the use of *sordes*, was an inherently ambiguous practice. Cicero will contemplate exploiting it when he thinks he can gain some advantage; but he will also mock its use by others. Likewise, despite the Roman familiarity with supplication as a cultural practice and its (possibly) quasi-scripted nature, its effectiveness was far from assured. The supplications of Clodius and Flaccus described above were both ultimately unsuccessful, as too were those of Cicero and his family in 58 BCE.[20] It would be mistaken, then, to view such appeals as empty

---

18. For detailed studies of the physical gestures involved in Greek and Roman supplication, see Freyburger (1988) 515–25; Naiden (2006) 240–49; 339–64; cf. Gould (1973). For other explicit references to physical prostration, see *Planc.* 50 (*prosternerent se*), Val. Max. 9.5.3 (*ad pedes prostratum*), and the examples below.

19. Cf. also *Sest.* 74: *socer ad pedes abiectus.*

20. On the supplications by Cicero's family, see *Red. sen.* 37–38; cf. Pompey's rejection of a public supplication by P. Plautius Hypsaeus described at Plut. *Pomp.* 55.10 and Val. Max. 9.5.3. Cicero himself also experienced a painful rebuff from Pompey; see *Att.* 10.4.3:

and predictable rituals. Again we need to beware the fallacy of conventionalization. Although some observers might regard an act of supplication with a degree of cynicism and detachment, the stakes involved for the participants in terms of personal face and public image were considerable.[21] This was an important factor for Cicero to consider as he tried to judge the urgency of his appeals in his judicial speeches. Indeed, as we have seen, for men such as Aquillius, the risk was so great that he refused to engage in any kind of plea at all.

## APPEALS AND SUPPLICATION IN THE COURTS

Two incidents in which Cicero was not directly involved illustrate the sort of supplication that was possible in Rome's courts—at least in certain circumstances. The first involves the trial of L. Piso, probably around 110 BCE (Val. Max. 8.1, abs. 6):[22]

> *item L. Piso a C. Claudio Pulchro accusatus, quod graves et intolerabiles iniurias sociis intulisset, haud dubiae ruinae metum fortuito auxilio vitavit: namque per id ipsum tempus quo tristes de eo sententiae ferebantur, repentina vis nimbi incidit, cumque prostratus humi pedes iudicum oscularetur, os suum caeno replevit. quod conspectum totam quaestionem a severitate ad clementiam et mansuetudinem transtulit, quia satis iam graves eum poenas sociis dedisse arbitrati sunt, huc deductum necessitatis ut abicere se tam suppliciter et attollere tam deformiter cogeretur.*

[Likewise L. Piso, prosecuted by C. Claudius Pulcher for the serious and quite unacceptable injuries he had inflicted on our allies, avoided the threat of certain ruin by fortuitous aid. For at the very moment when votes of guilty were being cast at his trial, a sudden storm of rain fell,

---

*alter, is qui nos sibi quondam ad pedes stratos ne sublevabat quidem, qui se nihil contra huius voluntatem facere posse.* Cf. Kaster (2009) 314.

21. Cf. Gould (1973) 95–96: "The element of [social] inversion of itself carries with it . . . a certain constraint and emotional charge for all those participating under any conditions."

22. For details of the trial, see Alexander (1990) 24 (no. 48) and 178 (no. 378). The identity of the prosecutor is disputed; Shackleton Bailey (2000) 192 prints C. Claudius, but considers the correct reading to be P. (see n. 6); contrast David (1992) 712–13. David (1992) 627 uses this incident to highlight the horror typically felt by Roman aristocrats toward the whole business of supplication.

and as he was prostrate on the ground kissing the jury's feet, he filled his mouth with mud. The sight turned the whole court from severity to mercy and leniency, since they thought he had already paid our allies penalty enough, brought to the necessity of casting himself down in such supplication and picking himself up in such a disgusting state.]

The account has all the features of a well-turned anecdote: note the dramatic onset of the thunderstorm, the memorable image of Piso's dirt-filled mouth, and the sudden reversal of the jurors' verdict. Nevertheless, there is no reason to doubt the basic veracity of the incident. As we have seen, full-length supplication (as indicated by the phrase *prostratus humi pedes iudicum oscularetur*) was a practice familiar in Roman society. For our present discussion, however, the most important detail is the timing of Piso's entreaty. Clearly this appeal did not take place during the speech of one of his advocates but at the very conclusion of the trial, as the jurors were casting their votes.[23] The incident provides a striking reminder, then, that the advocate's peroration was not the only occasion available for theatrics (or even the most effective one).

We find a second example of supplication at this same stage of proceedings at the trial of M. Aemilius Scaurus in 54 BCE (Asc. *Scaur.* 28C):[24]

*ad genua iudicum, cum sententiae ferrentur, bifariam se diviserunt qui pro eo rogabant: ab uno latere Scaurus ipse et M'. Glabrio, sororis filius, et L. Paullus et P. Lentulus, Lentuli Nigri flaminis filius, et L. Aemilius Buca filius et C. Memmius, Fausta natus, supplicaverunt; ex altera parte Sulla Faustus, frater Scauri, et T. Annius Milo, cui Fausta ante paucos menses nupserat dimissa a Memmio, et C. Peducaeus et C. Cato et M. Laenas Curtianus.*

[When the vote was being taken, Scaurus's supporters divided into two groups at the jurymen's knees: on one side Scaurus engaged in supplication along with M'. Glabrio (his sister's son), L. Paullus, P. Lentulus (son of Lentulus Niger the priest), the younger L. Aemilius Buca, and C. Memmius (son of Fausta); on the other side were Faustus Sulla (half-

---

23. If the trial is identified as Alexander (1990) 24–25 (no. 48), Piso's advocates were probably L. Licinius Crassus and M. Aemilius Scaurus; if identified with Alexander (1990) 178 (no. 378), their identity is unknown. On voting procedure during trials, see Greenidge (1901) 497–99, and Lintott (2004) 71, neither of whom mentions the possibility of supplication at this stage.

24. See Alexander (1990) 143 (no. 295); David (1992) 624–26; Marinone (2004) 132.

brother of Scaurus), T. Annius Milo (who a few months previously had married Fausta following her divorce from Memmius), C. Peducaeus, C. Cato and M. Laenas Curtianus.]

Some fifty years later, then, this type of supplication involves not just the defendant but numerous members of his family as well, carefully arranged on either side of the jurors as they cast their votes.[25] This entreaty is again separate from the speeches of the defense advocates; indeed, nothing in what remains of the oration that Cicero delivered on this occasion hints at this upcoming supplication. Without Asconius's information, we would have had no idea that this piece of judicial theater took place.[26]

An obvious question arises: how often did these voting-time supplications take place? At first glance, the existence of only two such examples in some fifty years of judicial activity suggests that the practice was highly unusual. And yet our extant evidence is so meager that it is difficult to be sure we have a fully representative picture of Roman practices. Moreover, surviving visual depictions of Roman trials suggest that physical supplication was a feature readily associated with the courts.[27] Quintilian also evidently regarded supplication as a viable tactic within the imperial courtroom, although he does not specify at what stage in the trial it is best deployed.[28] It is also debatable whether our two Republican incidents quoted above attracted comment in our sources because voting-time supplication was *unusual in itself* or because they involved other noteworthy elements (namely, the drama of Piso's mud-smeared face and the high number of prestigious participants in Scaurus's plea).

Against these considerations, however, has to be placed the antipathy toward public supplication that (as we have seen) still seems to have prevailed in some quarters during the Late Republic. In my view, this antipathy probably ensured that voting-time supplication was not standard practice in Cicero's time. To be sure, other examples may well have taken place that are not preserved in our extant evidence; but these were

---

25. On the identities of the individuals involved, see Marshall (1985) 127; 150–53; Lewis (2006) 228–30. In some instances, their association with Scaurus is not clear, but most had some kind of familial connection.

26. Cf. Dyck (2012), who makes no mention of the incident in his commentary on Cicero's *Pro Scauro*.

27. See Gabelmann (1984) plates 19 and 21.2; David (1992) figs. 3a, 3b, and 5. Discussion also in Bablitz (2008).

28. See Quint. *Inst.* 6.1.34 (*stratum denique iacere et genua complecti*); cf. Bablitz (2007) 53. Further discussion in chapter five.

probably not so frequent that they influenced significantly the theatrics that Cicero employed in his perorations.[29]

A further complication arises in this regard from the recent claim that relatives of the accused would have regularly supplicated jurors *before* a trial.[30] Certainly, as we saw in the previous chapter, relatives and supporters would often be present at trials, sometimes dressed *in sordibus*. It is not impossible then that they made gestures of entreaty to the jurors as the various parties gathered at the start of the trial's business. But there is little evidence to suggest full-length prostration at this stage. Indeed, the use even of more restrained appeals is far from certain.[31] Any such activity was very likely informal, ad hoc, and entirely separate from the appeals that Cicero planned to make during his actual oration.

### APPEALS IN CICERO'S JUDICIAL SPEECHES

One of the Roman advocate's basic tasks was to serve as intermediary between his client and the jurors. In this capacity, he often needed to find appropriate ways of framing requests and pleas on his client's behalf. In some instances, polite assertion might be the most suitable mode; in others, desperate entreaty. In *Pro Archia*, for example, where the accused is of relatively modest social status, Cicero keeps his language fairly restrained. To be sure, he raises his stylistic register in the speech's peroration, employing both an exhortatory imperative (*qua re conservate, iudices*) and a polite direct request (*petimus a vobis, iudices*) in section 31. Nevertheless, the tone is one of courteous deference rather than impassioned emotion. Indeed, the verb *peto* is one regularly used in Cicero's letters when requesting a favor from an aristocratic acquaintance.[32] A

29. For further discussion of the trial of Scaurus and its theatrics, see chapter five.

30. See Naiden (2006) 65: "In Rome, friends and family, including women, would circulate outside the court in Antony's case. These multiple acts, some by the defendant, some by others, all occur before the defendant utters even a word in the course of the trial." See also p. 67: "Pathos pours from many voices, both individual and chorus. Cicero does not neglect the fundamentals: knee clasps before the trial."

31. Naiden's main evidence for his assertion seems to be App. *B Civ.* 3.51 and Livy 3.58.1–4. But Appian is describing an appeal made by Antony's relatives *before a meeting of the senate*, not before a court case; and it is hazardous to take the scene depicted at Livy 3.58 as typical of what went on before trials in the Late Republic. The source of Naiden's reference to Cicero's "knee clasps before the trial" (see previous note) is unclear. As we have seen, Cicero engaged in public supplication in response to Clodius's legislation in 58 BCE; but this is not the same as knee clasps before a trial.

32. See, e.g., *Fam.* 5.9.1; 6.7.6; 13.7.5; 13.11.2; 13.21.2; 13.37.1. Cf. Risselada (1993) 250–51; Unceta Gomez (2009) 114–18. Naiden (2006) 91, n. 367 seems to be mistaken

similar tenor prevails at the conclusion of *Pro Balbo*. Cicero directly exhorts the jurors to show pity toward the defendant (*Balb.* 64: *miseremini eius*), but he does not attempt to develop this potentially emotional element at any length. The manner rather is one of urgent insistence as Cicero invokes the gods (*per deos immortales* at sect. 64) and piles up the imperatives (*Balb.* 64 and 65: *nolite iudices; nolite; proponite; cogitate; tenetote*).

We find a rather more plaintive form of appeal in Cicero's defense of Quinctius (a civil case pleaded before a single judge, C. Aquillius).[33] During the speech's introduction, Cicero outlines the difficulties confronting Quinctius in the present case and states (*Quinct.* 10):

> *te, C. Aquilli, vosque qui in consilio adestis, orat atque obsecrat ut multis iniuriis iactatam atque agitatam aequitatem in hoc tandem loco consistere et confirmari patiamini.*

> [Gaius Aquillius, and you who are his advisers: Quinctius begs and prays that you allow equity, which has been shaken and harassed by many acts of injustice, to find rest and strength at last in this tribunal.]

The same basic formula appears at the end of the speech as well (*Quinct.* 99: *itaque hoc te obsecrat, C. Aquilli, ut . . .* ). The religious connotations of the verb *obsecro* here endow it with a degree of force and impressiveness not present in *peto* and similar verbs of requesting;[34] but there is perhaps no need to conclude (as does Winterbottom) that, through such usage, "[g]ods and judges are put on much the same level."[35] We find similar expressions in urgent epistolary requests to Cicero made by M. Lepidus and M. Brutus (*Fam.* 10.35.2 and *Ad Brut.* 1.13.1, respectively). In such instances, there is no suggestion that Cicero is somehow on a par with the gods; the correspondents simply strive to convey their serious intent as petitioners and the importance that they attach to their requests.[36] In *Pro Quinctio*, then, the phrase endows the defendant's plea with a degree of earnestness and urgency, a tone that is reinforced by other elements

---

in classifying this request as an act of supplication. Cf. Naiden (2006) 342. On verbs of petitioning in Athenian courts, see Bers (2009) 87–89. Cf. Johnstone (1999) 117.

33. For a recent survey of this case, see Lintott (2008) 43–59.

34. On the original religious associations of the verb *obsecro*, see Unceta Gomez (2009) 68–72. On the use of *oro* to express urgency in Cicero's letters, see Risselada (1993) 253–55.

35. Winterbottom (2004) 226. See also 225: "where he can, [Cicero] brings his cases into closer relation with the divine."

36. Cf. Cicero's use of *oro et obsecro* at *Att.* 3.19.3.

in the peroration (see, e.g., *Quinct.* 95: *miserum . . . acerbum . . . calamito-sum . . . funestum*, etc.).

In cases involving more serious criminal charges, however, the language of appeal becomes more urgent still. In addition to *oro* and *obsecro*, we find the verbs *imploro* and *obtestor*, as well as the adjective *supplex*. The latter in particular has a strong connotation of submissiveness, and the main focus in the following discussion is on how (if at all) Cicero heightens the impact of these appeals with elements of judicial theater. As we shall see, his choice of strategy is influenced by a matrix of factors. First, given the aristocratic queasiness regarding supplication, he must decide in which voice to represent the appeal. Does he depict the defendant himself as the petitioner? Does he place the focus instead on the man's relatives and their appeals? Or does he try to bring his own authority to bear and offer an appeal in his own voice? Second, he must judge what physical actions can be incorporated with his remarks for greatest effect. These physical actions range from gestures of supplication to family tableaux involving friends and relatives. On occasions, too, tears were shed, a device that is given its own separate analysis in chapter four. Let us look, then, at some specific examples and the factors that shape Cicero's strategies.

## ADULT PROPS

One way in which Cicero heightens the emotive element in an appeal is to incorporate references to the defendant's family. If these relatives happen to be present in court, he will also try to integrate them directly in the physical action. The peroration on behalf of M. Fonteius (probably delivered in 69 BCE) represents perhaps the most ambitious example of this approach.[37] At the climax of the speech, Cicero exclaims (*Font.* 46): *dux Allobrogum ceterorumque Gallorum, num etiam de matris hunc complexu, lectissimae miserrimaeque feminae, vobis inspectantibus avellet atque abstrahet?* ("Surely the leader of the Allobroges and of the rest of the Gauls will not, as you all look on, wrench and tear away this man from the embrace

---

37. M. Fonteius was on trial for corruption while governor of Transalpine Gaul (probably from 74–72 BCE). See Alexander (1990) 94 (no. 186); Marinone (2004) 68. On his post as governor, see Broughton (1952) 104; 566. The dates of 74–72 for his governorship have been proposed most recently by Dyck (2012) 12. On the theatrics in this peroration, see also North (2000) 360–64; Winterbottom (2004) 221; 228. On the use of family members in the courts during the imperial period, see Bablitz (2007) 123–24.

of his mother, a most distinguished yet most unhappy woman?") From this remark, we can infer that Cicero brought forward Fonteius and his mother to stand in front of the jurors in an embrace, presumably making use of the same sort of space that was available to Antonius and M'. Aquillius in a similar context several decades earlier (see discussion in chapter one). Fonteius's sister (we learn) is also there, clinging to him on the other side (*Font.* 46): *praesertim cum virgo Vestalis ex altera parte germanum fratrem complexa teneat vestramque, iudices, ac populi Romani fidem imploret.* ("Especially since, on the other side, a Vestal Virgin holds her blood-brother in her embrace and implores your protection, gentlemen, and that of the Roman people.")[38]

The staging of this family tableau is clearly designed to heighten the impact of Cicero's emotive words. The physical presence of these distressed relatives right in front of the jurors makes their suffering difficult to ignore. This effect is augmented further by a direct appeal from Fonteius's sister (*Font.* 48): *tendit ad vos virgo Vestalis manus supplices easdem quas pro vobis dis immortalibus tendere consuevit.* ("To you a Vestal Virgin extends in supplication the very same hands that she has been accustomed to extend to the immortal gods on your behalf.") As we have noted, in some instances Cicero uses the vocabulary of supplication in the metaphorical, figurative sense of "plead desperately"; in this case, however, the explicitness of the phrase *manus supplices easdem, quas* suggests that Fonteia is literally stretching out her hands to the jurors in supplication, probably in a gesture similar to that used when praying to the gods.[39] (There is no indication, however, that she is engaging in full-length prostration.) The grand emotion of this scene then reaches a climax as Fonteius himself bursts into tears when confronted with this depiction of family piety (*Font.* 48): *videtisne subito, iudices, virum fortissimum, M. Fonteium, parentis et sororis commemoratione lacrimas profudisse?* ("Members of the jury, do you see how M. Fonteius—a very brave man—has suddenly poured forth tears at the mention of his parent and his sister?")

This example presents one of Cicero's most elaborate uses of judi-

---

38. Cf. Dyck (2012) 78–79.

39. Cf. Dyck (2012) 79: "This is doubtless staged so that Fonteia performs the act of supplication as C. describes it." Quintilian in his discussion of oratorical delivery refers to a gesture of supplication that involves stretching out both arms and lowering them slightly (*Inst.* 11.3.114–115): *sive in latus utramque distendimus sive satisfacientes aut supplicantes (diversi autem sunt hi gestus) summittimus.* Cf. also *Inst.* 11.3.86 on the use of the hands in supplication. For a visual representation of supplication involving an individual on his knees with arms extended (from Trajan's column), see Freyburger (1988) fig. 4.

cial theater. He coordinates embraces, tears, and supplicatory gestures involving three individuals into a single highly emotional scene. And yet we can see that this bold piece of showmanship was only possible because of several fortuitous circumstances. First, the defendant himself was clearly willing to take an active part in the appeal. As we have noted, this was not something the advocate could take for granted. A man such as M'. Aquillius was unwilling even to address a plea to the jurors, let alone burst into tears. Second, several relatives were prepared to assist in the spectacle. And, perhaps most useful of all, Fonteia's position as Vestal Virgin provided Cicero with rich material to exploit in his emotional pleas. In section 47, for example, he deftly elaborates upon her poignant position as one who cannot give birth to any male relatives of her own (*Font.* 47):

> nam ceterae feminae gignere ipsae sibi praesidia et habere domi fortunarum omnium socium participemque possunt; huic vero virgini quid est praeter fratrem quod aut iucundum aut carum esse possit?

[Other women can themselves produce offspring to support them, and can have at home a companion to share all their fortunes; yet for this virgin before you, who except her brother can bring her love and delight?]

Possibly, too, Fonteia's embrace of her brother helped to endow him with an aura of inviolability in the jurors' minds. We may compare the famous example of the Vestal Claudia, whose embrace of her father during his controversial triumphal procession in 143 BCE protected him from being manhandled by his opponents.[40] At the very least, her religious position endowed her appeal with a certain authority and helped to depict Fonteius's cause as quintessentially Roman (to be contrasted with the Gallic interests promoted by the prosecution).

Finally, the participants in these theatrics—as far as we can tell—played their roles competently and with conviction. This was important. A slight stumble or hesitation in such a scene could have had a disastrous effect. In this case, we can assume that Fonteius, as military commander, and Fonteia, as Vestal Virgin, had considerable experience with conducting themselves in front of a public audience. Nevertheless, some careful

---

40. See *Cael.* 34: *quae patrem complexa triumphantem ab inimico tribuno plebei de curru detrahi passa non est.* The father was Appius Claudius Pulcher (cos. 143); cf. Broughton (1951) 471–72; Austin (1960) 93; North (2000) 367.

preparation and rehearsal would still have been required. As we shall see in chapter five, this aspect of the advocate's preparation for a trial remains largely submerged in our ancient sources.

We do not find the same degree of orchestrated theatrics in any other peroration. The family tableau that Cicero stages in *Pro Caelio*, for example, strikes a very different tone (*Cael.* 79):

> *quod cum huius vobis adulescentiam proposueritis, constituitote ante oculos etiam huius miseri senectutem qui hoc unico filio nititur, in huius spe requiescit, huius unius casum pertimescit.*

[But, when you have contemplated the tender years of Caelius here, set also before your eyes the old age of this unhappy man, who relies on this his only son, who takes solace in his future, and whose only fear is that some harm will befall him.]

The repeated demonstrative *huius* confirms that Cicero is deploying Caelius and his father as visual props. It is worth noting, however, that he has excluded Caelius's mother from the scene, even though she was present in court.[41] His aim (we may assume) was to place emphasis on the intimacy of the relationship between father and son, a feature that the prosecution had spent considerable time discrediting.[42]

Nevertheless, although Cicero incorporates into the peroration some emotive phrases (note *miseri*, *unico filio nititur* and *pertimescit*), the judicial theatrics here seem rather muted overall, especially when compared with the performances at the trial of Fonteius. There is no reference to tears and no clear proof that father and son were engaged in an embrace, although such a gesture would perhaps have been natural and effective. It is also unlikely that the elder Caelius directly supplicated the jurors. Cicero seems to have preferred instead to suggest a degree of submissiveness *without* an actual entreaty (*Cael.* 79):

> *quem vos supplicem vestrae misericordiae, servum potestatis, abiectum non tam ad pedes quam ad mores sensusque vestros, vel recordatione parentum vestrorum vel liberorum iucunditate sustentate.*

---

41. See *Cael.* 4: *quid parentes sentiant, lacrimae matris incredibilisque maeror, squalor patris et haec praesens maestitia quam cernitis luctusque declarat.* The attire of Caelius, who spoke on his own behalf, is not explicitly described, but it seems reasonable to assume that he was dressed *in sordibus*. Cf. the garb of Scaurus, who likewise spoke in his own defense in the trial of 54 BCE (Asc. *Scaur.* 20C: *ipse quoque Scaurus dixit pro se ac magnopere iudices movit et squalore et lacrimis*).

42. See *Cael.* 4; 18. Cf. May (1995) 435; Winterbottom (2004) 221.

[And [Caelius's father], who is a suppliant to your compassion, a slave to your power, and prostrate not so much at your feet as before your hearts and minds, I urge you to raise up, either because of your recollection of your own parents or the delight you take in your children.]

The language is certainly emphatic; but since the elder Caelius is not literally a *servus* to the jurors' *potestas*, it is reasonable to suppose that the parallel adjective *supplicem* has a similarly metaphorical meaning. Likewise, the force of *abiectus* is mitigated by the phrase *non tam ad pedes quam ad mores sensusque vestros*, which shifts the emphasis toward the jurors' compassionate sensibilities.[43]

Cicero's phrasing thus required the old man to adopt an appropriately pitiful demeanor, but any gestures of anxious petition are difficult to establish. Certainly he did not engage as energetically in this piece of judicial theater as Fonteius and his family did. Indeed, the only direct plea comes from Cicero himself a little earlier (*Cael.* 78: *oro obtestorque vos, iudices*), where it is combined with fierce criticism of Sextus Cloelius's recent acquittal and of Clodia's *libido* in pursuing the present case. Moreover, the peroration concludes with a series of exhortatory imperatives rather than appeals (sect. 79: *nolite, iudices*; sect. 80: *conservate parenti filium*), and the very last phrase in the speech uses language more typical of Cicero's letters of recommendation than oratorical appeal (sect. 80: *fructus uberes diuturnosque capietis*).[44] The tone is thus one of insistent but polite deference rather than desperate entreaty. Most significant of all is the fact that Caelius himself seems to have played a very restrained role in this final scene. Perhaps he embraced his father—but there is no indication of tears and no obvious appeal to the jury.

Two factors may lie behind this constrained stance. First, like M'. Aquillius, Caelius may simply have been unwilling to adopt too submissive a pose. Several of his personal enemies (including Clodia) would have been present at the trial, and no doubt they were enjoying the discomfort and embarrassment that such proceedings brought.[45] Caelius, then, may have been determined not to give them the further satisfaction

---

43. Cf. Winterbottom (2004) 222.

44. See *Fam.* 13.22.2; 13.50.2; 13.64.1; 13.65.2. Cf. also Cicero's personal pledge at *Cael.* 77 (*promitto / spondeo*), which deploys the language of patronage between equals rather than submissive entreaty. Cf. Hall (2009a) 199.

45. In addition to Clodia, one of the speakers for the prosecution, L. Sempronius Atratinus, was the son of L. Calpurnius Bestia, with whom Caelius was engaged in a judicial feud. See *Cael.* 16; 76; Wiseman (1985) 67–68; Alexander (1990) 130–31 (nos. 268 and 269). Cf. the characterization of Caelius preserved at Sen. *De Ira* 3.8.6: *Caelium oratorem fuisse iracundissimum constat*. See also Geffcken (1973) 8–10.

of seeing him in a position of abject contrition. The second factor is perhaps more strategic. As scholars have noted, Cicero throughout his speech tries to depict the prosecution as nothing more than a malicious attack sponsored by a scorned woman.[46] The charges (he implies) are barely worth the court's time. From this perspective, then, too dramatic a conclusion would prove counterproductive. It would bestow too much credibility upon the prosecution. Cicero and Caelius thus need to show respect to the jurors and treat the situation seriously; but they also strive to diminish any hint of desperation.


CHILD PROPS


In three extant speeches, Cicero uses the son of the defendant as a prop in his judicial theater. The basic principle here is the same as in the two previous examples: Cicero directs the jurors' attention to innocent members of the accused's family and so broadens the scope of his appeal.[47] This aim appears most clearly in his defense in 62 BCE of P. Sulla, who had been charged with political violence in connection with the Catilinarian conspiracy.[48] The defendant's character was already tainted by an earlier conviction for corruption during the elections for 65 BCE (which subsequently led him to be ejected from the senate).[49] It is sensible, then, for Cicero to promote Sulla's family members—rather than Sulla himself—as figures deserving the jury's sympathy (*Sull.* 88): *neque enim nunc propulsandae calamitatis suae causa supplex ad vos, iudices, confugit, sed ne qua generi ac nomini suo nota nefariae turpitudinis inuratur.* ("[Sulla] has sought refuge as a suppliant before you, gentlemen, not in order to avert his own ruin, but to save his family and name from the stigma of criminal disgrace.") He then narrows the focus to Sulla's young son (*Sull.* 88): *id metuit, ne denique hic miser coniurati et conscelerati et proditoris filius nominetur.* ("His final fear is this—that this poor boy here be called the son of a conspirator, criminal and traitor.") Sulla's reputation as a politician may be dubious, but at least (Cicero implies) he is a caring and concerned father.

---

46. See Quint. *Inst.* 4.1.39; Tatum (2011) 165 and 177 (with references in n. 1).

47. Cf. Winterbottom (2004) 216: "the peroration did well to widen the focus." See also *Part. Orat.* 128.

48. See *Sull.* 11; 14; Alexander (1990) 114–15 (no. 234); Berry (1996) 10–11.

49. See Broughton (1952) 157; Berry (1996) 4–5; 167–68; cf. Alexander (1990) 101 (no. 201).

With this ground prepared, Cicero presents the boy as making his own plea to the jurors (*Sull.* 89): *hic vos orat, iudices, parvus, ut se aliquando si non integra fortuna, at ut adflicta patri suo gratulari sinatis.* ("This little boy, gentlemen, begs you to allow him at long last to congratulate his father so far as his battered fortune permits, even if he cannot do so with it intact.") There is no explicit indication here that the boy made any gesture of entreaty as Cicero spoke these words, or that he and his father engaged in an embrace. He was, however, positioned on the defense benches with other members of the family, whose solidarity is emphasized in a later entreaty (*Sull.* 89): *ut cum parente, cum liberis, cum fratre, cum his necessariis lugere suam calamitatem liceat, id sibi ne eripiatis vos, iudices, obtestatur.* ("[Sulla] entreats you, gentlemen of the jury, not to strip from him the right to mourn his misfortune in the company of his parent, his children, his brother and his relatives here in court.")

Here too we lack stage directions; perhaps the visual image of these individuals grouped together (all except the children presumably dressed *in sordibus*) was sufficient for Cicero's purposes.[50] But Sulla was desperate—or cynical—enough to allow himself to be depicted as submissive, as the phrases *supplex ad vos, iudices* (at *Sull.* 88 above) and *vos, iudices, obtestatur* (*Sull.* 89) indicate. (As we have seen, Caelius, by contrast, was reluctant to adopt such a pose at his trial.) It is not clear, however, whether Sulla reinforced this depiction with supplicatory gestures. Certainly the way in which Cicero breaks off his peroration because of his *dolor animi* suggests that he is striving for a high emotional tenor;[51] but the degree to which Sulla contributed to this by literal supplication or gestures of entreaty cannot now be recovered.

The defendant's son plays a rather more active role in events during the trial of P. Sestius (56 BCE).[52] In this instance, Cicero takes the unusual step of introducing the young man at an early stage in the speech, inviting him to read out a decree passed by officials in Capua in support of his father (*Sest.* 10):

---

50. See Berry (1996) 313 on these individuals. The *frater* was Sulla's (half-) brother, L. Caecilius Rufus (cf. *Sull.* 62: *hunc*); Sulla's mother is probably indicated by the reference to his *parens* (his father was by now deceased). A second child (his stepson, Memmius) is probably implicit in *cum liberis*. Also present were other associates (*his necessariis*). For the emotional potential of such a grouping, cf. Dixon (1991) 111 on the "sentimental ideal" of the Roman family: "The ideal, like our own, tended to focus on a particular stage of the life-cycle, that of the young family with small children or adolescents."

51. On Cicero's *dolor animi* here, see discussion in chapter four.

52. See Alexander (1990) 132 (no. 271); Marinone (2004) 118; Kaster (2006) 14–22.

*recita, quaeso, L. Sesti, quid decrerint Capuae decuriones, ut iam puerilis tua vox possit aliquid significare inimicis vestris, quidnam, cum se conroborarit, effectura esse videatur.*

[Lucius Sestius, please read out what the councillors at Capua decreed, so that your voice, although still boyish today, can give an indication to your enemies of what it is likely to achieve when it has matured.]

As Kaster notes, this tactic was designed to rouse compassion in the audience—and (perhaps we should add) admiration as well.[53] To most fathers in the audience, the young man's confident performance must have exemplified the kind of filial duty they hoped for in their own sons: he was appearing on a public stage, speaking with poise and assurance on behalf of his father, and willing to defend the honor of his family against its enemies.[54] Cicero thus begins the process of countering the prejudice stirred up by the prosecution against the defendant. Even if the jurors at this stage have doubts about the elder Sestius, they should at least respond warmly to this endearing picture of filial piety. Cicero seeks to engage their *benevolentia* using a device that derives, not from the rhetorical handbooks, but from his long practical experience in the courts.[55]

By comparison, the young man's role in the peroration of the speech is rather limited. Evidently he was expected to cry and look pleadingly at Cicero when required (*Sest.* 144: *oculis lacrimantibus me intuentem*), but there is little evidence in this case of a pitiful family tableau with his father. Indeed, the defendant seems (like Caelius) to have had no interest in presenting himself as *supplex* to the jury. He is not even depicted as making an entreaty. The suspicion arises, then, that Sestius, despite the strategic advantage of such a move, was unwilling to appear contrite and submissive in public—not surprising perhaps given his likely involvement in gang warfare during his year as tribune.[56]

Nevertheless, in this instance, unlike in *Pro Caelio*, Cicero seems to

---

53. Kaster (2006) 124.

54. Cf. Epstein (1987) 23: "A Roman was expected to avenge the wrongs he or his family received from their enemies."

55. There is no reference in the handbooks to this kind of ploy. Quintilian, however, does note that the methods used to stir pity at the start of a speech must be more restrained than those used in the peroration (Quint. *Inst.* 4.1.28): *in ingressu parcius et modestius praetemptanda sit iudicis misericordia.*

56. Cf. *Sest.* 78, 84 and 90 for the accusations that Sestius had hired bodyguards and henchmen. As noted by Kaster (2006) 14: "Cicero by design says almost nothing on [Sestius's tribunate]."

have been determined to incorporate a strong emotional element into the final appeal. To accomplish this goal without the assistance of the defendant, Cicero bases the plea around *his own* suffering. He invites the jurors to feel sympathy for himself as much as for Sestius.[57] This tactic was a potentially risky one. Any attempt to generate pity from his own position depended a good deal on the audience's goodwill toward him. The fact that he deploys such a strategy on numerous occasions (in some cases with theatrical tears as well, as we shall see in chapter four) attests to Cicero's confidence, both in the jurors' generally supportive attitude toward him and in his own ability to exploit it to good effect—or at least to his belief that this was the best available option in difficult circumstances.

It is no coincidence that most of these examples appear in speeches following Cicero's return from exile. Indeed, in *Pro Sestio*, Cicero's main approach is to associate the present trial with the traumatic events of that time. He highlights the crucial help that Sestius gave him during this period;[58] and he claims that the other prominent figures dressed *in sordibus* at the trial (including Milo and Lentulus Spinther) are now facing prosecution primarily because of the support they showed him during his absence from Rome.[59] This assertion is a tendentious one, but it enables Cicero to embark upon a lament that reminds the jury of his own recent sufferings (*Sest.* 145): *ac si scelestum est amare patriam, pertuli poenarum satis; eversa domus est, fortunae vexatae, dissipati liberi, raptata coniunx. . . .* ("And even if it is wrong to love one's fatherland, I have already suffered punishment enough. My home has been destroyed, my affairs thrown into confusion, my children put to flight, my wife assaulted. . . .")

Having thus put himself center stage, Cicero can now link his fate with that of Sestius (and Milo) (*Sest.* 146): *an ego in hac urbe esse possim his pulsis qui me huius urbis compotem fecerunt?* ("Could I remain in this city, if these men who granted me possession of it have been driven out?") A vote against Sestius (he implies) is in effect a vote against Cicero as well. And in the absence of emotional display from Sestius himself, Cicero tries to stir the jurors' feelings of pity via his own professions of distress.

---

57. Cf. Winterbottom (2004) 220, n. 24. See also Naiden (2006) 67: "Roman practice adds to all these elements a new one, the role of the advocate. . . . If the defendant cannot supplicate plausibly, the advocate supplicates for him." See also Thierfelder (1965) 407–8; Paterson (2004) 92–95.

58. *Sest.* 144: *video P. Sestium, meae salutis, vestrae auctoritatis, publicae causae defensorem, propugnatorem, actorem, reum.*

59. *Sest.* 145: *atque hic tot et talium civium squalor, hic luctus, hae sordes susceptae sunt propter unum me, quia me defenderunt, quia meum casum luctumque doluerunt. . . .*

Indeed, he concludes the speech with an appeal to the jurors in his own voice (*Sest.* 147): *qua re obtestor atque obsecro ut, si me salvum esse voluistis, eos conservetis per quos me recuperavistis.* ("So, then, if you wanted me to be saved from exile, I beg and entreat you, to protect those who restored me to you.")

Although most of the instances where Cicero attempts to stir up sympathy from his own plight date to the years following his exile, one does not. In his defense of Flaccus in 59 BCE, he utilizes instead the trials and tribulations of the Catilinarian conspiracy (63 BCE) as his emotional link with the defendant.[60] Flaccus was praetor at the time of this crisis, and Cicero claims that the man provided him with crucial assistance. This help (he asserts) established a special bond between the two of them, sanctified by oaths and promises that Cicero is now obliged to uphold (*Flac.* 103): *ego te, si quid gravius acciderit, ego te, inquam, Flacce, prodidero. o mea dextera illa, mea fides, mea promissa.* ("If you should suffer any greater harm, Flaccus, it will be I who have betrayed you. Alas for that handshake of mine, my promise, my pledges.")

Cicero further heightens the emotional intensity of the moment by representing Flaccus junior as suppliant to the jurors, and suggesting that they have the opportunity to serve as his mentor through their verdict (*Flac.* 106): *huic, huic misero puero vestro ac liberorum vestrorum supplici, iudices, hoc iudicio vivendi praecepta dabitis.* ("To this poor boy here, a suppliant to you and to your children, gentlemen, you will give through your judgement a guide on how to live.")[61] Indeed, Cicero depicts the boy as tearfully imploring him to live up to the promises made to his father (*Flac.* 106): *meam quodam modo flens fidem implorat ac repetit eam quam ego patri suo quondam pro salute patriae spoponderim dignitatem.* ("Somehow he pleads for my help with tears in his eyes and claims as his right that same position of rank that I once promised to his father for saving our country.") Cicero thus cleverly invites his audience to feel concern for both the son's tearful plight and his own inability to keep his promises if Flaccus is convicted.

Here, too, conspicuous by its absence is any element of entreaty from the defendant himself. Flaccus, like Sestius, seems to have been reluctant to adopt a pose of submission. Although the extended closing sentence

---

60. On the trial, see Alexander (1990) 122–23 (no. 247).
61. The term *supplex* must be metaphorical here, since the boy cannot literally be a suppliant to the jurors' children (who would not have been in court). The aim rather is to elicit the jurors' paternal instincts, as Cicero places them in the role of moral guides (*vivendi praecepta dabitis*).

of the speech calls for the jury's pity, it does so with dignified exhortatory imperatives rather than desperate appeals, and Cicero chooses to stress Flaccus's family, courage, and importance to the *res publica* rather than the catastrophic consequences of a conviction (*Flac.* 106): *miseremini familiae, iudices, miseremini fortissimi patris, miseremini fili; nomen clarissimum et fortissimum vel generis vel vetustatis vel hominis causa rei publicae reservate.* ("Pity the family, gentlemen, pity the redoubtable father, pity the son. Whether it be for his family's sake, or for his ancient lineage or for the man himself, preserve an illustrious and proud name for the Republic.")[62] Flaccus, we may suppose, was not inclined to contrition. As in *Pro Sestio*, Cicero's solution to this problem was to generate the emotion he needed from his own obligations to the defendant and his family.

In these three speeches, then, the role played by child props is relatively modest. Cicero refers to their distress in a few sentences during the peroration, but he does not base an extended scene around them (such as he does with Fonteius and Fonteia). At these moments, the children would have needed to adopt a sorrowful demeanor as Cicero drew attention to them, but, as far as we can tell, no other stage business was involved. This general restraint was presumably a matter of strategy. From a tactical point of view, Cicero was reluctant perhaps to place *too much* emphasis on such relatives. Although they broadened the range of emotional cues at his disposal, he was unwilling to make them the prime focus. Practical considerations of performance may have played a part in this approach. Just as the modern theatrical adage advises actors not to share the stage with animals or children, so Cicero may have recognized the potential perils of relying too heavily on youngsters as a source of pathos. The rewards were considerable if the performance went smoothly, but, as we shall see in chapter five, disaster could ensue if these human props did not play their part competently.

In this respect, it is frustrating that we know so little about Cicero's use of the two child props mentioned at *Orat.* 131 (quoted at the start of this book). Evidently in these instances the youngsters were small enough to pick up in his arms with ease (*Orat.* 131: *in manibus perorantes tenuerimus; sublato etiam filio parvo*).[63] His reference in the latter case to filling the forum with wailing and lamentation (*plangore et lamentatione*) suggests that the child constituted a significant focus of emotion. Per-

---

62. See Schöggl (2002) 91–100 on the use of *misericordia* and its cognates in Cicero's speeches.

63. As we saw in chapter one, Sulpicius Galba seems to have done the same with the son of Galus.

haps a readily portable child was easier to manage than a slightly older one. (Presumably the experienced orator could slyly attribute any crying or distress to the infant's awareness of the dangers currently facing the accused.) But, unfortunately for us, Cicero—perhaps deliberately—has drawn a veil over his technique in such instances. What may have been his most theatrically sentimental attempts to elicit pity from the assembled crowds are now hidden from view.

## PLEAS WITHOUT PROPS

Cicero's strategic options were naturally more constrained when such props were not available. Murena, for example, was evidently handicapped by a dearth of available relatives when accused of electoral corruption in 63 BCE. Cicero tries to compensate for this shortfall by at least invoking the man's family connections verbally, even if they are not present in person. He alludes to the family bust of his dead father (*Mur.* 88: *imaginem clarissimi viri, parentis sui*); to the kisses of his mother (*ad matrem, quae misera modo consulem osculata filium suum*);[64] and to his absent brother, who was overseas serving in the provinces (*Mur.* 89). In such situations, the presence of other supporters becomes all the more important. As we saw in the previous chapter, Cicero had arranged for a deputation from Murena's hometown of Lanuvium to attend the trial;[65] nevertheless, the means available for generating pity were limited. Fortunately, in this case the defendant himself was willing to be made the focus of the *miseratio* (*Mur.* 86):

> *nunc idem <in> squalore et sordibus, confectus morbo, lacrimis ac maerore perditus vester est supplex, iudices, vestram fidem obtestatur, vestram misericordiam implorat, vestram potestatem ac vestras opes intuetur.*[66]

[Now this very same man is before you as a suppliant, gentlemen, dressed in dirty, filthy clothes, exhausted by his illness, overwhelmed by tears and sorrow. He pleads for your protection, begs for your compassion, and looks to your power and resources to help him.]

---

64. *Mur.* 88 confirms that Murena's mother was still alive at the time of the trial, but, for some reason, unable to attend.

65. Cf. Winterbottom (2004) 227, n. 56.

66. For this textual reading, see, e.g., Berry (2000) xxxv.

The accumulation of submissive terms (*supplex, obtestatur, implorat, intuetur*) is emphatic, and this image is reinforced a short while later as Murena is portrayed again as directly entreating the jurors (*Mur.* 87: *ita vos L. Murena, iudices, orat atque obsecrat*). As we have noted, the use of the term *supplex* need not indicate literal supplication;[67] nevertheless, Cicero's emphasis on Murena's entreaties would be counterproductive if they were not matched by an appropriate demeanor. Some kind of supplicatory gesture of the arms such as Fonteia's seems plausible in this instance, although proof is lacking.

Cicero had faced similar challenges in the two murder trials of Roscius of Ameria and Aulus Cluentius. Both cases involved deadly disputes within the family, and in both instances the defendants lacked support from their immediate kin. To bolster Cluentius's position, then, Cicero packed the court with seven delegations of supporters from various districts, including one from the man's hometown of Larinum (*Clu.* 197–98). Indeed, his attempts to create a positive impression of Cluentius go a step further. In a move not paralleled elsewhere, he invites these fellow townsmen to stand up as a court official reads out their testimonial on Cluentius's behalf (*Clu.* 196: *vos quaeso, qui eam detulistis, adsurgite*). These supporters—like good family members—then proceed to shed tears as they listen (*Clu.* 197: *ex lacrimis horum, iudices, existimare potestis omnes haec decuriones decrevisse lacrimantes*). Even if Cluentius's own family is highly dysfunctional, Cicero can at least create an impression of the accused as a man tightly integrated into the social networks around him.[68]

Having thus established an image of Cluentius as loved by his friends and deserving of a decent person's pity, Cicero can go on to depict the man himself in a supplicatory pose (*Clu.* 200): *sin autem, id quod vestra natura postulat, pudorem, bonitatem virtutemque diligitis, levate hunc aliquando supplicem vestrum, iudices. . . .* ("If, however, as your nature demands, gentlemen, you love honor, virtue and goodness, lift up this man who is at last a suppliant to you. . . .") Cicero's use of *levate* here need not imply that Cluentius has actually prostrated himself. He uses a similar term (*sustentate*) metaphorically in *Pro Caelio* with reference to Caelius's father

---

67. So too Vasaly (2000) 462, who argues for a metaphorical interpretation of the phrase. Less convincing, however, is the claim that the verbal appeals at section 87 are placed in Murena's mouth "both as *pro forma* and as a reflection of a potent public ritual of humility demanded by the Roman public of all who underwent trial." As we have seen, some aristocrats were less prepared than others to engage in shows of humility.

68. Note also Cicero's rather forced references at *Clu.* 198 to supporters of high rank who have not been able to attend the trial. On the tears of the townsmen from Larinum, see chapter four.

(see above).[69] Nevertheless, Cluentius, like Murena, seems to have engaged energetically in this submissive role, shedding tears as he made his pleas (*Clu.* 201): *orat vos Habitus, iudices, et flens obsecrat, ne se invidiae . . . ne matri . . . ne Oppianico . . . condonetis.* ("Habitus [i.e., Cluentius] begs and beseeches you in tears, gentlemen, that you do not deliver him up to maliciousness . . . nor to his mother . . . nor to Oppianicus.") Again, some sort of supplicatory gesture seems plausible.

Cicero's peroration on behalf of Roscius of Ameria shares some similarities in approach. Toward the end of the speech he does his best to present the defendant in the company of respected and influential individuals, referring in particular to the support of Caecilia (*Rosc. Am.* 147: *spectatissima femina*) and a certain Messalla (*Rosc. Am.* 149).[70] Indeed, as the rhetoric rises toward its conclusion, Cicero even describes Roscius as a son esteemed by his family (*Rosc. Am.* 152: *probatum suis filium*). Nevertheless, the fact remained that Roscius, like Cluentius, had no *close* relatives upon whom an effective appeal could be based. In this case, however, there is no apparent entreaty from the defendant. Indeed, Cicero steers clear of direct appeals altogether. The only plea incorporated into the peroration involves a rather unusual trope, as he apostrophizes the absent figure of Chrysogonus (*Rosc. Am.* 144):[71]

> *rogat oratque te, Chrysogone, si nihil de patris fortunis amplissimis in suam rem convertit . . . anulumque de digito suum tibi tradidit . . . ut sibi per te liceat innocenti amicorum opibus vitam in egestate degere.*

[Roscius requests and entreats you, Chrysogonus, that, if he has taken nothing from his father's extensive riches into his own estate . . . and has given to you the very ring from his finger . . . that you allow him, innocent as he is, to live out his life in poverty supported by the assistance of his friends.]

The absence of Chrysogonus necessarily imparts to the appeal an element of artificiality, but there is a bitter edge to the phrasing as well: despite all of Chrysogonus's terrible crimes against him, Roscius is asking only to be allowed to live the rest of his life in poverty. This is far more oblique than a direct plea to the jurors begging for acquittal.

---

69. Cf. Winterbottom (2004) 222. For the act of raising up a suppliant to signify a positive response to a plea, see, e.g., Livy 39.13.3 (*attollere*); Val. Max. 5.1.8 (*adlevavit*); Suet. *Ner.* 13 (*adlevatum*). Cf. Gould (1973) 78.

70. Probably M. Valerius Messalla Niger (cos. 61); see Dyck (2010) 203 for discussion.

71. On the absence of Chrysogonus, see n. 68 in chapter two.

Any sympathy, then, that Cicero hopes to generate for Roscius depends on presenting him as a victim of Chrysogonus's cruel abuse of power. To develop this portrayal, Cicero uses another unusual device, speaking in the voice of Roscius himself in another imagined address to Chrysogonus.[72] Again, the tone steers clear of desperate appeal, as Roscius is presented initially as a man of forebearance in the face of injustice (e.g., *Rosc. Am.* 145: *mea domus tibi patet, mihi clausa est; fero*). He goes on, however, to express his indignation at Chrysogonus's actions in a series of vigorous rhetorical questions (*Rosc. Am.* 145). Cicero pursues a similar tactic in his defense of Cluentius, prefacing the accused's appeal with an extended attack on the man's mother, Sassia, and her vindictive attempts to harm her son (*Clu.* 199–200). But in this peroration on behalf of Roscius, the focus is kept even more insistently on the unfair treatment experienced by the defendant. Even when Cicero introduces the concept of the jury's *misericordia* at section 150, he does not apply it directly to Roscius. He describes it as a quality required by the state as a whole, and contrasts it with the *crudelitas* of recent times.[73]

Cicero thus virtually omits the element of appeal altogether.[74] His reason for this is not entirely clear. His tactic in the trial of Cluentius some years later suggests that he did not regard it as entirely inappropriate for a man accused of family murder to seek pity from a jury. Perhaps then his decision to dispense with such an appeal in Roscius's case was simply an ad hoc judgement. In the aftermath of Sulla's proscriptions, he may have believed the jury would be more easily persuaded by resentment at Chrysogonus than pity for the accused. But perhaps the personality of Roscius was a factor too. If there was any truth to the prosecution's exaggerated depiction of him as a surly rustic, Cicero may not have trusted him to play his part successfully in an appeal; indeed, Roscius may have been unwilling even to try to do so.[75]

But perhaps Cicero's greatest challenge in constructing an emotional appeal arose in his defense of Milo.[76] As we saw in chapter two, Milo re-

---

72. See Dyck (2010) 200 on this device of *sermocinatio*; cf. Quint. *Inst.* 6.1.26; Lausberg (1998) 366–69, sections 820–24.

73. See *Rosc. Am.* 150 with reference to *ea crudelitas quae hoc tempore in re publica versata est*.

74. See Craig (2010) 84 on *indignatio* in this peroration: "Cicero's attack upon Chrysogonus . . . blurs the line between the complaint of a *patronus* appealing for pity and the *indignatio* of a prosecutor." Cf. also Craig (2010) 86: "This is virtually a prosecutor's peroration"; Dyck (2010) 197.

75. On the prosecution's depiction of Roscius, see n. 104 in chapter one.

76. As noted by Quintilian (*Inst.* 6.1.25): *nam quis ferret Milonem pro capite suo supplicantem qui a se virum nobilem interfectum quia id fieri oportuisset fateretur?* ("Who would have put up with Milo begging for his life, when he had admitted that he had slain a man of high status because it had been right to do so?")

fused to adopt *sordes* or express any sense of remorse at Clodius's death. Moreover there are no references to relatives of Milo providing support for him at the trial. Cicero thus had no props at his disposal to utilize in an appeal, and he had to contend with a truculent defendant unwilling to sue for mercy. On the side of the prosecution, by contrast, was a grieving widow who presented her testimony in a highly theatrical manner.[77]

Cicero's first step in this difficult situation is to present Milo's impassive demeanor as the admirable staunchness of a political martyr.[78] He depicts the defendant as resolutely accepting the consequences of his actions because they have brought benefit to the state (*Mil.* 93). But having imparted this positive spin to Milo's outer appearance, Cicero cleverly goes on to suggest that there is in fact emotional turmoil within, attributing to him several *imaginary* exclamations (*Mil.* 94: *o frustra, inquit, mei suscepti labores, o spes fallaces, o cogitationes inanes meae!*). As Quintilian notes, these laments are designed to be consistent with the wider depiction of Milo as a staunch individual; they thus carefully avoid any note of self-pity.[79] Milo's professed regrets concern not himself but the failure of his plans to rescue the state from danger. Having established Milo's matyrdom for the republic, Cicero can then go on to suggest in more plaintive language that the man has been unjustly forsaken by his political allies (*Mil.* 94: *ubi nunc senatus est quem secuti sumus . . . ?*). Cicero deftly softens Milo's ostensibly uncaring façade.[80]

But there was a limit to how far this device could be extended, and the rest of the peroration is devoted to the strategy that we have already identified in *Pro Sestio* and *Pro Flacco*: Cicero tries to generate sympathy from his own plight rather than the defendant's.[81] As in those earlier speeches, the first step is to draw attention to the profound obligations that exist between Cicero and the accused. And again, the point of emo-

---

77. On Fulvia's dress and comportment during the trial, see chapter two.

78. Cf. Dyck (1998) 227–33, who suggests that this depiction of martyrdom incorporates Stoic influences as well. See also the remarks of Axer (1989) 308–11 on Cicero's comparison of Milo with a gladiator; and more generally Clark and Ruebel (1985); May (1988) 132–38.

79. See Quint. *Inst.* 6.1.27: *itaque idem Cicero, quamquam preces non dat Miloni eumque potius animi praestantia commendat, accomodavit tamen ei convenientis etiam forti viro conquestiones: 'frustra' inquit* etc. Cf. Tzounakas (2009) 129–30.

80. Cf. Tzounakas (2009) 129–30.

81. Cf. Quint. *Inst.* 6.1.24: *nonnumquam etiam ipse patronus has partes subit (ut Cicero pro Milone: o me miserum . . .) maximeque si, ut tum accidit, non conveniunt ei qui accusatur preces.* See also Casamento (2004) 55–58; Heckenkamp (2010) 179.

tional reference is Cicero's exile. As early as section 94, for example, Cicero puts the following remark in Milo's mouth (*Mil.* 94):

> *ego cum te . . . patriae reddidissem, mihi putarem in patria non futurum locum?*
> *. . . ubi denique tua, M. Tulli, quae plurimis fuit auxilio, vox atque defensio?*

[When I had restored *you* to the fatherland, could I have imagined that there would be no place for *me* in that same country? . . . Where, Marcus Tullius, is your eloquent advocacy, which has helped so many others?]

Cicero thus highlights the profound debt that he owes Milo with regard to his exile, and he goes on to claim that this debt brings him to tears (*Mil.* 95: *nec vero haec, iudices, ut ego nunc, flens*).

These obligations come to the fore again a few sections later (*Mil.* 100): *quid habeo quod faciam pro tuis in me meritis nisi ut eam fortunam quaecumque erit tua, ducam meam?* ("What return can I make to you for your services to me, except that whatever fortune befalls you I should count it as my own?") This sense of duty in turn becomes the catalyst for Cicero's first direct appeal to the jury (*Mil.* 100):

> *non abnuo, non recuso vosque obsecro, iudices, ut vestra beneficia quae in me con-*
> *tulistis aut in huius salute augeatis aut in eiusdem exitio occasura esse videatis.*

[I do not reject this fate, I do not spurn it, and I implore you, gentlemen, either to add to those kindnesses that you have bestowed upon me by saving Milo, or to realize that, by ruining him, you will destroy them.]

The stark formulation of this dilemma (*aut . . . aut*) identifies Milo's cause closely with Cicero's own. If the jurors do not help Milo, then the benefits that they have granted Cicero will be lost.

This notion that a vote against Milo is a vote against Cicero informs the rest of the peroration as well. Cicero himself now takes center stage and invites the jury to feel compassion for his plight at having failed to fulfil his moral obligation, should Milo be convicted (*Mil.* 102): *o me miserum, o me infelicem! revocare tu me in patriam, Milo, potuisti per hos, ego te in patria per eosdem retinere non potero.* ("O how wretched and unfortunate am I! You, Milo, were able to restore me to my fatherland with the assistance of these gentlemen—but through their help I shall not be able to keep you in yours.") Instead of referring to the plight of the accused's family at this point, Cicero invokes the sorrow of his own (*Mil.* 102): *quid respondebo liberis meis qui te parentem alterum putant? quid tibi, Quinte frater* . . . *?* ("What shall I reply to my children, who regard you as a father? What shall I say to you, brother Quintus . . . ?") We may note too the portrayal of Milo as a kind of surrogate father to Cicero's own children (*te parentem alternum putant*).

These same conceits are developed further as Cicero makes his second direct plea (*Mil.* 103):

> *nolite, obsecro vos, acerbiorem mihi pati reditum esse quam fuerit ille ipse discessus. nam qui possum putare me restitutum, si distrahor ab his per quos restitutus sum?*

[I beg you, do not allow my restoration from exile to be even more bitter than my actual departure was. For how can I regard myself as restored when I am torn from those who restored me?]

Following several further highly emotional exclamations, Cicero claims to be overwhelmed by tears (*Mil.* 105) and brings the speech to a swift conclusion, with a final plea for the jurors to have the courage to vote according to their feelings (*Mil.* 105: *vos oro obtestorque, iudices, ut in sententiis ferendis, quod sentietis, id audeatis*).

In this peroration, then, it is Cicero who takes on the burden of entreating the jury and of generating high emotion.[82] Without any help from the defendant or other human prop, he is forced (yet again) to use his own experiences in exile as the prompt for the audience's sympathy and pity. As we have seen, this was a strategy that he had used in previous cases, although this example is particularly elaborate.

There are several possible reasons for the extended nature of the appeal in this instance. It may be that the challenge posed by Milo's plight was especially great. In such unpromising circumstances, Cicero had to work particularly hard to secure the desired effect. But other factors may have shaped the text as well. We know, for example, that our extant version of the speech diverges in some significant respects from the one that Cicero actually delivered at the trial.[83] It is possible, then, that our text represents an idealized literary version of the kind of plea

---

82. Cf. Quint. *Inst.* 6.5.10: *quod illi preces non dedit et in earum locum ipse successit?*

83. See Asc. *Mil.* 41C and contrast the extant text of *Mil.* 72–89. For discussion, see Settle (1962) 237–60; Stone (1980); Riggsby (1999) 105–12; Lintott (2008) 119–20.

that Cicero strove for, rather than a precise record of what he was able to achieve under the fraught and raucous conditions of the trial.[84] Whatever the case, it is worth noting that, although the text includes several direct pleas to the jurors, there is no suggestion that Cicero engaged in any type of formal supplication before them. Evidently the advocate will engage in theatrically emotional appeals, but he does not himself supplicate.

## SUPPLICATION AND DICTATORSHIP

So far, then, we have found little evidence for defendants and their relatives engaging in full-length supplication during Cicero's speeches on their behalf. Fonteia, as we have seen, almost certainly engaged in some theatrical entreaties during the peroration on behalf of her brother, and Murena and Aulus Cluentius may well have adopted a similarly submissive pose. Our final example, however, involves a trial conducted under very different circumstances. In this particular case, there is good reason to suppose that supplication (including prostration) played a crucial part in Cicero's presentation of his case.

Cicero's speech on behalf of Q. Ligarius (*Pro Ligario*) was delivered during Caesar's dictatorship in 46 BCE, at a time when it was still unclear how he would treat those who had taken up arms against him in the civil wars.[85] It was also unclear how the senate was to function under his leadership. Nevertheless, a notable incident that took place in early October of that year hinted at the existence of a disturbing new dynamic. During a meeting of the senate, the respected consular L. Piso raised the issue of the continued exile of one of Caesar's enemies, M. Marcellus (*Fam.* 4.4.3: *a L. Pisone mentio esset facta de Marcello*). As he did so, the exile's brother, Gaius Marcellus, threw himself at Caesar's feet in supplication (*C. Marcellus se ad Caesaris pedes abiecisset*). Although such dramatic gestures were not unknown during the previous decades (as we have seen), what happened next was remarkable (*Fam.* 4.4.3): *cunctus [sc. senatus] consurgeret et ad Caesarem supplex accederet.* ("The whole senate rose as a group and approached Caesar in supplication.") It is difficult to imag-

---

84. On the difficulties in delivery that Cicero faced at the trial, see discussion in chapter five.

85. On Caesar's appointment as *dictator* for ten years, see Dio Cass. 43.14. By February 44 BCE he had been given the title *dictator perpetuo* (*Phil.* 2.87); see also Yavetz (1983) 38–45; Hall (2009b).

ine that each senator threw himself at Caesar's feet, as C. Marcellus had
done. It seems more likely that they moved toward Caesar as a group
with hands outstretched in entreaty, while a few perhaps went down on
bent knee before him. Whatever the precise details, the stunt conveyed
succinctly the fundamental shift in power that had taken place in the
wake of the civil war. Caesar was now Rome's grand patron dispensing
favors according to personal whim. This was not how the senate traditionally made decisions.

Nevertheless, Cicero attempted to put an optimistic gloss on events.
He celebrated the dictator's decision to allow Marcellus to return to
Rome and, in the following months, lent his support to others who were
likewise seeking the restoration from exile of their relatives.[86] These included the family of Q. Ligarius, and Cicero describes in a letter to the
man their recent attempts to plead his case before Caesar (*Fam.* 6.14.2):

> cum a. d. V Kal. intercalaris priores rogatu fratrum tuorum venissem mane ad
> Caesarem . . . cum fratres et propinqui tui iacerent ad pedes et ego essem locutus
> quae causa, quae tuum tempus postulabat. . . .

[On November 26, when, at the request of your brothers, I went to Caesar's morning reception . . . and when your brothers and relatives threw
themselves at his feet and I gave a speech appropriate to your situation
and circumstances. . . .[87]]

Having to engage in such supplication must have been dispiriting for traditional republicans, but presumably the potential benefits outweighed
any scruples. Indeed, Cicero was optimistic about Ligarius's restoration
in the near future (*Fam.* 6.14.2: *hac opinione discessi ut mihi tua salus dubia
non esset*). Unfortunately, however, a new obstacle quickly arose: one of
Ligarius's enemies (the younger Aelius Tubero) now sought permission
from Caesar to prosecute him.

Some scholars have viewed this prosecution itself as a form of political theater—a show trial designed to advertise publicly Caesar's *clemen-*

---

86. For Cicero's celebration of Caesar's decision, see, e.g., *Marcell.* 1: *tantam enim
mansuetudinem, tam inusitatam inauditamque clementiam; Marcell.* 12: *at haec tua iustitia et
lenitas florescet cotidie magis.* The aims and intentions of the speech have been debated; see
especially Winterbottom (2002), arguing against the extreme view of Dyer (1990), who
regards Cicero's praise of Caesar as essentially ironic and subversive. See most recently Dugan (2013). For Cicero's efforts in the cause of other exiles, see, e.g., *Fam.* 4.13, 6.5, 6.10b.
87. Cf. *Lig.* 13–14. See also Crawford (1984) 241–43.

*tia.*[88] This view seems to me overly cynical. A plausible motive for the judicial attack can be found readily enough in Tubero's resentment at the treatment he had suffered at Ligarius's hands in Africa.[89] Indeed, the recent supplication at Caesar's house had raised the possibility that Ligarius might even be restored to favor. Caesar for his part may well have approached the trial with an open mind. On the one hand, he was perhaps uneasy about dismissing too hastily the grievances of a man such as Tubero. Staging a formal trial thus gave him the chance to display his commitment to judicial transparency. Yet he would have been aware too that the occasion potentially offered him the chance to advertise his friendly disposition to former enemies.[90]

Whatever the precise motives, Cicero cleverly exploits Caesar's position as sole judge at the trial. His whole defense (he claims) is directed toward the dictator's sense of compassion (*Lig.* 1: *omnis oratio ad misericordiam tuam conferenda est*). Later too he asserts that, in this particular court, Caesar is more like a father than a juror. Cicero therefore needs to follow a different line of argument (*Lig.* 30): *sed ego apud parentem loquor:* "*erravit, temere fecit, paenitet; ad clementiam tuam confugio, delicti veniam peto, ut ignoscatur peto.*" ("But in the presence of a parent I argue like this: 'He has strayed, he has acted rashly, he is sorry. I appeal to your sense of mercy, I seek pardon for this fault, I plead for forgiveness.'")[91] Cicero thus suggests that the usual rules of advocacy do not apply in this situation: his arguments aim, not at proving Ligarius's innocence, but at securing Caesar's *clementia.*[92]

As Quintilian recognized, Cicero's professions in this respect are disingenuous; the speech in fact contains much more than just a plea for

---

88. See Kumaniecki (1967) 455–56; Craig (1984) 195, n. 6; 199; Johnson (2004); Gildenhard (2011) 234–35. On the *clementia Caesaris*, see the convenient summary in Griffin (2003).

89. Note the references to Tubero's *ira* (*Lig.* 22), his *iniuriae* (*Lig.* 24, 25, 29), and *querella* (*Lig.* 23). This personal animosity probably arose from Ligarius's refusal to help him when sick during the civil war, an event that Caesar regards as important enough to record at *B Civ.* 1.31 (although responsibility is assigned in the first place to Attius Varus). Cf. Bringmann (1986) 78–79; Gotoff (1993a) xxxiv.

90. See Gotoff (1993a) xxxii–xxxvii.

91. For this textual reading, see, e.g., Gotoff (1993a) 103.

92. Cf. also *Lig.* 29: *quicquid dixi, ad unam summam referri volo vel humanitatis vel clementiae vel misericordiae tuae.* As will become clear, my interpretation of Cicero's tactics here differs significantly from that recently offered by Gildenhard (2011) 233–40. In my view, although Cicero considered dictatorship objectionable, he regarded Caesar's policy of *clementia* positively, at least in the short term; cf. Winterbottom (2002). His aim in *Pro Ligario*, then, is narrow and specific: to gain Ligarius's restoration, using whatever strategies will aid this cause. Depicting Caesar as *pater* was one of these. I thus do not regard Cicero's *deprecatio* either as "a subversive snipe" or as "hilarious"; cf. Gildenhard (2011) 236–37.

mercy.[93] But Cicero's emphasis on *clementia* is shrewd. His references to fatherly indulgence and forgiveness create a context in which petition and supplication are entirely appropriate.[94] Thus, when Cicero at section 36 describes Ligarius's brother as petitioning Caesar as a suppliant (*Lig.* 36: *nunc a te supplex fratris salutem petit*), there are good grounds for interpreting the phrase literally. As we have seen, the man had already supplicated Caesar at his house, and the senate likewise had shown that submissive entreaty was an appropriate way to negotiate business with the dictator (or, as Cicero was careful to depict him, with the city's *parens*).[95] Indeed, in section 37, Cicero urges Caesar to act now in front of the people in the same way he had done in the senate house when supplicated there on behalf of Marcellus (*Lig.* 37: *fac igitur, quod de homine nobilissimo et clarissimo fecisti nuper in curia, nunc idem in foro. . . . ut concessisti illum senatui, sic da nunc populo*). An energetic supplication by Ligarius's relatives at this moment would have provided strong visual reinforcement for these remarks—as well as a propaganda coup that Caesar could exploit to the fullest.


CONCLUSIONS

As this analysis has shown, Cicero's judicial theatrics were carefully calibrated according to the needs of the moment. Various factors played a part in his calculations. When willing props such as Fonteius and Fonteia were at hand, he was prepared to base appeals on them and contrive a relatively complex form of stage action (including embraces, tears, and supplicatory gestures). He was keen also to involve child props where possible, although in our three extant examples, their roles in the peroration seem to have been kept fairly brief. Where no such accomplices were available, defendants sometimes placed themselves center stage as figures deserving pity (as we saw in the cases of Murena and Cluentius). In these instances, in particular, the precise extent of their submissive theatrics is difficult to gauge. Both context and language point to some

---

93. Note, for example, the skewed presentations of events and motives in sections 2–4; the criticisms of the prosecutor Tubero at 9–11 and 21–25; and the discussion of senatorial decrees at section 20. Cf. Craig (1984) 198; Montague (1992) 562. For Quintilian's view, see *Inst.* 7.4.17 with reference to Cicero's statement at *Lig.* 30.

94. For important comments on the Greek and Roman conceptions of "forgiveness," see Konstan (2010) 22–58.

95. Cf. the title *parens patriae* bestowed upon Caesar (probably) a year or so later; see Dio Cass. 44.4.4; App. *B Civ.* 2.106; Ramsey (2003) 208; Stevenson (2008) 104–10.

pose of humble entreaty, but formal, full-length prostration seems unlikely. Conversely, in the peroration to *Pro Roscio Amerino*, Cicero eschews appeals entirely. In this variety of approach, we can discern a lively rhetorical intelligence and impressive flexibility in technique.

No less fascinating, however, are those instances where Cicero seems to have been obliged to work around the defendant's reluctance to undertake an appeal. In *Pro Caelio*, as we have seen, he contrives a heartwarming scene of father-and-son unity but eliminates anything that might smack of desperation or submissiveness on the part of Caelius. In other cases, by contrast, Cicero takes on the burden of the appeal himself. Faced with the apparent reluctance of Flaccus, Sestius, and Milo to entreat the jurors directly, he strives to generate emotion from his own (supposed) distress at their plight. This was a matter of rhetorical strategy, not conceit.

Unfortunately, the paucity of our evidence makes it difficult to appraise in detail the appeals that *prosecuting* advocates integrated into their speeches. We know the bare outline of one example: in *Pro Cluentio*, Cicero asserts that Sassia, who was allegedly the driving force behind the prosecution of Cluentius, engaged in *vota* and *preces* during the trial (*Clu.* 201: *ne matri, cuius vota et preces a vestris mentibus repudiare debetis . . . condonetis*). But it is not entirely clear what form these took. If the prosecutor (the younger Oppianicus) followed the same basic technique that Cicero used in his defense perorations, he may well have brought Sassia forward in front of the jurors and put into her mouth a number of emotional prayers and appeals. Perhaps she also engaged in some form of supplicatory gesture. Indeed, since the prosecutor was her stepson, the potential existed for an effective depiction of family sorrow and solidarity. Yet, in the end, the details elude us, not least because our only glimpse of the scene is via the distorting lens of Cicero's own speech. Nevertheless, the incident is an important reminder that the pleas and entreaties that Cicero orchestrates in his defense speeches would sometimes have been operating as a counterweight to the earlier pleas and entreaties of his opponents.[96]

These appeals and their associated theatrics, however, always formed a *supplementary* strategy of persuasion within the speech as a whole. Cicero never relies upon these emotional arguments alone. This point was

---

96. Cf. Cicero's appeal based upon the *sordes* of the Sicilian provincials at *Verr.* 2.5.126–28. At the very end of the second *actio*, however, he focuses rather upon prayers to the gods. See *Verr.* 2.5.188: *vos etiam atque etiam imploro et appello sanctissimae deae*; and *ceteros item deos deasque omnes imploro et obtestor.*

well established in traditional rhetorical theory and is important for our understanding of the purpose of such appeals.[97] They were not designed to offer a humble admission of fault; they aimed rather to broaden the range of issues that jurors were to consider as they weighed their verdict.[98] The sight of distressed petitioners helped to shift attention away from rational argument and toward the realm of personal relationships (along with all the emotions they entail).

But while these emotional concerns were well understood by rhetorical theorists, the practical issue of how to stage such performances most effectively remained beyond the handbooks. For Cicero, it was the daily life of the Roman politician that provided the best grounding in such techniques. He would have observed his contemporaries engaging in supplication at election time and noted the risks and benefits involved in such posturing. He would also have witnessed rivals and allies deploying similar stunts in the senate, and he and his family themselves resorted to such measures before and during his exile. Appeals and supplication thus formed a familiar part of the general theatricality of life as a patron and grandee in Rome. Nevertheless, although Cicero integrates such elements into his defense speeches, his theatrics do not—except perhaps in the exceptional circumstances of *Pro Ligario*—go to the extremes that we have observed in the voting-time supplications of Piso (c. 110 BCE) and Scaurus (54 BCE). Although Cicero's attempts to generate high emotion often go beyond what we are familiar with today, there seem to have been some boundaries that he crossed only rarely and with good reason.

---

97. See *Inv. Rhet.* 2.104; *Rhet. Her.* 1.24; *Part. Orat.* 122; Quint. *Inst.* 7.4.17; cf. Arist. *Rhet.* 1.6; Konstan (2010) 26; 38.

98. Cf. Naiden (2006) 88: "But both Greek and Roman law court speeches show that defendants who supplicate do assert their innocence—and that they often assert their innocence at the very moment when they supplicate." See also Konstan (2001) 43; Bers (2009) 92.

# CHAPTER 4

# SHEDDING TEARS IN COURT
## When Crying Is Good

Jane Clifton, New Zealand Listener, July 12–18 (2008), p. 13: "As a former education chief, Maris O'Rourke, once reproached an executive who was aghast at her weeping during a meeting: 'Yes, I'm crying. Why aren't you?'"

Cicero in several orations develops his emotional theatrics to such an extent that he affects to break down in tears as he speaks.[1] Although such overt emotionality is not unknown in modern courtrooms, the image of a weeping male advocate is one that raises important questions, both about Roman cultural practices in general and Cicero's technique as a pleader in particular.[2] It has been suggested, for example, that public expressions of grief in Roman society were typically viewed as "woman's work," with men being expected to exhibit a contrasting degree of emotional restraint.[3] At first glance, then, the tears of a Roman advocate would seem to expose him to criticisms of acting in an unmanly fashion. In order to understand how Cicero could use such tears for oratorical advantage, we thus need to investigate Roman attitudes toward crying in some detail. Once we have established when and why public expressions of distress were acceptable in Rome, we can go on to examine the

---

1. See *Planc.* 104; *Mil.* 105; *Rab. Post.* 47–48; *Cael.* 60. Evidently Cicero also shed tears in his defense of Cispius, a speech that he did not publish (see further discussion below). As noted in chapter three, Cicero at *Sull.* 92 claims to be unable to continue speaking because of his *dolor animi*, a phrase that may or may not indicate tears; again, further discussion below.

2. For the (occasional) use of tearful pleading in the English courts of the Victorian and Edwardian periods, see Birkett (1961) 17: "but without the background of that harrowing scene where Marshall was throwing his protecting arms around this sobbing woman to shield her, without that face of tears and that pleading voice, instinct with compassion, it is quite impossible at this distance of time really to appreciate the effect." Cf. Powell and Paterson (2004) 18.

3. See Corbeill (2004) 69: "women take on themselves the public self-degradation that accompanies funerary rites . . . while men normally avoid such extremes." Any such displays "undermine the *gravitas* of elite males." Cf. Johnstone (1999) 122–24, and Bers (2009) 77–85 and 91–93, on tearful pleading in the Athenian courts.

speeches themselves in order to appreciate how Cicero integrates tears into his defenses in a plausible and effective manner.[4]

## TEARS IN ROMAN SOCIETY

Although Classical scholars in recent decades have shown considerable interest in the sociology of crying, the role of tears in Roman oratory remains largely unexplored.[5] Thorsten Fögen's recent collection of essays, for example, runs to nearly five hundred pages, yet it refers in its *index locorum* to only one of Cicero's speeches.[6] We need, then, to undertake our own study of Roman attitudes toward crying, focusing in particular on the extent to which it was acceptable for men of the aristocratic class to shed tears in public. This kind of investigation does not require (in my view) an especially complex theoretical framework. If we can identify specific examples where a positive value was attributed to male tears, we can infer that men in Roman society *sometimes* had licence to cry. Indeed, as we shall see, on occasion they were even admired for doing so. Male tears did not always signify an effeminate weakness of spirit; at times they could be construed as a sign of the individual's deep concern for friends and family.

The topic, however, is a complex one, especially since Cicero himself was sharply criticized on at least two occasions during his career for indulging excessively in tears. Several of his friends, for example, censured the extent of his grief following the death of his daughter, Tullia, in 45 BCE. In general, it was of course entirely appropriate for a man to shed tears of distress at the death of friends and family. Thus we find Pliny the Younger readily admitting to having wept on hearing news of the deaths of various acquaintances (*Ep.* 5.21.6; 8.23.8; cf. 8.16.5). Even Seneca the Younger in ascetic philosophical mode accepts that *some* tears are to be

---

4. Standard discussions of highly emotional passages in Cicero generally show little interest in wider Roman attitudes toward crying. See, e.g., Austin (1960) 122; Berry (1996) 316. Winterbottom (2004) 221–22 notes the role of tears in Cicero's perorations but engages with the subject only via litotes: "The words, here as elsewhere, dwell much on weeping, and it is not to be imagined that the tears failed to flow."

5. The brief remarks by Kroll (1933) 225–26 and MacMullen (1980) demonstrate a keen awareness that ancient and modern attitudes differ significantly; only recently, however, has this important point been explored with any rigor. See in particular van Wees (1998); Casamento (2004); Corbeill (2004) 67–106; Fögen (2009) with bibliography; Heckenkamp (2010). For useful discussions of crying in modern societies, see Lutz (2001) and Shields (2002).

6. See Fögen (2009) 479, with one reference to *De Haruspicum Responso.* Cicero's treatises receive greater attention.

expected in cases of bereavement.[7] Cicero, however, seems to have persisted in his grief far longer than was customary. From the perspective of his colleagues, the longer he stayed away from Rome in mourning, the more he seemed to be putting his private emotions before his public obligations as patron and politician.[8]

A similar principle underlies the criticisms launched at Cicero for a lack of staunchness during his period of exile. Several extant letters to his wife and family during this period refer explicitly to tears prompted by his own emotional distress. In April 58 BCE, for example, Cicero writes (*Fam.* 14.4.1):

> *ego minus saepe do ad vos litteras quam possum propterea quod cum omnia mihi tempora sunt misera, tum vero, cum aut scribo ad vos aut vestras lego, conficior lacrimis sic ut ferre non possim.*

> [I send off letters to you less often than I am able to, because every moment is a misery for me; then too, when I do write to you or read your letters, I am so overwhelmed by tears that I cannot bear it.]

Such tears shed at a time of distress on behalf of his family are, up to a point, what the Romans would expect of a good father. They demonstrate his paternal affection and sense of duty. But this weeping takes on a more questionable character if it threatens to hamper the vigor and initiative also expected of the Roman *paterfamilias*. It is not encouraging then that Cicero displays much the same distress some six months later (*Fam.* 14.1.5; November 58 BCE):

> *quid, obsecro te (me miserum!), quid futurum est? et si nos premet eadem fortuna, quid puero misero fiet? non queo reliqua scribere, tanta vis lacrimarum est; neque te in eundem fletum adducam.*

> [What, in the name of heaven—wretch that I am—what does the future hold? And if there is no change of fortune for me, what will become of

---

7. See Sen. *Ep.* 99, especially section 19: *his indulgemus, illis vincimur; Ep.* 63.1: *lacrimandum est, non plorandum.* Cf. Wilson (1997) 59–60.

8. See, e.g., the letter of L. Lucceius (*Fam.* 5.14). Atticus had made similar remarks as early as March 45 (*Att.* 12.20.1). By May, M. Brutus too had written to him in the same vein, and criticisms were being voiced by others as well (*Att.* 12.38a.1). Cicero offers a stubborn justification of his actions at *Fam.* 5.15, but this will have done little to alter the general perception of his behavior. For Servius Sulpicius's well-known letter of consolation at this time, see *Fam.* 4.5. Cf. Erskine (1997) 39.

my poor boy? I cannot write anything else; the tears are so overwhelming, and I don't want to call forth the same tears in you.]

It is possible that there is an element of calculation behind this self-presentation;[9] but if so, it was not a pose that was universally admired. As early as May, Atticus had privately criticized him for showing a lack of spirit.[10] And passages in his letters seem to have contributed to the ambivalent judgments on Cicero's character that appeared following his death. Indeed, Dio Cassius develops this theme at some length, introducing into his history a fictional episode in which the philosopher Philiscus gives Cicero a stern lecture on the need to show fortitude in misfortune.[11]

Male tears, then, could be construed negatively, and the origins of this cultural attitude probably reside in Roman views of masculinity. As Craig Williams has noted, Romans typically associated masculine behavior with rationality and the exercise of control (over oneself and others).[12] Emotional restraint was thus often regarded as an admirably male quality, while overt displays of feeling were viewed as effeminate and weak.[13] This matrix of values can be seen in Cicero's own criticisms of the tears shed by his friend, Servius Sulpicius Rufus, during a private meeting in May 49 BCE. In a letter to Atticus, Cicero describes their discussion of a particularly fraught question: should they throw in their lot with Caesar's

---

9. See, e.g., Lintott (2008) 179: "tears and sorrow form a refrain in the surviving letters to Terentia and his children, but there is more than a hint of artistic contrivance, suggesting that that [sic] this was a position adopted to deflect criticism." Cf. Hutchinson (1998) 25–48. In general, see Garcea (2005).

10. See Att. 3.10.2: me tam saepe et tam vehementer obiurgas et animo infirmo esse dicis. For Cicero's thoughts of suicide during this whole period, see Q Fr. 1.4.4; Att. 3.3; 3.4; 3.7.2; 3.9.1.

11. Dio Cass. 38.18.1–38.29.4 (especially 38.18.1: οὐκ αἰσχύνῃ . . . ὦ Κικέρων, θρηνῶν καὶ γυναικείως διακείμενος). See Millar (1964) 49–51; Claassen (1996). Cf. Livy's judgment reported at Sen. Suas. 6.22: omnium adversorum nihil ut viro dignum erat tulit praeter mortem. Also Asinius Pollio's exclamation (Sen. Suas. 6.24): utinam moderatius secundas res et fortius adversas ferre potuisset! For criticism among Cicero's contemporaries, see the remark of Laterensis, reported at Planc. 90: mortem me timuisse dicis.

12. See most succinctly Williams (1999) 141: "Masculinity was not fundamentally a matter of sexual practice; it was a matter of control." Cf. Alston (1998) 220: "Most views of the vir emphasized potestas as a characteristic." Cf. Casamento (2004) 48.

13. See Williams (1999) 135–38, with the references in n. 50. Greek and Roman philosophers in particular seem to have pushed this desire for ascetic, manly restraint to its extreme; see van Wees (1998) 16–18 on the influence of Plato; also Erskine (1997). For someone like Seneca, the control of the emotions often becomes an end in itself, a sort of philosophical test; see Wilson (1997) 59–61.

invading forces or support Pompey's resistance instead? Cicero depicts Sulpicius as breaking into tears in the course of their conversation (*Att.* 10.14.1: *atque haec ita multis cum lacrimis loquebatur ut . . .*) and makes it clear that these tears derived, not so much from Sulpicius's love and concern for the *patria*, as from simple fear: *numquam vidi hominem perturbatiorem metu.* ("Never have I seen a man so panicstricken!") Although Cicero admits that Sulpicius's anxieties are not unfounded (*neque hercule quicquam timebat quod non esset timendum*), he expresses sardonic surprise that the catalogue of miseries that the man related had not dried up his tears long before now (*ut ego mirarer eas tam diuturna miseria non exaruisse*).

This is hardly a sympathetic reaction. To weep because of grief or familial piety (it seems) is one thing; to cry out of *metus* and *timor* quite another. (Cicero refers to Sulpicius's *timor* later in the letter as well.) As a result, Cicero now had doubts about the man's resolution and reliability and was inclined to exclude him from his future plans (*Att.* 10.14.3: *ut iam celandus magis de nostro consilio quam adhiben<dus> videretur*).[14]

In short, context mattered. But if this was the case, a further question naturally arises: if tears were viewed negatively when they conveyed fear, weakness, or a lack of restraint, in what circumstances could they be interpreted more positively?

We may begin with an example from the imperial period. In his *Panegyricus*, Pliny the Younger recounts the emotions of the emperor Trajan at the departure of a friend who was retiring from his post as prefect of the Praetorian Guard. Here is how he describes their final farewell (*Pan.* 86.3):

> *quam ego audio confusionem tuam fuisse, cum digredientem prosequereris! prosecutus es enim nec temperasti tibi, quo minus exeunti in litore amplexus, in litore osculum ferres.*

> [What distress you felt, I am told, when you saw him onto the boat as he departed. Yes, you saw him off, and there on the shores you were not ashamed to give him your embrace and kiss of farewell.]

Pliny's language here—in particular the phrase *nec temperasti tibi*—suggests that this show of affection was something that in other circumstances could have been omitted quite appropriately. But Pliny wants to

14. For another striking example of inappropriate tears, note the grief attributed to Hortensius and Crassus at the death of their pet fish. See Plin. *HN* 9.172; Macrob. *Sat.* 3.15.4; Plut. *Mor.* 976A; Higginbotham (1997) 45.

depict Trajan as a man for whom personal affection matters more than propriety. The passage then continues (*Pan.* 86.4):

> *stetit Caesar in illa amicitiae specula, stetit precatusque est abeunti prona maria celeremque, si tamen ipse voluisset, recursum nec sustinuit recedentem non etiam atque etiam votis et lacrimis sequi.*

[There on a watchtower, the witness of his friendship, stood Caesar, and prayed for a calm sea for his departing friend, prayed too for a speedy return (if that was to be his desire); nor could he help following him into the distance with repeated prayers and tears.]

It is this last detail that is significant for the present discussion. Pliny depicts the emperor as a man who cries—tears of anxiety perhaps at the perils of his friend's journey, but probably also tears of affection and sorrow. The important point is that these tears are meant to reflect positively on Trajan: Pliny could quite easily have omitted them from his narrative. Their inclusion, then, seems intended to present Trajan as a man of admirable compassion. Here is an emperor who cares about his friends.[15]

A similar sensibility appears in several episodes mentioned in Cicero's letters. Atticus, for example, is reported as shedding tears as he wished the orator well on his departure for his provincial command in Cilicia (*Att.* 6.1.8): *flens mihi meam famam commendasti; quae epistula tua est in qua mentionem <non> facias?* ("You appealed to me with tears in your eyes to take care of my good name. Is there a single one of your letters which does not mention it?") Cicero clearly takes these tears as proof of Atticus's profound affection for him. Some six years later, another parting led to a similar reaction (*Att.* 15.27.2: *te, ut a me discesseris, lacrimasse moleste ferebam*).

The compassion implied by such tears could extend beyond concern for close friends and convey instead a wider sense of *humanitas*. The point is best illustrated by the various anecdotes that depict powerful Romans shedding tears at momentous historical events. Scipio Aemilianus, for example, is famously said to have wept at the sight of the destruction of Carthage.[16] Although different accounts interpret these tears in slightly different ways, the anecdote's piquancy derives primarily from Scipio's

---

15. See also Plin. *Pan.* 73.4, where Trajan is again depicted as shedding tears, in this case probably tears of pride. Cf. Suet. *Aug.* 58 on Augustus weeping in the senate.
16. See App. *Pun.* 132; Polyb. 38.22.1–3; Diod. Sic. 32.22.24.

apparent grief at a moment when a triumphant, even gloating reaction might have been expected.[17] The general's tears thus suggest that he has some sense of the greater human tragedy beyond this moment of military success. They are a sign not of weakness or cowardice but of compassion and magnanimity. Livy in similar fashion presents Marcellus as shedding tears at the capture of Syracuse in 212 BCE.[18] And Caesar cries when presented with the signet ring of Pompey (his adversary and former son-in-law) following the man's assassination in Egypt.[19]

These examples, then, suggest that there were numerous contexts in which the shedding of tears could be construed positively in Roman society. But perhaps the best evidence comes from Cicero himself, when he describes various individuals offering social support to others. In the course of the fourth Catilinarian, for example, he depicts several of his allies (including his brother) shedding tears as they sit nearby offering their assistance.[20] Likewise, when P. Sulla went to ask Cicero to speak in his defense, he was supported in his petition by the tears of two Marcelli, who were also present in court when the case went to trial.[21] As we saw in chapter three, Cluentius was likewise aided in court by representatives from various towns who wept as their testimonial was presented.[22] Similarly the tears of Ligarius's brothers furnished proof of their admirable sense of fraternal affection.[23]

These examples allow us to formulate the hypothesis that tears were accorded great respect in Roman society when they conveyed a sense

---

17. See discussion by Astin (1967) 282–87.

18. See Livy 25.24.11, who explicitly notes the complex emotions behind Marcellus's tears: *inlacrimasse dicitur partim gaudio tantae perpetratae rei, partim vetusta gloria urbis.* For Marcellus then (unlike Scipio) there is indeed a sense of joy at his achievement. But Marcellus also has the greatness of mind to see beyond his own personal success and appreciate the tragedy of Syracuse's precipitous reversal of fortune. Cf. Rossi (2000).

19. Plut. *Pomp.* 80.7: τὴν δὲ σφραγῖδα τοῦ Πομπηίου δεξάμενος ἐδάκρυσεν. Cf. Kroll (1933) 225–26. In this case, Caesar's tears seem to be tears of compassion and regret, and these prevail over any sense of triumph as his main opponent in the civil war is eliminated. Cf. also Livy 45.4.2 on Aemilius Paullus: *et ipse inlacrimasse dicitur sorti humanae.*

20. *Cat.* 4.3: *nec tamen ego sum ille ferreus qui fratris carissimi . . . maerore non movear horumque omnium lacrimis a quibus me circumsessum videtis.* Whatever the historical accuracy of Cicero's assertion, the fact that he chooses to represent the scene in this fashion tells us much about cultural attitudes.

21. *Sull.* 20: *neque eosdem Marcellos pro huius periculis lacrimantes aspicere . . . potui.* The elder Marcellus was praetor in 80; his son was consul in 50; see Berry (1996) 171. *his . . . Marcellis* at *Sull.* 19 confirms their presence in court at Sulla's trial.

22. *Clu.* 197: *ex lacrimis horum, iudices, existimare potestis omnes haec decuriones decrevisse lacrimantes.*

23. *Lig.* 33: *moveant te horum lacrimae, moveat pietas, moveat germanitas.* Cf. also the tears of Caelius's mother at *Cael.* 4: *lacrimae matris incredibilisque maeror.*

of social solidarity with family and friends. In certain contexts, proving this loyalty through tears took precedence over any concerns with manly restraint. For the Roman audience, the tears of friends signified, not a disturbing lack of self-control, but a laudable commitment to one's social obligations. When friends or family in Rome were in difficulty, it was entirely proper, and even expected, that one should put all available resources at their disposal—resources that included both one's physical presence at court and (if necessary) one's tears.[24]

The existence of such a principle helps us to make sense of an ostensibly curious incident that took place during a debate in the senate on 1 January 57 BCE. At this meeting, P. Servilius Vatia (cos. 79 BCE) tried to persuade the incoming consul, Metellus Nepos, not to hinder attempts to recall Cicero from exile. To this end, he engaged in a piece of highly emotional oratory that involved an elaborate invocation of Metellus's dead ancestors, and in particular the example of Metellus Numidicus, who had, like Cicero, spent time in exile.[25] The result, Cicero claims, was that Nepos burst into tears and agreed to Servilius's pleas (*Sest.* 130): *conlacrimavit vir egregius ac vere Metellus totumque se P. Servilio dicenti etiam tum tradidit.* ("That outstanding gentleman—a true Metellus—burst into tears and right then gave himself over entirely to P. Servilius as he was speaking.")[26] As Robert Kaster observes, "To suppose Metellus' emotion eccentric or extreme would be to mistake an important element of Roman culture."[27] As our working hypothesis suggests, Nepos's tears would have been viewed as an admirable indication of his deep concern for his family name, and of his worthy sense of compassion and fairness. In other words, this was not random emotionalism. Nepos was behaving according to a socially approved script that placed a positive cultural value on tears shed on behalf of family and friends.

Now, there is in fact good reason to suppose that this exchange as a whole was a prearranged political stunt. We know from Cicero's letters that private negotiations some two months earlier had led to Nepos

---

24. The remarks of David (1992) 73 point in a similar direction: "Larmes de convention? Sûrement pas. Larmes d'une émotion socialement convenue, bien davantage." Cf. Casamento (2004) 51–52.

25. See *Sest.* 130: *cum ille omnes prope ab inferis evocasset Metellos.* Also: *cumque eum ad domestici exempli memoriam et ad Numidici illius Metelli casum vel gloriosum vel gravem convertisset.*

26. The compound form of the verb *conlacrimavit* need not perhaps imply that Servilius himself was in tears as he made his speech. See *TLL* vol. 3, col. 1575, line 16 (s.v. *collacrimo*): *deinde evanida vi praepos. idem q. flere, valde lacrimare.* Cf. *Sest.* 123; *Rep.* 6.9.

27. Kaster (2006) 369.

agreeing to adopt such a course (*Att.* 3.23; cf. *Att.* 3.22.2). The first day of his consulship, then, may have seemed an appropriate occasion on which to declare publicly this significant change of attitude toward a former *inimicus*.[28] But the spontaneity (or otherwise) of the incident does not alter its relevance for our understanding of Roman cultural values. Indeed, Servilius and Nepos presumably chose this form of performance because they believed it operated comfortably within the parameters of aristocratic behavior.

The tearful theatrics at the trial of M'. Aquillius (see chapter one) also accord with our proposed principle. In the first place, Marius's weeping provides further proof that tears and military manliness were not mutually exclusive in Rome (*De or.* 2.196: *cum C. Marius maerorem orationis meae praesens ac sedens multum lacrimis suis adiuvaret*). Second, this public display of distress was acceptable because Marius and the accused had enjoyed a close political relationship, serving as consuls together in 101 BCE—a detail to which Antonius as advocate drew attention repeatedly (*De or.* 2.196: *ego illum crebro appellans collegam*). He was able, then, to characterize Marius's tears as tears of obligation, and he seems to have exploited this same principle with regard to his own performance as well. As a close ally of both Marius and Aquillius at this time, he could himself plausibly shed tears as he delivered the peroration (*De or.* 2.196: *non fuit haec sine meis lacrimis*). It is against this cultural background that we need to assess Cicero's own use of tears in his judicial oratory.[29]

Before we turn to the speeches, however, we need to address one further matter. In chapter three it was noted that Cicero on occasion uses adjectives such as *supplex* in a metaphorical rather than literal sense. By doing so, he conveys an individual's generally submissive attitude rather than any use of physical supplication. To what extent, then, does Cicero follow a similar usage in the vocabulary of weeping and laments? Is there any reason to suppose that references to *lacrimae* and the like are intended to convey an individual's highly distressed state *in general* rather than their shedding of actual tears?

Certainly the verb *flere* can be used in the more general sense of "bewail" or "lament"—an action that might or might not involve actual

---

28. Cf. Kaster (2006) 281.

29. This principle of "friends cry on behalf of friends" meant that pleas and supplications were regularly accompanied by tears, both from the actual suppliant and from supporters. For tears in supplications in nonjudicial contexts, see *Verr.* 2.2.95; 2.3.69; *Red. pop.* 12. Cf. De Libero (2009).

tears.[30] Cicero, for example, describes in the following terms the opposition of the younger Cato to the consuls of 58 BCE (*Sest.* 60): *tamen
voce ipsa ac dolore pugnavit, et post meum discessum iis Pisonem verbis flens
meum et rei publicae casum vexavit ut. . . .* ("Nevertheless, [M. Cato] fought
against the consuls with indignant speeches and, after my departure into
exile, verbally harassed Piso, lamenting both my misfortune and that of
the republic, in such a way that. . . .") It seems reasonable enough to
view the participle *flens* here as a convenient way of conveying the generally impassioned nature of Cato's oratory. It need not imply that he
actually broke down in tears as he gave his speech—although we must
be wary of preferring this intepretation simply because it more readily conforms with our own cultural conceptions regarding appropriate
comportment.[31]

The same word, however, probably has a more literal application in a
passage from Suetonius, which describes an emotional speech delivered
by Caesar to his troops by the Rubicon in 49 BCE (Suet. *Iul.* 33): *pro con-
tione fidem militum flens ac veste a pectore discissa invocavit.* ("[Caesar] at an
assembly called upon the loyalty of his troops, weeping and tearing his
robe from his breast.")[32] In this case, Suetonius points to specific facets
of Caesar's oratorical technique, including his appeal to the soldiers'
loyalty and protection (*fidem . . . invocavit*) and the ripping of his clothes
(*veste a pectore discissa*). In this context, then, *flens* refers most naturally to
a third element of manipulation: his exploitation of tears.[33] It is difficult
to know whether Suetonius's portrayal has any historical veracity; but it
does imply that the shedding of (actual) tears was regarded as an oratorical device often deployed by Roman politicians.

Other evidence likewise suggests that we need to take literally the
references to tears in Cicero's speeches, especially as far as the orator's
own performance is concerned. In Book 2 of *De Oratore*, Cicero stresses
the commitment required of the orator when undertaking an emotional
style of speaking. In general, the manner must be forceful (*De or.* 2.211:
*intenta ac vehemens*) and the style of delivery intense (*De or.* 2.214: *simili*

---

30. See the distinction drawn at *TLL* vol. 6, col. 899, line 10 (s. v. *fleo*): *proprie i. q.
lacrimas effundere;* and col. 900, line 69: *transitive, i. q. deplorare, complorare, deflere.* Cf. Casamento (2004) 42.

31. Note that Gardner (1958) 117 and Kaster (2006) 68 both avoid specific reference
to tears in their translations ("deploring" and "lamenting" respectively).

32. Cf. Dio Cass. 41.4. For the use of tears by Pompey in a similar context, see Plut.
*Pomp.* 3.5. For other examples of Roman commanders engaging in highly emotional displays in front of their troops, see Makhlayuk (2008).

33. Cf. Rolfe (1998) 77.

*contentione actionis*). This emotional conviction must also be evident from various aspects of the orator's physical appearance (*De or.* 2.190): *neque ad misericordiam adducetur, nisi tu ei signa doloris tui verbis, sententiis, voce, vultu, conlacrimatione denique ostenderis.* ("Nor will the juror be led to feel pity, unless you show him clear evidence of your own distress, through your words, sentiments, voice, facial expression and even crying.")[34] The phrasing here is explicit and unambiguous: the orator on occasions goes beyond conveying general emotional distress through voice and facial expression (*voce, vultu*); at times he resorts to actual tears (*conlacrimatione*). Quintilian likewise emphasizes the physical manifestations of distress—including tears—that sometimes accompanied his perorations (*Inst.* 6.2.36: *frequenter <ita> motus sum ut me non lacrimae solum deprenderent, sed pallor et veri similis dolor*). In the following examples, then, there is every reason to suppose that Cicero intended the references to his tears to be taken literally. So let us turn now to the texts of these speeches themselves, in order to examine how exactly he presented these tears in order to gain the persuasive impact that he wanted.

TEARS IN CICERO'S SPEECHES

## *Pro Plancio and Pro Cispio*

In the course of his defense of Cn. Plancius in 54 BCE, Cicero spends some time justifying his style of pleading in an earlier trial, that of P. Cispius, tribune in 57 BCE.[35] Our evidence regarding Cispius's trial is limited, in part because Cicero seems not to have published the speech that he made on this occasion.[36] It is clear, however, that he had attempted a tearful appeal at the end of his speech—a device that was ridiculed by his opponent (M. Laterensis) in the later trial of Plancius (*Planc.* 76): *et mihi lacrimulam Cispiani iudici obiectas. sic enim dixisti: "vidi ego tuam*

---

34. Cf. also the remarks on delivery at *Rhet. Her.* 3.25 and 3.27.

35. On the trial of Plancius, see Alexander (1990) 142–43 (no. 293). The charge was brought under the *lex Licinia de sodaliciis* (*Planc.* 36) in connection with Plancius' campaign for the post of aedile. Cf. Holden (1881) xxx–xxxviii. On Cicero's use of tears during the trial, see Casamento (2004) 50–55; Heckenkamp (2010) 180–82.

36. On Cispius's trial, see Crawford (1984) 170–72; Alexander (1990) 136 (no. 279). Its precise date is uncertain. Marinone (2004) 117 suggests that the prosecution could have been as early as the final weeks of 57, immediately after Cispius left office. Münzer (1889) col. 2589 assumes a slight delay and places it in 56 BCE. An even later date, however, would give greater relevance and impact to Laterensis's reference to it in 54 BCE. Cf. Lintott (2008) 219; also Gruen (1974) 304.

*lacrimulam.*" ("You reproach me with the 'one little tear' I shed at the trial of Cispius. For this is what you said: 'I saw that one little tear of yours.'") Laterensis's criticism, it seems, was neatly phrased. The diminutive, singular form *lacrimula* cleverly suggested that Cicero's weeping was so forced that he could manage only one paltry tear.[37]

Laterensis appears to have asserted the artificiality of Cicero's entreaty in another remark too (*Planc.* 75): *atque etiam clamitas, Laterensis: "quo usque ista dices? nihil in Cispio profecisti; obsoletae iam sunt preces tuae."* ("And you even loudly demand, Laterensis: 'How much longer are you going to speak in that way? You gained no advantage from it in the case of Cispius. Your entreaties are threadbare now.'") With the word *quousque* Laterensis evidently implied that Cicero had recently been engaged in a tedious sequence of such defenses, and that this repetition had rendered his entreaties (*preces*) clichéd and useless (*obsoletae*).[38] Moreover, if the phrase *nihil profecisti* is evidence for Cispius's conviction, Laterensis deftly reminded the jurors that others before them had not been swayed by such tricks. He thus encouraged them likewise to regard with skepticism any tearful appeal that Cicero might attempt to mount in his upcoming defense of Plancius.

Laterensis, it seems, also drew the jurors' attention to another occasion on which Cicero had embarked upon a pitiful plea. For Cicero asserts (*Planc.* 83): *te idcirco in ludos causam conicere noluisse, ne ego mea consuetudine aliquid de tensis misericordiae causa dicerem, quod in aliis aedilibus ante fecissem.* ("Your motive in trying to prevent this trial from synchronizing with the games was that I might not introduce some pitiful references to the carriages in the procession, as you said was my practice when I was defending other aediles.") We can infer that, in some earlier trial, Cicero had drawn the audience's attention to the public games then in progress in order to heighten his emotional appeals. (This speech likewise does not survive, nor is its precise occasion known.)[39] Moreover, Laterensis also suggested wittily that Cicero in 63 BCE had fixed a penalty of exile to

---

37. Cf. Holden (1881) 167. The connotation of artificiality may have been strengthened by Terence's use of *lacrimula* in the phrase *falsa lacrimula* at *Eun.* 67. It is just possible that Laterensis had himself quoted the Terentian saying, which Cicero now judiciously misquotes. On the Romans and the notion of "fake" tears (*lacrimae simulatae*), see De Libero (2009). Cf. Casamento (2004) 44–46.

38. Alexander (2002) 143–44 has suggested that the main focus of Laterensis's ridicule was the tendency at this time for Cicero to depict prosecutions of his acquaintances as attacks on himself. See, however, Stangl (1912) 165 (lines 20–21): *Laterensis in Tullium dixerat epilogos eius inridens, quos eum constat nimium flebiles et miserationis plenos in iudiciis semper habuisse.*

39. See Holden (1881) 176.

his antibribery laws in order to provide himself with greater opportunities for such theatrics.[40]

Cicero's tearful judicial antics thus seem to have been a prime target for the prosecution as they presented their case. Presumably their aim was a kind of preemptive strike—to discredit beforehand the very technique that Cicero was likely to employ on behalf of Plancius. Indeed, Laterensis and fellow prosecutor, L. Cassius, clearly understood how Cicero went about constructing his appeals.[41] We learn, for example, that they vigorously challenged the notion that Cicero enjoyed a close emotional bond with the defendant (*Planc.* 4): *merita Cn. Planci erga me minora esse dicerent quam a me ipso praedicarentur.* ("[The prosecutors] said that Plancius' kindnesses to me are not as great as I myself proclaimed them to be.") As we saw in chapter three, asserting an intimate tie with the client was an important step in Cicero's attempts to generate high emotion. If the prosecutors could undermine such claims at the outset, they could disarm one of Cicero's most potent weapons.

And yet, since Laterensis and Cassius spoke before Cicero in the trial, we need to ask when exactly they had heard his assertions regarding Plancius's *merita.* One solution is to suppose that there had already been a preliminary hearing of the case.[42] This is not impossible, but an alternative explanation is available. Writing to his brother in 56 BCE, Cicero states that, in the course of his ongoing defense of Bestia in the courts, he had made a point of bestowing high praise upon Sestius. His purpose in doing so was to prepare the ground for his likely defense of Sestius in the near future.[43] It is quite plausible, then, that he did something similar two years or so later with regard to Plancius. During a speech in the courts (we may suppose) or in the senate, he had gone out of his way to praise Plancius and the many services he had performed on the orator's behalf. Such tactics (if this reconstruction is correct) give us a fascinating glimpse into the jockeying for position that could take place prior to the start of a trial.

---

40. See *Planc.* 83: *hic etiam addidisti me idcirco mea lege exsilio ambitum sanxisse, ut miserabiliores epilogos possem dicere.*

41. Note that Cassius admitted during the trial to having studied some of Cicero's published speeches (*Planc.* 66).

42. See Humbert (1925) 176–89, who suggests that the prosecution and defense each made (at least) two set-speeches during the trial.

43. See *Q Fr.* 2.3.6: *hic προῳκοδομησάμην quiddam εὐκαίρως de iis quae in Sestium apparabantur crimina et eum ornavi veris laudibus magno adsensu omnium.* ("At this point I exploited the moment to lay down a foundation for my defence of Sestius against the charges that are being prepared against him and contrived a well-deserved eulogy, which was received with great approval by all.")

But Laterensis and Cassius were determined not to be outmaneuvered. Indeed, they worked hard throughout their speeches to discredit Cicero's claims to a special intimacy with Plancius. Cassius, for example, evidently asserted that Cicero owed no more to Plancius than he owed to any of his other supporters in the senate (*Planc.* 68: *nam quod ais, Cassi, non plus me Plancio debere quam bonis omnibus*).[44] And Laterensis ended his speech with two emphatic images designed to make the same point (*Planc.* 95):

> *nunc venio ad illud extremum, in quo dixisti, dum Planci in me meritum verbis extollerem, me arcum facere e cloaca lapidumque a sepulchro venerari pro deo.*

> [I now come to that final passage in your speech—your claim that when I built up with fine phrases Plancius' services toward me, I was making an arch from a sewer, venerating as a god a mere stone from a tomb.[45]]

Laterensis cleverly depicts Cicero's relationship with Plancius as perfunctory and quotidian. The great orator's defense of the man is thus not a case of loyally rescuing a close friend from danger; it is simply a hack piece of judicial pleading.[46]

In the course of his reply, then, Cicero needed to reassert his emotional authenticity as an advocate. He achieves this aim in part by countering Laterensis's critique of his performance at the trial of Cispius. He admits to having cried during the speech, but this weeping (he claims) did not consist of a single tear—there was a whole flood of them (*Planc.*

---

44. Cicero's reference to Cassius's *oratio* at *Planc.* 58 confirms that these remarks were made during the prosecutor's set-speech, and so an attempt to anticipate Cicero's tactics in his peroration. See also *Planc.* 69: *quaeris a me, Cassi, quid pro fratre meo qui mihi est carissimus . . . amplius quam quod pro Plancio facio facere possim.*

45. The phrase *ad illud extremum* here refers most naturally to the final, climactic argument in Laterensis's own *oratio*. At section 85, however, Cicero refers to an exchange whose context may well have been different again (*Planc.* 85: *admonuisti etiam, quod in Creta fuisses, dictum aliquod in petitionem tuam dici potuisse; me id perdidisse*). Lintott (2008) 223 considers assigning the exchange to the case's *altercatio*. This option is closed to Humbert (1925) 185, who does not believe that trials during the Late Republic featured a formal *altercatio*; see also 60–66. Stroh (1975) 44 imagines an occasion from Laterensis's election campaign. In my view, it is not impossible that Laterensis in the course of his oration had engaged Cicero in some banter, resulting in his triumphant claim that Cicero had missed the opportunity for a witticism.

46. These strategies were complemented by wider attacks on Cicero's character and political career in general, including criticisms of how he had handled the political situation before his exile (see the rebuttals at *Planc.* 86–89); criticisms of his personal courage (*Planc.* 90); and criticisms of his political compromises, in particular his relationships with Pompey and Caesar (*Planc.* 91–94).

76): *non modo lacrimulam, sed multas lacrimas et fletum cum singultu videre potuisti.* ("You could see on that occasion, not just 'one little tear', but many tears and weeping mixed with sobs.") Cicero here not only refuses to be embarrassed by his crying; he even brandishes its effusiveness as proof of his integrity.

The next argument, however, is the most important (*Planc.* 76):

> *an ego, qui meorum lacrimis me absente commotus simultates quas mecum habebat deposuisset, meaeque salutis non modo non oppugnator, ut inimici mei putarant, sed etiam defensor fuisset, huius in periculo non significarem dolorem meum?*

[Or would you have me show no symptoms of grief when danger threatened one who had been so affected by the tears of my dear ones, when I myself was faraway, that he waived his old differences with me, and, so far from being my assailant (as my enemies had anticipated), had even been my champion?]

Cicero here depicts his tears as a moral obligation. Since Cispius had responded sympathetically to his family's plight during his exile, it was only appropriate that he in turn respond sympathetically to Cispius's misfortune. His weeping at the man's trial was thus not a manipulative oratorical strategy but part of Cicero's ethical duty to an ally.[47]

He adopts a similar approach as he sets up his emotional appeal on behalf of Plancius. As early as section 25, Cicero asserts that Plancius had been a sort of father (*quasi parens*) to him (*Planc.* 25):

> *neque enim ego sic rogabam ut petere viderer, quia familiaris esset meus, quia vicinus, quia huius parente semper plurimum essem usus, sed ut quasi parenti et custodi salutis meae.*

[I canvassed on his behalf in a way that made it seem not that I was petitioning because he was a friend, or a neighbor, or because I had always enjoyed a very close connection with his father, but because he was himself, in a sense, a father and protector to me.]

---

47. Cf. Stangl (1912) 165 (lines 24–26): *adseverat Cispium hoc suae orationis adfectu non indignum fuisse, cum quo post amicitiae reconciliationem ita participatu fortunae suae dolorem senserit, ut inpense diligi mereatur.* It is clear enough that Cispius in his capacity as tribune had helped with Cicero's recall from exile (see *Red. sen.* 21; *Sest.* 76); but it is difficult to tell how far Cicero exaggerated this support in order to justify his defense of the man. See also Casamento (2004) 52–53.

This claim is embellished further toward the end of the speech, when Cicero describes Plancius's assistance to him during his exile in particularly grand and noble terms. Here too he has to counter the astutely querulous claims of the prosecution, who had asserted that Cicero was not actually in mortal danger from his enemies while he was in exile.[48] As he launches into the peroration, he insists that he was indeed in great peril when he entered Greece: the country was packed with wicked men who hated him.[49] Plancius's support was thus crucial to his welfare, and Cicero sketches a dramatic scene (*Planc.* 98): *simul ac me Dyrrachium attigisse audivit, statim ad me lictoribus dimissis, insignibus abiectis, veste mutata profectus est.* ("As soon as he heard that I had reached Dyrrachium, Plancius immediately set out to see me, dressed *in sordibus*, with his lictors dismissed and his marks of office laid aside.")[50] Cicero's relationship with Plancius (he wants the jurors to believe) is based on a profound sense of duty and obligation—a point he also makes quite explicitly (*Planc.* 98): *audi, audi atque attende, Laterensis, ut scias quid ego Plancio debeam.* ("Listen to this, Laterensis, listen and pay close attention, so that you may know how much I owe to Plancius.")

Cicero further heightens the emotional element of his account by depicting Plancius himself as shedding tears at this encounter in Greece (*Planc.* 99): *o acerbam mihi, iudices, memoriam temporis illius et loci, cum hic in me incidit, cum complexus est conspersitque lacrimis nec loqui prae maerore potuit!* ("How bitter to me, gentlemen, is the memory of that time and place, where he fell upon me, embraced me, sprinkled me with his tears, and could not speak because of his grief.") Perhaps this really was how events unfolded; but the scene suits Cicero's oratorical purposes so well that we may suspect some artistic embellishment, if not downright fabrication. For Plancius's tears and embrace in Greece can now be presented as a *beneficium* that Cicero must repay in kind at the present trial. Cicero sets up this notion of reciprocity with a melodramatic exclamation (*Planc.* 101):

---

48. See *Planc.* 95: *neque enim mihi insidiarum periculum ullum neque mortis fuisse.*
49. See *Planc.* 98: *cognovi . . . refertam esse Graeciam sceleratissimorum hominum ac nefariorum, quorum impium ferrum ignesque pestiferos meus ille consulatus e manibus extorserat.*
50. Plancius was serving as quaestor to L. Appuleius Saturninus in the province of Macedonia; see Broughton (1952) 197. Saturninus himself was less generous in his support of Cicero (*Planc.* 99).

*memini enim, memini neque umquam obliviscar noctis illius, cum tibi vigilanti assidenti maerenti vana quaedam miser atque inania falsa spe inductus pollicebar, me, si essem in patriam restitutus, praesentem tibi gratias relaturum.*

[For I remember, I remember and never will forget that night when, as you kept watch, sat beside me, and grieved, I, poor wretch that I was, was led by some empty hope to make idle, worthless promises: that if ever I were restored to my homeland, I personally would repay this kindess to you.]

The repetition here of *memini*, the dramatic emphasis of *neque umquam obliviscar*, the three participles in asyndeton, and the collocation of the adjectives *vana, miser, inania* and *falsa*, all raise the emotional tone of the passage, thus endowing Cicero's promise to Plancius (*pollicebar*) with a special grandeur and significance. This impressiveness in turn bestows a certain moral gravity upon the scene that follows. Cicero tries to make the jury believe that they are witnessing, not some contrived piece of judicial theater, but the formal exchange of an ethical obligation.

Having laid this foundation, Cicero can now perform the climax of his peroration with conviction (*Planc.* 102): *quid enim possum aliud, nisi maerere, nisi flere, nisi te cum mea salute complecti? salutem tibi iidem dare possunt qui mihi reddiderunt.* ("What else can I do except grieve, except weep, except embrace you along with my salvation? Those same men who brought salvation to me can bestow it upon you.") The remark that follows confirms that the embrace implied by *complecti* is in fact a very real, physical one (*Planc.* 102): *te tamen—exsurge, quaeso—retinebo et complectar.* ("But whatever the case—stand up, I beg—I shall preserve you and hold you close.") This literal embrace complements the one that Plancius gave him at his own time of need (*Planc.* 99 *complexus est*). Cicero thus presents himself as fulfilling a promise made long ago to his friend, and the phrasing is designed to stress the element of reciprocity (*iidem . . . qui . . .*).

But this is not the end of the theatrics. Cicero also refers to the presence of Plancius's father in court and depicts the two of them as jointly appealing to the jurors on behalf of the defendant (*Planc.* 102): *mecumque vos simul hic miserrimus et optimus obtestatur parens, et pro uno filio duo patres deprecamur.* ("Together with me, this most excellent yet unfortunate father entreats you—and together as two fathers we appeal to you on behalf of one son.") As we saw earlier, Cicero in section 25 suggested that he had viewed Plancius as a sort of *parens* and protector to him;

now the roles are reversed (*pro uno filio duo patres*). Cicero thus grants himself yet further licence for his tears. It is now his duty as quasi-*parens* to cry on Plancius's behalf, and he can draw the peroration as a whole to a close with the claim that he is overwhelmed by his weeping (*Planc.* 104: *plura ne dicam tuae me etiam lacrimae impediunt vestraeque, iudices, non solum meae*).[51]

We can well imagine the exasperation and growing consternation of the prosecutors as they witnessed Cicero's performance. They had gone to considerable lengths to try to scupper any such use of tearful appeals, and yet Cicero had managed to contrive an elaborate peroration nevertheless—one that incorporated a dramatic embrace, pleas from both himself and the defendant's father, and copious tears. His determination to stage such a scene confirms his conviction in the effectiveness of these strategies, even though they were all too familiar to his contemporaries, and even though they had not brought success (apparently) in his earlier defense of Cispius.

But this example is most important perhaps because it allows us to identify several key elements in Cicero's technique. The effective deployment of these emotional theatrics relied on various factors: his ability to depict a sense of obligation to, and intimacy with, the accused; his careful contrivance of a link with his exile—an event that provided a credible source of emotion from which to generate tears; and a narrative facility that enabled him to present these elements in a highly wrought manner in the course of building to an emotional climax. As we shall see, these elements recur in various combinations in his other tearful defenses.

## Pro Rabirio Postumo

In the final months of 54 BCE—or perhaps at the start of 53—Cicero found himself reluctantly speaking in defense of his old foe, Aulus Gabinius, who was being prosecuted *de repetundis*.[52] The defense was

---

51. The wider implications of this remark, especially its reference to the tears of the president of the court (*tuae . . . lacrimae*), are discussed further below. See also David (1992) 638 on the peroration of *Pro Plancio*.

52. See Crawford (1984) 188–97; Alexander (1990) 148 (no. 303). On the difficulties in reconstructing the timing of this trial, see Lintott (1974) 67 and (2008) 246; Fantham (1975) 442–43; Marinone (2004) 133 and 496. Siani-Davies (2001) 73–81 provides a judicious assessment of the relevant issues. An earlier trial *de maiestate* in October had ended in Gabinius's acquittal; see Alexander (1990) 145 (no. 296). On Cicero's dislike of Gabinius at this time, see *Q Fr.* 3.1.24; 3.5.5; 3.7.1–2; cf. also *Rab. Post.* 19; 33; Val. Max. 4.2.4.

not successful, and, following Gabinius's conviction, a prosecution was launched against one of his associates, Rabirius Postumus, in an attempt to recover some of the fines that Gabinius was unable to pay (*Rab. Post.* 8–10). Cicero was persuaded to take on this case too.[53]

His speech on behalf of Rabirius is relatively short (only forty-eight sections) and addresses itself primarily to rather dry financial arguments. Nevertheless, here too Cicero decided to conclude on a note of high emotion, a strategy made particularly challenging by Rabirius's apparent lack of close relatives upon whom the advocate could base an appeal.[54] Here as elsewhere, Cicero's solution is to base his appeal on his own unfortunate circumstances.

His first gambit involves a rather forced conceit (*Rab. Post.* 45): *tua, Postume, nummo sestertio a me addicuntur? o meum miserum acerbumque praeconium!* ("Am I, Postumus, to be the one who auctions off your property at a single sesterce? O what a wretched and bitter role for me to play!") Certainly, the loss of Rabirius's family estates had emotive potential as far as the male upper-class jury was concerned. One of the main expectations of a Roman aristocrat was that he protect (and if possible increase) his family's wealth.[55] And yet the notion of Cicero as an auctioneer helping to sell off Rabirius's property seems a rather contrived description of the situation. (It is not clear that anyone would have viewed Cicero's role in these terms, if he had not himself chosen to depict it so.)[56] But this slant invites the jurors to feel pity for Cicero's predicament, and so enables him to make a direct appeal for their indulgence (*Rab. Post.* 46: *quod, iudices, ne faciatis oro obtestorque vos*).

Cicero then goes on, as in *Pro Cispio* and *Pro Plancio*, to portray his speech as part of an ethical obligation owed to the defendant. His tears thus spring from a sense of reciprocal duty (*Rab. Post.* 47):

> *sed iam quoniam servo fidem quam praestiti, Postume, reddam etiam lacrimas quas debeo; quas quidem ego tuas in meo casu plurimas vidi.*

---

53. Alexander (1990) 149 (no. 305); Marinone (2004) 133–34; Lintott (2008) 246–49.

54. For references to Rabirius's absent family members, see *Rab. Post.* 45: *hem, Postume, tune es C. Curti filius, C. Rabiri iudicio et voluntate filius, natura sororis filius? tune ille in omnes tuos liberalis?* On Cicero's use of tears during this speech, see Casamento (2004) 48–49.

55. See the speech of Q. Metellus in honor of his father Lucius, quoted at Plin. *NH* 7.140: *pecuniam magnam bono modo invenire.* The reference to "respectable means" (*bono modo*) is important; see Earl (1967) 24; 31–32; Rosenstein (2006) 373–75.

56. Cf. Siani-Davies (2001) 214–15.

[But now, since I am fulfilling the promise of loyalty that I gave to you, Postumus, I shall also return to you the tears that I owe you—those countless tears that I saw you shed during my own misfortune.]

It is not entirely clear here what promise Cicero refers to with his phrase *servo fidem quam praestiti*; in this respect, the speech is perhaps not quite so carefully honed as his defense of Plancius.[57] Nevertheless, as in *Pro Plancio*, it is Cicero's exile that provides his best source of high emotion (*Rab. Post.* 47):[58]

> *versatur ante oculos luctuosa nox meis omnibus, cum tu totum te cum tuis copiis ad me detulisti. tu comitibus, tu praesidio, tu etiam tanto pondere auri, quantum tempus illud postulabat, discessum illum sustentasti.*

[Before my eyes appears the night that was so grievous to my whole family, when you offered yourself to me unreservedly, together with your resources. You supported my departure with your companions, your protection, even with as much gold as the occasion demanded.]

Was Rabirius's help really that crucial to Cicero's departure from Rome? (Note the emphatic four-fold repetition of *tu*.) Perhaps—although the jurors were probably in no better position to verify the details than we are today. Cicero's skill lies in constructing a plausibly dramatic scene that emphasizes the ethical obligations he owes to Rabirius.

Indeed, Cicero then goes on to heighten the emotional significance of Rabirius's help (*Rab. Post.* 47): *tu numquam meis me absente liberis, numquam coniugi meae defuisti.* ("During my absence never did you fail to help my children or my wife.") And finally, with a concluding reference to Rabirius's dead father, Curtius, and to the accompanying weeping of Rabirius's *necessarii*, he can claim to be overwhelmed by tears of his own. Cicero is a good friend crying at the distress of a close acquaintance (*Rab. Post.* 48): *sed iam omnia timeo, bonitatis ipsius invidiam reformido. iam indicat tot hominum fletus quam sis carus tuis et me dolor debilitat intercluditque vocem.* ("But now everything is a source of dread to me. I shudder at the ill-will that this man's very goodness will provoke. Now the weeping of so many people here shows how dear you are to your family, and my grief paralyzes me and chokes my voice.")

---

57. Cf. Siani-Davies (2001) 219: "Presumably, this refers to Cicero's promise to defend Postumus." This assumption is probably correct, but Cicero leaves the point underdeveloped.

58. Cf. Winterbottom (2004) 228; Casamento (2004) 51.

Nevertheless, Cicero contrives a recovery from this theatrical trauma, and having demonstrated his close emotional association with Rabirius, he concludes by formulating a final direct appeal to the jurors in his own voice (*Rab. Post.* 48: *vos obsecro, iudices, ut*). As we saw in chapter three, when no other options are available, he is prepared to throw his own personal authority behind the cause of the defendant.

Overall, then, although the stage action involved in this peroration is much simpler than that deployed in *Pro Plancio*, Cicero exploits two of the same elements: his supposed debt to the defendant and the emotional trauma of his exile.

## Pro Milone

These elements appear also in Cicero's defense of Milo. As we saw in chapter three, his tearful appeals refer repeatedly to the ethical obligations that he owes to the defendant.[59] And his exile serves again as the catalyst for his emotional reflections, although in this case he does not focus on one particular scene from this dreadful time (as he does in *Pro Plancio* and *Pro Rabirio Postumo*). Instead he relies on a series of more generalized exclamations and rhetorical questions in his attempts to raise the emotional tenor.[60] Thus, at the conclusion of this extended climax, he can at last claim to be overcome by tears (*Mil.* 105: *sed finis sit; neque enim prae lacrimis iam loqui possumus, et hic se lacrimis defendi vetat*).

## Pro Caelio

Not every example of judicial crying, however, follows this pattern. In *Pro Caelio*, Cicero's tearful lament appears not in the peroration but in his rebuttal of the allegation that Caelius had plotted to poison Clodia (*Cael.* 58–60). Its function thus has little to do with generating pity for the defendant; rather, it aims rather to stir up resentment and indignation against Clodia, who (it was rumored) had poisoned her husband—the prominent politician Metellus Celer—several years earlier.[61]

To achieve this goal, Cicero again draws upon his facility with vivid narrative. Claiming to have been personally present at Celer's deathbed,

---

59. See, e.g., *Mil.* 94: *ego cum te . . . patriae reddidissem, mihi putarem in patria non futurum locum?* And *Mil.* 100: *quid habeo quod faciam pro tuis in me meritis nisi ut eam fortunam quaecumque erit tua ducam meam?*

60. See, e.g., *Mil.* 104, which includes two exclamations, three rhetorical questions and a brief instance of *sermocinatio*.

61. Note, e.g., the comment at *Cael.* 60: *nonne ipsam domum [sc. Clodia] metuet ne quam vocem eiciat . . . ?*

he presents a melodramatic account of the man's demise (*Cael.* 59): *vidi enim, vidi et illum hausi dolorem vel acerbissimum in vita, cum Quintus Metellus abstraheretur e sinu gremioque patriae.* ("For I saw with my own eyes, saw and drank in that sorrowful sight, the bitterest in my life, when Quintus Metellus was torn from the breast and embrace of his fatherland.") Although this eyewitness point of view lends Cicero's grief a degree of authenticity, at times the details strain credulity. Celer's dying words, for example, are described as faltering (*interruptis*), yet somehow the man was strong enough to strike the wall shared with his neighbor, call upon Cicero and Catulus, and articulate some stirringly patriotic sentiments (*Cael.* 59):

> *extremum sensum ad memoriam rei publicae reservabat, cum me intuens flentem significabat interruptis ac morientibus vocibus quanta impenderet procella mihi, quanta tempestas civitati et cum parietem saepe feriens eum qui cum Quinto Catulo fuerat ei communis, crebro Catulum, saepe me, saepissime rem publicam nominabat, ut non tam se emori quam spoliari suo praesidio cum patriam tum etiam me doleret.*

> [With his last thoughts he remembered the republic, and, fixing his gaze upon me as I wept, in broken and dying words he indicated to me how great a storm was hanging over me, and how great a tempest threatened the State; then, knocking several times on the wall which divided his house from the one where Quintus Catulus had lived, he frequently called on the name of Catulus, often on mine, and most often on that of the republic, grieving not so much that he was dying, as that his country and I also should be robbed of his protection.]

The scene is carefully calculated to provoke the jurors' indignation. Cicero depicts Clodia's supposed crime as more than just a domestic matter; her murderous actions had far-reaching consequences for the whole state. (Note the references to the *res publica* and *patria*.) But Celer's death also affected Cicero personally: the phrase *quanta impenderet procella mihi* alludes to his exile and the struggles that preceded it. Celer's death (he suggests) robbed him of a valuable ally. The high emotional register of these reflections also allows Cicero to contrive a tearful, stuttering conclusion to the passage (*Cael.* 60): *sed revertor ad crimen; etenim haec facta illius clarissimi ac fortissimi viri mentio et vocem meam fletu debilitavit et mentem dolore impedivit.* ("But I return to the accusation; indeed the mention I have made of that illustrious and gallant man has choked my voice with tears and dazed my mind with sorrow.")

This example is important for two reasons. First, it demonstrates Cicero's flexibility in technique. He can, when necessary, generate tears in a context quite distinct from the peroration and its usual emphasis on the plight of the defendant.[62] Second, it highlights the various factors that shaped his design of *Pro Caelio* as a whole. As we saw in chapter three, Cicero seems to have had specific strategic reasons for not engaging in a highly emotional appeal in the peroration. This decision, however, had an interesting consequence. It opened up the possibility of deploying tears elsewhere in the speech. There was of course no obligation for Cicero to do so. But the very fact that he did indeed choose to break down crying at this earlier point attests once again to his belief in the effectiveness of this form of pleading. He finds a way of exploiting tears, even though Caelius had apparently ruled out their use in the peroration.

## Pro Sulla

Our final example poses a problem of interpretation. As we saw in the previous chapter, Cicero in the peroration of *Pro Sulla* deploys several devices designed to heighten its emotional impact. He exploits the presence in court of Sulla's son by inviting the jurors to sympathize with the boy's suffering (*Sull.* 88–89); and he represents Sulla himself as making an entreaty (*Sull.* 89: *vos, iudices, obtestatur*). Other tropes appear as well, most notably the reversal-of-fortune motif. Eventually these remarks are brought to a faltering conclusion (*Sull.* 92): *sed iam impedior egomet, iudices, dolore animi ne de huius miseria plura dicam.* ("But, for my part, gentlemen, I am now prevented from speaking further about this man's suffering by my *dolor animi*.")[63] As we have seen, this kind of claim is often made when Cicero presents himself as breaking down in tears. In this case, however, there is no specific reference to *lacrimae* or *fletus*. Instead Cicero refers to his emotional state with the words *dolor animi*. What are we to make of this choice of phrase?

---

62. The use of emotional strategies in contexts other than the peroration coincides to a degree with rhetorical theory; see Quint. *Inst.* 6.1.51.

63. For the reversal-of-fortune motif, see, e.g., *Sull.* 91: *o miserum et infelicem illum diem quo consul omnibus centuriis P. Sulla renuntiatus est, o falsam spem, o volucrem fortunam, o caecam cupiditatem, o praeposteram gratulationem!*

D. H. Berry seems to regard this scene as essentially no different from others where Cicero breaks down in tears.[64] Arguably then we should treat the phrase *dolor animi* as a simple synonym for *lacrimae*. The *Thesaurus Linguae Latinae*, however, classifies the usage at *Sull.* 92 under a more generalized sense of emotional distress and glosses it with the Greek terms πονοψυχία and συμπάθεια.[65] Moreover, it is clear that Cicero's construction of this emotional climax differs significantly from those that we have just analyzed. He does not attempt to entreat the jurors directly; he does not express any great obligation to Sulla that requires reciprocal tears; and he does not assert an especially close friendship with the man. The best that Cicero can manage is a solemn oath that Sulla was not, to his knowledge, involved in the Catilinarian conspiracy (see *Sull.* 86). Nor apparently is there any physical contact between Cicero and the defendant (such as an embrace) that might serve as a cue for the onset of tears.

Cicero, then, does not identify himself so completely with Sulla's cause—and this difference may well account for his assertion of generalized grief (*dolor animi*) rather than actual tears. Nevertheless, a further subsidiary motive may have underpinned Cicero's reference to his sense of mental anguish. In his final remarks, he turns the jurors' attention to the trial's political context: the aftermath of the Catilinarian conspiracy. In particular, he refers to the reputation for *severitas* that he himself acquired in the wake of his execution of the conspirators, and he urges the jurors not to acquire their own reputation for cruelty by convicting Sulla (*Sull.* 93: *falsam a nobis crudelitatis famam repellamus*). Instead, they should show leniency and compassion (*Sull.* 92: *severitatem . . . lenitate ac misericordia mitigate*). To a degree, then, Cicero's presentation of himself as a man of powerful empathy—one who feels *dolor animi* at the fate of his client—may have had a political as well as an oratorical dimension to it. He shows the people of Rome that there is far more to him than the *severitas* that he was obliged to exercise against the criminals (*improbos*) involved in the conspiracy (*Sull.* 92).

---

64. See Berry (1996) 316. Cf. 305: "there is no reason to doubt that, when he spoke, Cicero was genuinely affected by the pathos of Sulla's plight."

65. See *TLL* vol. 5, col. 1842, lines 70–74 (s. v. *dolor*). In other instances *dolor animi* denotes the resentment provoked by insult and personal abuse. See, e. g., [Caes.] *B Afr.* 46.1; *Sest.* 88. Cf. *TLL* vol. 5, col. 1841, line 25 (s.v. *dolor*): *orta ex iniuria (saepe prope i. q. ira, indignatio)*. In yet others, it denotes what we understand as sorrow. See, e.g., *Dom.* 98 and *Fam.* 4.6.1. Cf. *TLL* vol. 5, col. 1840, lines 3–4 (s.v. *dolor*): *orta ex damno, iactura, rebus adversis . . .* (syn. *luctus, maeror, tristitia* sim.).

CRYING IN COURT

It is clear from our discussion so far that Roman trials regularly involved expressions of high emotion. On some occasions, it was the advocate who shed tears, on others, the defendant.[66] In some instances, too, relatives, friends and witnesses might contribute to the weeping.[67] But these displays of emotion at times extended even further. As we saw in chapter one, judicial oratory in Rome was highly interactive. The skilled advocate knew how to elicit shouts, applause, and laughter from the assembled crowd. Indeed, in his depiction of the star advocate, Cicero even suggests that he could bring the audience to tears (*Brut.* 290: *cum velit fletus*).

We should pause before dismissing this phrasing as mere hyperbole. At the start of this book we encountered an image of Cicero holding a child in his arms and filling the forum "with lamentation and wailing" (*Orat.* 131: *plangore et lamentatione*). It is possible perhaps that these nouns refer to the tears and laments of Cicero alone. But they more likely refer to the emotional reaction that he stirred up among the audience as a whole. The main focus of the passage is on the emotions of jurors (*Orat.* 131: *mens iudicum permovenda est*), and it is a simple step to suppose that his theatrics influenced the mood of the surrounding crowd as well. As he states, the forum was filled with noise *completely* (note the prefix *com-* in *compleremus*).

The possibility of widespread tears and wailing during a legal trial is disturbing perhaps to modern sensibilities. Yet, as we have seen, the protocols of the Roman courts were very different from our own. Indeed, the physical presence of large audiences may have enabled the skilled advocate to exploit the phenomenon labelled by today's behavioral psychologists as "emotional contagion"—the process whereby one person's emotional state readily reproduces itself in another person situated nearby.[68] The grand scale of these events thus facilitated attempts to whip up

---

66. For the tears of defendants, see, e.g., Fonteius (*Font.* 48), Murena (*Mur.* 86) and Cluentius (*Clu.* 201).

67. For relatives, see, e.g., *Flac.* 106 (*meam quodam modo flens fidem implorat*); *Sest.* 144 (*filium oculis lacrimantibus me intuentem*) and 146 (*qui his lacrimis qua sit pietate declarat*); *Lig.* 32 (*huius T. Brocchi . . . lacrimas squaloremque ipsius et fili vides*) and 33 (*quid de fratribus dicam? . . . moveant te horum lacrimae*). On friends and supporters, see *Rab. Post.* 48 (*iam indicat tot hominum fletus*); *Clu.* 197 (*ex lacrimis horum, iudices*). On witnesses, see, e.g., *Verr.* 2.1.93 (*Malleolus a me productus est et mater eius atque avia, quae miserae flentes eversum a te puerum patriis bonis esse dixerunt*) and *Verr.* 2.3.74 (*lacrimantem testari*). At *Clu.* 166–68 the father of a dead man may have wept in court as his testimony was read out (note *maeror tuus*).

68. As experimental science has shown, there is often a strong physiological element to emotional arousal. One person's distress (or joy) can produce measurable physical re-

the emotions of the crowd. And the intensity of these reactions in turn explains Cicero's desire to deploy theatrics whenever possible. If successful, they could significantly influence the dynamics of the whole trial.[69]

But no less disturbing to our sensibilities is the possibility that Roman jurors also wept openly in the course of an advocate's speech. And yet this is exactly what Quintilian seems to envisage when he describes the orator's effect on a jury (Quint. *Inst.* 6.1.23): *plurimum tamen valet miseratio, quae iudicem non flecti tantum cogit, sed motum quoque animi sui lacrimis confiteri.* ("What carries most weight, however, is the appeal to pity, which forces the juror not only to be moved, but also to express openly this emotion through his tears.")[70] Indeed, Cicero toward the end of *Pro Plancio* suggests that his emotional appeal has been so powerful that he has brought not only some of the jurors to tears but even the *quaesitor* of the court (C. Alfius Flavus) as well (*Planc.* 104):[71]

> *teque, C. Flave, oro et obtestor, qui meorum consiliorum in consulatu socius, periculorum particeps, rerum quas gessi adiutor fuisti, meque non modo salvum semper, sed etiam ornatum florentemque esse voluisti, ut mihi per hos conserves eum per quem me tibi et his conservatum vides. plura ne dicam tuae me etiam lacrimae impediunt vestraeque, iudices, non solum meae.*

[Gaius Flavus, during my consulship you supported my policies, shared in my dangers and assisted in my achievements. You always wished not just for my safety but also for my recognition and prosperity. I beg and implore you to save for my sake, with the assistance of these jurors, the man with whose assistance you see that I have been saved, both for your benefit and the benefit of these jurors. Your tears, Flavus, stop me from speaking further, as do those of you, gentlemen, as well as my own.]

---

sponses in another. See Hatfield, Cacioppo, and Rapson (1994) 7–78. How this emotional contagion manifests itself in public depends a good deal on social and cultural *mores;* but the basic elements of shared physiological arousal are usually present. See Hatfield, Cacioppo, and Rapson (1994) 147–82. For a (possible) example of Roman familiarity with this phenomenon, see Sen. *De Ira* 2.2.5: *inde est quod adridemus ridentibus et contristat nos turba maerentium et effervescimus ad aliena certamina.* Cf. Casamento (2004) 47–55.

69. Note, however, the fascinating account at *De or.* 2.197–204 of the way in which M. Antonius was able to win over a hostile crowd to his side during the trial of Norbanus; cf. May (1994).

70. Cf. Bablitz (2007) 117: "on two occasions Quintilian speaks of tears as a reality rather than as a possibility, and views the tears as evidence of the advocate's successful emotional appeal."

71. On Flavus, see *Planc.* 43: *hunc C. Alfium.* He was probably praetor in 54, and had served as *quaesitor* at the earlier trial of Gabinius in that year; see *Q Fr.* 3.1.24. He had been tribune in 59; see Broughton (1952) 227, n. 3. Cf. Holden (1881) 202.

It is tempting perhaps to discount the claim as nothing more than a manipulative fabrication. We could hypothesize, for example, that Cicero invented the detail when writing up the speech for publication, in order to exaggerate the extent of his oratorical impact. Or it may have been a bold bluff perpetrated at the time of delivery, as Cicero audaciously tried to persuade onlookers that he had won the support of Flavus and the jury. Or perhaps—if we prefer an even more jaundiced view of Cicero and his contemporaries—Flavus and Cicero were complicit in these theatrics; the two men had arranged this striking emotional climax beforehand.[72]

Collusion is certainly possible. The courts in 54 BCE were the site of much political maneuvering, as opponents of the triumvirs attempted to settle scores.[73] In several instances we know that bribery and political influence were brought to bear to try to influence the outcome of these events.[74] And yet, although Flavus himself has been described as hostile to the triumvirs, the prosecution of Plancius does not seem to have been motivated primarily by these wider political concerns. Laterensis's grudge at being defeated in the elections by Plancius provides all the motivation we need.[75] If, then, there was a degree of complicity between Cicero and Flavus, it most likely derived from personal obligations between the two men, rather than widespread corruption.

There remains, however, a fourth possible option: that the tears of Flavus and the jurors were a genuine reaction to Cicero's emotional pleas. At first glance, this possibility strains credibility. It seems difficult to believe that these educated men were really willing to empathize so deeply with advocates who were patently aiming to manipulate them. And yet the passage from Quintilian quoted above suggests that jurors could indeed become emotionally involved in proceedings. Indeed, he makes the same claim elsewhere in similarly emphatic terms (*Inst.* 6.2.7): *an cum ille qui plerisque perorantibus petitur fletus erupit, non palam dicta sententia est? huc igitur incumbat orator, hoc opus eius, hic labor est.* ("When

---

72. Cf. *Planc.* 43 where Cicero refers to a perception that the *quaesitor* was especially well disposed to Plancius.

73. See, e.g., Gruen (1974) 311–31; Fantham (1975) 436–37; 443; Siani-Davies (2001) 65–73.

74. See, e.g., *Q Fr.* 3.2.3; 3.3.3. Gruen (1974) 324–25; Fantham (1975) 435; Siani-Davies (2001) 68.

75. See Siani-Davies (2001) 67, where Flavus is described as a member of the "Catonian faction." Gruen (1974) 319–22 is the exception in regarding the prosecution of Plancius as motivated by broader political enmities. Cf. Gelzer (1969) 199; Alexander (2002) 144.

that weeping which is the goal of most perorations breaks forth, isn't the verdict declared openly for all to see? Let this then be the orator's aim; this is his task, this the toil.") There is no suggestion here that jurors who react in this way are somehow foolish or failing to live up to some ideal of detachment and impartiality (nor indeed that they are colluding with the advocate). They are simply behaving as many individuals do when presented with scenes of distress, powerfully and movingly presented.


CONCLUSIONS

Cicero's judicial tears demand our attention in the first place because they raise questions of oratorical technique. How did the master orator set up his emotional appeals so that the accompanying weeping did not seem forced and false? As we have seen, several important devices can be identified: his assertion of a special degree of intimacy with the accused; his claim that the present tears are a kind of debt owed to the accused for kindnesses shown in the past; and his linking of these kindnesses (where possible) to his time in exile—an undeniably traumatic event in his life that furnished a source of plausibly authentic tears. Finally, Cicero's skill in portraying melodramatic scenes—such as his fraught meeting with Plancius in Greece and the death of Metellus Celer—helps him to raise his pleading to a high emotional pitch.

It is unlikely, however, that Cicero gleaned this technique from the rhetorical handbooks. In general, such treatises have little to say about the exploitation of tears. (Crying was, after all, essentially an aspect of delivery.) In several works, we find the sensible maxim that the orator should keep tearful appeals brief. (See, for example, *Rhet. Her.* 2.50: *commiserationem brevem esse oportet. nihil enim lacrima citius arescit.*) But, as Kellogg demonstrated many years ago, this is essentially an ethical proverb deriving from Greek comedy rather than a highly developed rhetorical principle.[76] It seems likely, then, that Cicero learned his technique, not from books, but from his observation of contemporary orators. Although he was too young to have witnessed at first hand Antonius's tears (and those of Marius) on behalf of Aquillius, he had the opportunity to ques-

---

76. Kellogg (1907). Cicero at *Inv. Rhet.* 1.109 attributes the tag to the rhetor Apollonius; but the teacher himself was probably doing no more than quoting a familiar saying. Quintilian, as often, expounds upon the implications of the advice in rather more detail than the previous handbook treatments (*Inst.* 6.1.27–29). But much is still left to the orator's personal judgement.

tion him about his techniques during their later conversations.[77] More generally, too, he would have observed other kinds of tearful performance in the context of private and public supplications (and in other forms of social and political theater as well).

It may well be no coincidence that Cicero's most emphatic tearful appeals all date to the period following his return from exile. To be sure, he exploits various types of judicial theatrics early in his career as advocate; but only after 57 BCE does he deploy *his own tears* for rhetorical effect. Perhaps only this late in his career did he feel confident enough in his prestige and credibility to execute these stunts successfully (although, as we have seen, he was not immune from ridicule for trying to do so). Possibly, too, he came to appreciate that his exile provided him with a reliably plausible *topos* from which to generate oratorical tears (one that, for obvious reasons, was not available to him previously).

The other important issue raised by Cicero's exploitation of tears is the cultural value attached to crying in ancient Rome. As we have seen, the atmosphere of the Roman court was very different from that of modern legal proceedings. The open display of emotion by defendant, family, and relatives is best explained (I have suggested) by the existence of social principle that regarded public weeping as an admirable means of expressing loyal support for family and friends. We have seen tears deployed in this way both in private social contexts and in public venues such as the senate. Their prevalence at judicial trials was a natural extension of this cultural practice. As we saw in chapter one, the court's presiding official seems to have had no great interest in curbing such displays; indeed, to try to do so may have been viewed as an unreasonable intrusion upon traditional social customs.

The third category of weepers—the jurors and wider public audience—is perhaps the most difficult for the modern reader to comprehend. Jurors in particular are expected to maintain a degree of outward composure and neutrality when hearing the different sides of a case. We might also expect in Roman jurors some curmudgeonly resistance to the oratorical tricks that they themselves had learned during their own rhetorical education. And yet, as we have seen, the evidence suggests that this was not the case. This aspect of behavior warrants further investigation. As Andrew Riggsby has demonstrated, many Roman jurors probably took their seats at a trial intending to vote according to

77. Cf. May (2001) on Antonius' influence on Cicero in the matter of emotional pleading.

principles of justice and fairness.[78] But this basic intent need not have precluded them from getting involved in the drama of the moment and showing their reactions to the unfolding situation. Like the members of the *corona*, the jurors too—in the right conditions—seem to have felt a strong participatory impulse. Indeed, engaging closely with events may have been precisely what was expected of a conscientious member of the jury.

---

78. See Riggsby (1997).

# CHAPTER 5

# JUDICIAL THEATRICS BEYOND CICERO

As we saw in chapter one, a broad tradition of oratorical theatrics was well established by the time Cicero embarked upon his career in the courts. But how widespread was the use of such showmanship among his own contemporaries? Was he unusual in integrating these techniques into his judicial pleading? Or were such tricks the norm? In this final chapter, I consider some of the examples of judicial theater that we can discern in the speeches of other Late Republican orators. As we shall see, significant methodological obstacles arise when we try to generalize from the limited evidence available to us. Nevertheless, Quintilian's discussion of oratorical showmanship in the imperial period seems to suggest a strong continuity in judicial theatrics across the centuries.

We may begin with the advocate Erucius, who acted as prosecutor in the trial of L. Varenus (Cicero spoke for the defense).[1] From remarks made by Quintilian, we can infer that Erucius brought into court a man swathed in bandages, whose wounds he proceeded to reveal in the course of his speech (*Inst.* 6.1.49: *subinde vulnus in iudicio resolvebatur*). This stunt recalls the long-established practice of displaying scars in court for heightened oratorical impact (discussed in chapter one). But since Erucius was speaking for the prosecution, his purpose may have been primarily evidentiary: this visual presentation helped to support the allegation that a violent assault had taken place. Nevertheless, we can assume that Erucius was well aware of the theatrical value of his human prop. The sight of the man's wounds had an emotional directness as powerful as any words.[2]

---

1. The date of Varenus's trial is uncertain. See Alexander (1990) 175 (no. 368), under "Trials of Indefinite Date." Marinone (2004) 274 seems to favor a date of 77/76 BCE. Cicero's speech survives only in fragments; see Crawford (1994) 7–18. On Erucius, who also served as prosecutor in the case against Roscius of Ameria, see Malcovati (1976) 284–86 (no. 79); David (1992) 762–63.

2. Note that Quintilian regards Erucius's actions as calculated stagecraft (*Inst.* 6.1.49: *eius modi scaenae*). For references to other aspects of the trial, see Quint. *Inst.* 4.2.26; 5.13.28; 7.1.9; 7.2.36.

Erucius, however, seems to have overplayed the device. Quintilian's use of *subinde*, combined with the imperfect tense (*resolvebatur*), suggests that the advocate could not resist making repeated use of the stooge and his bandages. This heavy-handedness gave Cicero the opportunity to make several witty remarks (Quint. *Inst.* 6.1.49: *multa dixit urbane*) that spoiled the intended effect. Indeed he may even have contrived a cleverly disparaging comparison between Erucius's performance and that of Antonius at the trial of Aquillius.[3] Nevertheless, the incident is an important one. It confirms that other advocates toward the start of Cicero's career were deploying judicial theatrics. It is worth noting too that these tricks were not confined to the peroration of a defense.

Further concrete examples, however, are difficult to find. One scrap of evidence from Charisius (a fourth century CE grammarian) suggests that Q. Hortensius, Cicero's great oratorical rival and colleague, exploited the facial scars of C. Rabirius in a speech in the man's defense in 63 BCE (probably at a *iudicium populi* on a charge of *perduellio*).[4] Indeed, Hortensius seems to have adopted the persona of the defendant during this passage (hence *mearum* in the phrase *mearum cicatricum*), a device that we have seen Cicero himself use in his defenses of Milo and Roscius of Ameria. But the evidence fails us when we try to reconstruct further details of his performance.[5]

Other uses that Hortensius made of judicial theatrics are even less clear.[6] Cicero describes the man's general style of delivery as forceful and animated, especially early in his career, and this manner apparently suited well the bustle that orators encountered in the forum.[7] Any ac-

3. This may be the point behind Cicero's phrase reported at Prisc. *Inst.* 3.40: *Erucius hic noster Antoniaster est.* For the text, see Keil (1855) 112. Cf. Quint. *Inst.* 8.3.22; Crawford (1994) 15 (fragment 10); 17.

4. For the text, see Barwick (1964) 159, lines 6–8: *cicatricum, non cicatricium. Hortensius pro C. Rabirio "cicatricum mearum," quod emendate dictum sit.* Cf. Malcovati (1976) 322. On the possible format of the trial, see Jones (1972) 40–44. As noted by Alexander (1990) 110, n. 1, "This case . . . constitutes the most difficult legal conundrum of all the trials in this period." Cf. Lintott (2008) 120–21. On Hortensius's contribution to the legal process, see also *Rab. Perd.* 18.

5. Note that Cicero himself, speaking at a later stage in this trial, likewise referred to the battle-scars on Rabirius's face (*Rab. Perd.* 36: *qui hasce ore adverso pro re publica cicatrices ac notas virtutis accepit*). Evidently such tropes could be recycled effectively by different orators.

6. On Hortensius's oratory in general, see *Brut.* 301–8; 317–29; Malcovati (1976) 310–30; Dyck (2008).

7. For Hortensius's lively and forceful delivery, see *Brut.* 317: *verborum et actionis genere commotior.* Cf. *Brut.* 317: *acrem enim oratorem, incensum et agentem et canorum, concursus hominum forique strepitus desiderat.* As noted in chapter one, the impressiveness of Hortensius's language as a young man often provoked cheers and shouts from his audience (*Brut.* 326:

tual stunts in the courts, however, go unreported. Cicero, it is true, does claim in his *Verrines* to be worried that Hortensius, as speaker for the defense, will attempt a tearful plea on behalf of the defendant, using the same tricks as M. Antonius did on behalf of Aquillius (*Verr.* 2.5.3–4). But this assertion is designed in part to set up a witty jibe: if Hortensius does attempt such a trick (Cicero claims), he will reveal on Verres's exposed body, not battle scars, but the bite-marks of the governor's lovers (*Verr.* 2.5.32: *cicatrices populus Romanus aspiciat, ex mulierum morsu vestigia libidinis atque nequitiae*). Nevertheless, behind this bravado there may have been a very real concern that Hortensius had the ability to stage an effective emotional plea on Verres's behalf. Indeed, since Aquillius, like Verres, had been governor of Sicily and had achieved worthy military success there, the parallel would have been a productive one for Hortensius to exploit.[8] And yet, of course, in this instance we cannot progress beyond speculation, since Hortensius never got the chance to deliver a final peroration.[9]

One incident reported by Cicero, however, confirms that his contemporaries did on occasion try to integrate human props into their appeals. In *Pro Cluentio*, Cicero describes an attempt in an earlier trial by the advocate Caepasius (the elder) to generate pity for the defendant, Fabricius (*Clu.* 58):[10]

> *itaque cum callidissime se dicere putaret et cum illa verba gravissima ex intimo artificio deprompsisset: "respicite, iudices, hominum fortunas, respicite dubios variosque casus, respicite C. Fabrici senectutem." cum hoc "respicite" ornandae orationis causa saepe dixisset, respexit ipse. at C. Fabricius a subselliis demisso capite discesserat.*

---

*itaque Hortensius utroque genere florens clamores faciebat adulescens*). On the changes in his style over time, see *Brut.* 320.

    8. See Broughton (1951) 577 on Aquillius's governorship in 100 BCE. For his success against the slaves in Sicily, see, e.g., *Verr.* 2.5.5; 2.5.14. On this likely line of argument, cf. van der Blom (2010) 179, n. 18.

    9. Cf. *Orat.* 129: *nobis pro familiari reo summus orator non respondit Hortensius*. Quintilian, however, notes the existence in his day of a *Pro Verre* (*Inst.* 10.1.23), which was perhaps a schoolroom exercise, or perhaps a version of Hortensius's planned defense, circulated after the trial had concluded. For a variety of views, see Settle (1962) 99–111; Alexander (1976); Frazel (2004).

    10. On the trial of C. Fabricius in 74 BCE, see Alexander (1990) 74–75 (no. 148). Gaius and Lucius Caepasius both spoke for the defense; the advocate in the anecdote is described as *maior Caepasius* (*Clu.* 58). See *Brut.* 242; Malcovati (1976) 373–75; David (1992) 782. The incident is also mentioned at Quint. *Inst.* 6.1.41. Cf. Classen (1985) 52–53.

[And so, when he thought he was speaking really skillfully and had brought out from the secret recesses of his craft the following weighty words: "Look back upon the fortunes of mankind, gentlemen, look back upon all the uncertain and changeable outcomes, look back upon the old age of Gaius Fabricius"; when, in order to embellish his oration, he had uttered the phrase "look back" several times, he looked back himself. But Gaius Fabricius had abandoned the benches with his head hanging low.]

The incident provides an important reminder of the risks involved in attempting judicial theatrics—a point stressed by Quintilian in particular and one to which we shall return later in this chapter.[11] Presumably in this case we are to imagine Caepasius standing more or less in front of the jurors, with the defense benches behind him to one side. (Such an arrangement explains why he was not aware of Fabricius's absence as he made his initial remarks.)[12] In general, his intended effect seems rather modest in scope. There is no sign, for example, of a family tableau or a desperate embrace between relatives, such as we find in some of Cicero's speeches (see chapter three). He seems merely to have planned to integrate Fabricius into his appeal with a dramatic flourish. Yet he managed to botch even this simplest of arrangements. As Cicero reports, the jurors burst out laughing at his gaffe, and the whole effect was ruined.[13]

Nevertheless, these were risks that other orators too were prepared to take, and the trial of Scaurus in 54 BCE provides our best example of the ambitious theatrics that some of Cicero's contemporaries attempted. In chapter three, we noted the remarkable supplication by some ten members of Scaurus's extended family as the jurors went to cast their votes.[14] Although it is possible that Cicero was the architect of this stunt, the defense case as a whole involved such a curious assemblage of advocates

11. Note, however, that Cicero himself does not use this incident to illustrate the pitfalls of judicial theatrics (as Quintilian does at *Inst.* 6.1.41). Its immediate rhetorical point is to prove Fabricius's awareness of his own guilt. It was his sense of shame (Cicero claims) that led him to skulk away from the benches *demisso capite* (*Clu.* 59: *ita tum Fabricius primum suo iudicio, quod est gravissimum . . . est condemnatus*). Fabricius's unscheduled departure from his seat illustrates again the relaxed protocol that seems to have prevailed at these occasions.

12. Cf. Lintott (2004) 63–64.

13. The jurors' mirth was heightened yet further by Caepasius's evident irritation at the situation (*Clu.* 59: *hic iudices ridere, stomachari atque acerbe ferre patronus, causam sibi eripi et se cetera de illo loco "respicite, iudices" non posse dicere*).

14. See Asc. *Scaur.* 20C; Alexander (1990) 143–44 (no. 295); David (1992) 624–26; Lewis (2006) 216–31.

(six in all) that we should hesitate before making such an assumption.[15] Moreover, Asconius tells us that Scaurus himself, dressed *in sordibus*, utilized tearful appeals when speaking in his own defense (Asc. *Scaur.* 20C: *magnopere iudices movit et squalore et lacrimis*); and his half-brother, Faustus Sulla, wept as he gave testimony at the trial (Asc. *Scaur.* 28C: *is in laudatione multa humiliter et cum lacrimis locutus non minus audientes permovit quam Scaurus ipse permoverat*). Overall, then, Cicero seems to have played only a minor role in the defense's extensive showmanship, and the trial suggests that other advocates rivalled him in their use of theatrics. Indeed, the group supplication by Scaurus and his allies may represent an experimental attempt to develop and extend existing practices yet further.[16]

Manipulative theatrics also continued to be used in oratorical contexts outside the courts.[17] Indeed, Asconius's account of events immediately following the murder of Clodius in 52 BCE suggests that an understanding of these techniques extended to aristocratic women as well.[18] He depicts Fulvia, Clodius's widow, displaying the corpse to a crowd gathered at her house and pointing out the various wounds it had suffered (Asc. *Mil.* 32C: *augebat autem facti invidiam uxor Clodi Fulvia quae cum effusa lamentatione vulnera eius ostendebat*). Such grief and indignation were of course exactly what the Romans would have expected from a wife who had just heard of her husband's violent death. Nevertheless, Asconius's phrasing suggests an element of oratorical calculation in Fulvia's actions: this was a performance specifically designed to heighten the outrage of the assembled crowd. As we saw in chapter two, the role of distraught widow was also one that Fulvia pursued energetically at the ensuing prosecution of Milo.[19]

---

15. See Asc. *Scaur.* 20C on the six advocates involved (Q. Hortensius, P. Clodius, M. Marcellus, M. Messalla Niger, M. Calidius, and Cicero himself). For the motives of Scaurus's supporters (both his advocates and others), see Courtney (1961), who argues for the influence of political vendettas from earlier decades; and Gruen (1974) 333–36, who regards the group as uniting to support a general principle; see also Marshall (1985) 127; 150–53; Lewis (2006) 228–30; Dyck (2012) 97–98.

16. See chapter three for discussion of the likely frequency of voting-time supplications at Roman trials.

17. For the use of tears at a *iudicium populi* in 74 BCE, see *Clu.* 137 (discussed in chapter one). For their use in the senate, see *Red. pop.* 12.

18. On these and subsequent events, see Sumi (1997), esp. 96.

19. Asc. *Mil.* 40C: *ultimae testimonium dixerunt Sempronia, Tuditani filia, socrus P. Clodi, et uxor Fulvia, et fletu suo magnopere eos qui assistebant commoverunt*. It is possible that Asconius's account is distorted by a tradition hostile to Fulvia; but such influence is difficult to identify explicitly. We might hypothesize that Fulvia had learned some demagogic tricks from her husband. Yet, although Clodius himself was an effective manipulator of the *populus*, it remains unclear how far he exploited tears and other theatrics in his oratory. For one

The demagogic potential of Clodius's body was further exploited the following day, when it was carried to the forum and placed on the Rostra in order to display its wounds (Asc. *Mil.* 33C: *ut vulnera videri possent*). Once there, the corpse provided a powerful means for stirring up opprobrium, as T. Munatius Plancus and Q. Pompeius Rufus delivered speeches at a *contio* (Asc. *Mil.* 33C: *invidiam Miloni fecerunt*). Following this raucous assembly, Clodius's body was given an impromptu cremation in the senate house, causing a fire that eventually burned down the whole building.[20]


ANTONY AT CAESAR'S FUNERAL

This rhetorical exploitation of a corpse in the wake of a murder brings us to another notorious example of oratorical theatrics: the speech of Mark Antony at Julius Caesar's funeral in March 44 BCE. Readers of Shakespeare will be familiar with one device that Antony supposedly exploited in the course of his oration: the displaying of Caesar's bloodied and dagger-rent robes.[21] As we shall see, this emotive prop is attested in several of our ancient accounts of the event. One source, however, describes a far more elaborate *coup de théâtre*. According to Appian, Antony arranged for a wax effigy of Caesar to be raised above the funeral couch for all to see (*B Civ.* 2.147: ἀνέσχε τις ὑπὲρ τὸ λέχος ἀνδρείκελον αὐτοῦ Καίσαρος ἐκ κηροῦ πεποιημένον· τὸ μὲν γὰρ σῶμα, ὡς ὕπτιον ἐπὶ λέχους, οὐχ ἑωρᾶτο).[22] This remarkable stunt supposedly involved a crane, which

---

possible use of oratorical tears in July 54, see the emendation of Shackleton Bailey (1965) 208 at *Att.* 4.15.4: *Publius sane diserto epilogo <la>crim[in]ans mentis iudicum moverat.* But, as Tatum (1999) 229–30 has argued, the reading *criminans* is plausible enough, especially if we accept the political reconstruction of Linderski (1971) and (1995) 115–36. For the trial, see Alexander (1990) 138 (no. 284). On Clodius's oratory, see Malcovati (1976) 430.

20. The high emotion surrounding these events may lead us to wonder how far such devices were incorporated into the later prosecution of Milo as well. As we have seen, Fulvia and Sempronia certainly provided tears at one point in the trial; and the main prosecutor's close relationship with the deceased (he was Clodius's nephew), combined with the trauma of the event itself, would in theory have offered a fertile context for further theatrics—yet positive evidence fails us. For the nephew's role in the prosecution, see Asc. *Mil.* 41C; David (1992) 890; Lewis (2006) 239–40.

21. Shakespeare *Julius Caesar* Act 3, Scene 2, 170–78: "You all do know this mantle: I remember / The first time ever Caesar put it on; / 'Twas on a summer's evening, in his tent, / That day he overcame the Nervii: / Look, in this place ran Cassius' dagger through: / See what a rent the envious Casca made: / Through this the well-beloved Brutus stabb'd; / And as he pluck'd his cursed steel away, / Mark how the blood of Caesar follow'd it." For recent discussions, see Ramage (2006) 48–51; Wills (2011) 98–114; Mahy (2013) 339–40.

22. For the text of Appian, see Mendelssohn (1881).

then turned the effigy around so that its many wounds were clearly evident (*B Civ.* 2.147: τὸ δὲ ἀνδρείκελον ἐκ μηχανῆς ἐπεστρέφετο πάντῃ, καὶ σφαγαὶ τρεῖς καὶ εἴκοσιν ὤφθησαν ἀνά τε τὸ σῶμα πᾶν καὶ ἀνὰ τὸ πρόσωπον θηριωδῶς ἐς αὐτὸν γενόμεναι). In terms of ingenuity, planning, and showmanship, this scene far outstrips any performance that we have considered so far. If we accept Appian's version of events, Antony must be regarded as a true innovator in both political and oratorical theatrics.

But how reliable is Appian's account? Several prominent scholars have been willing to believe that events similar to those that Appian describes took place. Weinstock, for example, concludes: "[Appian's account] proves to be the closest to the historical events and is in agreement with Cicero's brief allusions."[23] Likewise, Harriet Flower's reconstruction of Caesar's funeral assumes that Appian's account is accurate.[24] And George Kennedy asserts: "Appian must be thought to have some basis for his account for the very reason that it is unusual."[25]

Certainly, the exploitation of an effigy at such a funeral is not implausible *in itself.* As scholars have noted, effigies of the deceased were a familiar feature of this kind of event.[26] Arguably, then, it would have been relatively easy for Antony to acquire such a prop for use in his oratorical showmanship. Cranes too (one assumes) would have been easily obtainable in the metropolis of Rome. Yet an important distinction needs to be drawn: the availability of such items by no means proves that Antony actually made use of them.

The strongest argument *against* the authenticity of Appian's crane and effigy is the fact that they do not appear in any other account of Antony's speech. They do not feature, for example, in Plutarch's biographies of Cicero, Brutus, and Antony.[27] And this absence is made all the more disconcerting by the fact that Plutarch, like Appian, is often said to have been influenced by the history written by Asinius Pollio. If Appian came across the crane and effigy in Pollio, why has Plutarch consistently ignored these remarkable details?[28]

---

23. Weinstock (1971) 352.

24. See Flower (1996) 125–26. Cf. Gregory (1994) 93–94; Sumi (2002a); (2005) 109. The recent discussion by Carotta and Eickenberg (2011) similarly accepts Appian's details.

25. Kennedy (1968a) 106.

26. Dio Cassius, for example, claims that three wax effigies played a part in Augustus's funeral ceremonies some years later (56.34.1). Cf. Drumann and Groebe (1899) 417; Weinstock (1971) 360–61; Bodel (1999) 272; Sumi (2005) 108–9. See also Sumi (2002b) 421 on Sulla's funeral. For the apparent use of an effigy in a funeral procession for a very different reason, see Dessau (1955) 738 (no. 7212).

27. See Plut. *Brut.* 20.4; *Cic.* 42.4; *Ant.* 14.6–8, discussed below.

28. On the influence of Pollio on Appian's account of the funeral, see Weinstock

The omission of these same items by Quintilian is no less suspicious.[29] In Book 6, for example, Quintilian discusses some of the props that an orator can exploit for emotional effect, and in this connection refers to Caesar's bloodied robes at his funeral (Quint. *Inst.* 6.1.31):

> *quarum rerum ingens plerumque vis est velut in rem praesentem animos hominum ducentium, ut populum Romanum egit in furorem praetexta C. Caesaris praelata in funere cruenta.*

[These things commonly make an enormous impression, because they confront people's minds directly with the facts, as when Caesar's blood-stained toga, brought forward at his funeral, drove the Roman people to fury.]

It is curious that Antony's role in these events is not explicitly stated, and it may be that Quintilian here has in mind the effect of Caesar's robes during the funeral procession, rather than during Antony's speech. Donald Russell, for instance, translates the phrase *praelata in funere* as "carried in his funeral," although a meaning of "brought forward [sc. by Antony] at the funeral" is perhaps no less likely.[30] Nevertheless, there is also no explicit mention of Antony in the passage that follows (Quint. *Inst.* 6.1.31):

> *sciebatur interfectum eum, corpus denique ipsum impositum lecto erat, vestis tamen illa sanguine madens ita repraesentavit imaginem sceleris ut non occisus esse Caesar sed tum maxime occidi videretur.*

[Everyone knew that Caesar had been killed; his very corpse had been placed on the bier. Nevertheless, it was those robes, wet with blood, that presented an image of the crime so powerfully that Caesar seemed not to have been slain already, but was being slain then and there.]

---

(1971) 352: "[Appian's] source, direct or indirect, was no doubt Asinius Pollio." Cf. Peter (1914) lxxxvii–lxxxxvii (on Pollio's influence on both Appian and Plutarch); Gabba (1956) 244–49; Pelling (1979) 84–86; (1988) 153–54; Gowing (1992) 40. But see the cautionary remarks of Badian (1958a). On the limits of source criticism in the study of Appian, see the useful summary in Carter (1996) xxxi–xxxii.

29. For Quintilian's knowledge of Asinius Pollio, see *Inst.* 10.1.113.

30. Russell (2001) 33. Cf. Butler (1921) 403: "carried at the head of his funeral procession."

Certainly, if Quintilian is referring here to Antony's exploitation of the robes, his account involves considerable ellipse (just explicable, perhaps, if the orator's stunt was so well known that it did not need explicit mention). But, whatever the case in this respect, the more glaring omission is that of Antony's use of crane and effigy. The whole thrust of Quintilian's discussion is the way in which props can aid the orator's rhetorical impact. If Antony's performance was as novel and creative as Appian claims, it is difficult to explain why Quintilian simply omitted these sensational and noteworthy details.

Given these inconsistencies, the modern critic has two basic options: the first is to assume, on the basis of what we think we know about Appian's working methods, that he must have found the crane-and-effigy detail in *some* source or other, and so engage in speculation as to its identity. The second is to conclude that, for some reason or other, Appian himself invented the detail.[31]

This second option naturally entails the conclusion that Antony was not in fact as inventive a showman as Appian's account implies. His final theatrical flourish with the effigy is simply a literary fabrication. But it is important to note too that the first option does not guarantee the authenticity of Antony's crane-and-effigy either: the source from which Appian drew the detail may itself have been inaccurate. (Since the identity of this source remains mere speculation, so too must its degree of reliability.) In my view, then, it is unwise to place too much weight on Appian's evidence in our attempt to reconstruct the history of oratorical theatrics in Rome.

This conclusion, however, does not mean that his account of Antony's speech is of no interest to us. On the contrary: it offers a fascinating depiction of the way in which an orator might use elements of performance to manipulate the mob. For the speech in fact is not a set-speech of the type we find elsewhere in Appian. At various points the historian

---

31. As scholars have noted, Suetonius's account of the funeral (*Iul.* 84) complicates matters yet further. This version asserts that Antony did not in fact deliver a formal *laudatio*, and that his performance as a whole was rather understated. Deutsch (1928) has argued that this account is fundamentally correct and, as Pelling (1988) 153–54 notes, his line of interpretation has found favor among some eminent historians, including Syme (1939) 98, n. 1, and Yavetz (1969) 66–69. But the impression created by Suetonius's account—that Antony played only a very modest role in proceedings—diverges sharply from the portrayals of Cicero and Plutarch. There is no easy way to reconcile these differences. Kennedy (1968a) 105 is perhaps right to regard Suetonius's version as incomplete and marred by "assumptions and obscurities." Cf. Osgood (2006) 12, n. 1. Yet again, however, there is no sign in Suetonius of a crane or effigy.

interrupts Antony's words in order to describe the different theatrical devices that he employed. Toward the start of the account, for example, Appian refers to the severe and thunderous countenance that Antony adopted as he read out the various honorific decrees awarded to Caesar during his life (*B Civ.* 2.144: τῷ μὲν προσώπῳ σοβαρῷ καὶ σκυθρωπῷ). This effect was heightened (he claims) through the use of effective pauses and gestures (2.144):

> ἐφ᾽ ἑκάστῳ δὲ τούτων ὁ Ἀντώνιος τὴν ὄψιν καὶ τὴν χεῖρα ἐς τὸ σῶμα τοῦ Καίσαρος ἐπιστρέφων ἐν παραβολῇ τοῦ λόγου τὸ ἔργον ἐπεδείκνυ.

[With each decree Antony turned his face and his hand toward Caesar's body comparing the deed with the word.]

And a little later, Appian describes Antony raising his voice and stretching out his arm toward the Capitoline hill as he expressed his continued allegiance to Caesar (2.145: ἐφ᾽ ὅτῳ δὴ μάλιστα τὴν φωνὴν ἐπιτείνας, καὶ τὴν χεῖρα ἐς τὸ Καπιτώλιον ἀνασχών).

This deftly orchestrated performance did not end there, however. According to Appian, Antony went on to arrange his toga so that he had free use of his arms as he bent down in front of Caesar's bier and offered up ostentatious prayers (*B Civ.* 2.146):

> τοιάδε εἰπὼν τὴν ἐσθῆτα οἷά τις ἔνθους ἀνεσύρατο, καὶ περιζωσάμενος ἐς τὸ τῶν χειρῶν εὔκολον τὸ λέχος ὡς ἐπὶ σκηνῆς περιέστη κατακύπτων τε ἐς αὐτὸ καὶ ἀνίσχων, πρῶτα μὲν ὡς θεὸν οὐράνιον ὕμνει καὶ ἐς πίστιν θεοῦ γενέσεως τὰς χεῖρας ἀνέτεινεν.

[Having said this, he gathered up his robes like one inspired by religious fervor, and wrapping them around him so that his hands were free, he stood next to the bier as if he were on stage. He bent toward it and then raised himself again, first singing a hymn to Caesar as if to a heavenly god, and then raising his hands in the air to testify to Caesar's divine birth.]

The reference here to stage performance (ὡς ἐπὶ σκηνῆς) casts Antony as a chorus-leader shaping the emotions of those around him and guiding their actions. Indeed, as part of this process, he adopted a low, mournful tone (ἐς τὸ θρηνῶδες) and deployed oratorical tears, weeping for the injustices suffered by his friend (ὠδύρετο καὶ ἔκλαιε).

The speech builds to its climax with a further piece of oratorical theater. Antony strips Caesar's body of its garment, which he then lifts up on a pole (ἐπὶ κοντοῦ), displaying the rents wrought by the assassins' daggers (λελακισμένην ὑπὸ τῶν πληγῶν καὶ πεφυρμένην αἵματι). This emotive device provokes the desired effect: taking its lead from Antony like a dramatic chorus, the mob grows restless with fury (*B Civ.* 2.146: ἐφ' οἷς ὁ δῆμος οἷα χορὸς αὐτῷ πενθιμώτατα συνωδύρετο καὶ ἐκ τοῦ πένθους αὖθις ὀργῆς ἐνεπίμπλατο).

The appearance of crane and effigy at this climactic moment neatly completes the theatrical analogy, evoking the use of the *mechane* in Greek drama.[32] The sight of these emotive props pitch the assembled crowd into a frenzy of violence (*B Civ.* 2.147): τήνδε οὖν τὴν ὄψιν ὁ δῆμος οἰκτίστην σφίσι φανεῖσαν οὐκέτι ἐνεγκὼν ἀνώμωξάν τε καὶ διαζωσάμενοι τὸ βουλευτήριον, ἔνθα ὁ Καῖσαρ ἀνήρητο, κατέφλεξαν. ("So the people were no longer able to bear the pitiful sight presented to them, and, having uttered a groan and hitched up their clothes, they burned down the senate chamber where Caesar was slain.")[33]

Appian's account, then, presents a memorable example of oratorical manipulation, with an emphasis not just on the content of Antony's speech but on its style of delivery as well. He portrays the consul as a consummate demagogue who brings the crowd to a crescendo of fury through a series of carefully contrived, theatrical devices. And this may well be the best way to view the episode: as a cleverly embellished portrait—almost a pointed caricature—of the kind of oratorical deceptions that a political puppet master such as Antony was able to perpetrate in Late Republican Rome. Certainly, to regard the crane and effigy as a rhetorical fiction runs counter to the traditional view of Appian as essentially an artless compiler who added little to what he found in his sources. But recent studies have argued for a greater degree of conscious literary shaping within his writings.[34] At the very least, this depiction of the

---

32. This similarity between the crane in Appian's account and the *mechane* regularly used in Greek theatrical productions led Weinstock (1971) 354 to consider (and then reject) the possible influence of theatrical productions on Appian's narrative. Although such influence is hard to prove conclusively, the possibility should not perhaps be dismissed outright; cf. Wiseman (1998) 52–59; Beness and Hillard (2001).

33. Caesar was not in fact slain in the Curia but in Pompey's theater. Cf. Carter (1996) 377, n. 186.

34. For a convenient summary of the debate, see Bucher (2000) 411–15. Cf. Gowing (1990); (1992) 241–44; Bucher (2005). Also Carter (1996) xxxii: "It is much safer to credit Appian with some critical intelligence and some familiarity with how a historian was supposed to go about his work."

funeral speech in Book 2 seems designed to tie in with Antony's claim in Book 3 that he had deployed "sly emotional manipulation of the people" (ἀσήμῳ δημοκοπίᾳ) during the oration (App. *B Civ*. 3.35).[35]

The elements of invention in Appian's account, however, should not lead us to overlook Antony's skillful performance as a whole. On the evidence of Plutarch, it seems clear enough that the man engaged in some form of theatrics with Caesar's bloodied robes, and that this succeeded in provoking the mob into a violent and destructive frenzy.[36] Presumably in this regard he had learned much from the friends and relatives of Clodius Pulcher in 52 BCE: Antony almost certainly observed these dramatic events at first hand, and he was himself now married to Fulvia.[37] Moreover, the use of oratorical theatrics ran in the family. (His grandfather was the same M. Antonius who defended M'. Aquillius.) Although Cicero (and later Octavian) tried to paint Antony as an oratorical buffoon, on this occasion at least he seems to have lived up to his grandfather's impressive example—albeit without the use of a crane and effigy.[38]

---

35. Cf. Antony's claim that he exploited the corpse's wounds and clothes in order to inflame the passions of the mob (*B Civ*. 3.35: τάδε γάρ μου τὰ ἔργα καὶ ῥήματα ἠρέθισε τὸν δῆμον). Moreover, in the senatorial debate that immediately followed Caesar's death, Appian portrays Antony as deliberately steering his peers away from a calm and rational consideration of the situation in order to ignite instead a conflagration (δαλὸν ἐξάψας) of anxious self-interest (*B Civ*. 2.128–29). Antony then goes on to manipulate the mob assembled outside the senate house. By revealing that he is wearing a breastplate (θώραξ) beneath his tunic, he rouses the crowd's indignation at the dangers facing him, and stirs to action those demanding vengeance for Caesar's death (*B Civ*. 2.130). On Appian's depiction of deceit in Roman politics, see further Cowan (forthcoming).

36. On Antony's antics with the robes, see the broadly consistent accounts at Plut. *Brut*. 20.4, *Cic*. 42.4 and *Ant*. 14.7, although there are minor differences in detail. Pelling (1988) 153–54 suggests Asinius Pollio as a possible source for these versions (see also 27–28). This is plausible enough, but, as noted above, it is awkward to claim Pollio as the source for both Plutarch and Appian without explaining why Plutarch has omitted the crane and effigy. See also *Att*. 14.10.1 and *Phil*. 2.91. The account at Plut. *Caes*. 68.1 makes no reference to Caesar's robes, mentioning only the wounds on his body (ταῖς πληγαῖς διαλελωβημένον). Dio dispenses with the garment and has Antony point to the wounds on the corpse itself (44.35.4): τόν τε νεκρὸν . . . προθέμενος ἡματωμένον τε, ὥσπερ εἶχε, καὶ τραύματα ἐκφαίνοντα.

37. Antony served as subscriptor to the prosecution of Milo, a short while after Clodius's murder; see Asc. *Mil*. 41C. Plut. *Brut*. 20.5 draws a comparison between the rioting that broke out at Caesar's funeral and that following Clodius's murder. Cf. Welch (1995); Sumi (1997) 84, n. 21; Lewis (2006) 236–37.

38. See in particular *Phil*. 2.42: *vide autem quid intersit inter te et avum tuum*; also *Phil*. 3.21–22; Suet. *Aug*. 86.2–3. Cf. Plut. *Ant*. 2.8. See also Calboli (1997); Ramsey (2010) 162; Mahy (2013).

## CICERO AND HIS CRITICS

This survey of our limited evidence suggests that Cicero was not alone in his use of judicial theatrics, although it is difficult to quantify exactly how deeply these techniques permeated the oratory of his contemporaries. Nevertheless, there is evidence to suggest that, in the mid-fifties BCE, Cicero's repeated performances began to attract comment and criticism from those around him. Most intriguing perhaps is a remark that Cicero assigns to M. Antonius in *De Oratore* (written in November 55 BCE) on the subject of emotional pleading (*De or.* 2.191):

> *ac ne hoc forte magnum ac mirabile esse videatur, hominem totiens irasci, totiens dolere, totiens omni motu animi concitari, praesertim in rebus alienis, magna vis est earum sententiarum atque eorum locorum, quae agas tractesque dicendo, nihil ut opus sit simulatione et fallaciis.*

[And in case it seems perhaps a great and remarkable thing that an individual gets angry on so many different occasions and is moved so often by distress and every type of emotion, especially with regard to other people's business—there is such great power in the thoughts and tropes that you use and exploit when pleading that there is no need for pretence and deception.]

As Wisse notes, the orator's authenticity is not a topic that features prominently in rhetorical theory prior to Cicero.[39] So its place here (Wisse suggests) may owe something to the Atticist/Asianist controversy, whose origins can perhaps be traced back to this period.[40]

Although this explanation is plausible, it remains speculative.[41] An alternative solution is perhaps to be found in the querulous reactions of Cicero's contemporaries to the numerous performances that they saw him give in the courts during this period. In the year before he wrote *De*

---

39. Wisse (1989) 263–68, esp. 264–65: "The genuineness of the emotions to be displayed, however, is not discussed, neither by Aristotle nor by school rhetoric. None of the surviving material until Quintilian shows any awareness of the problem." See also Narducci (1997) 77–96; Cavarzere (2004) and (2011) 122–41.

40. Wisse (1989) 268; see also Wisse (1995) on the possible origins of the controversy. On the various views presented regarding this question, see the useful bibliography in Narducci (2002) 409, n.14.

41. Cf. Wisse (1989) 268 regarding further questions "that seem impossible to answer."

*Oratore*, Cicero seems to have spoken in the courts in defense of Bestia, Sestius, Asicius, Caelius, Balbus, Bestia again, (possibly) Cispius, as well as (possibly) Milo at a *iudicium populi*.[42] This energetic activity would have involved him in a variety of theatrical pleas conveying a range of emotions (cf. *totiens omni motu animi concitari* above). Moreover, as we saw in chapter four, Laterensis in 54 BCE spent considerable time mocking Cicero's use of tearful appeals in his defense of Cispius. Other onlookers (we may suppose) made similarly caustic observations.[43] Indeed, as we saw in chapter three, Cicero himself remarked sardonically on the oratorical theatrics of Cn. Oppius Cornicinus (with regards to his trick in the senate of casting off his toga and throwing himself at the feet of his son-in-law).[44] It would be no surprise, then, if Cicero felt rather defensive about his ability to cry on so many different occasions, on behalf of so many defendants (note the emphatic repetition of *totiens . . . totiens . . . totiens* at *De or.* 2.191 quoted above).[45]

Cicero responds by presenting in *De Oratore* a public façade of emotional integrity. He makes Antonius claim that his impassioned appeals in court have all been founded upon genuine feeling; there was thus no need for *simulatio* or *fallacia*. Given Cicero's ongoing activities as a practising advocate, this assertion of authenticity is understandable. Any admission to the contrary would have been gleefully exploited at future trials by shrewd opponents such as Laterensis.[46] It is in Cicero's interests, then, to draw a veil over the manipulative elements of his techique. It

42. See Marinone (2004) 117–20. Cf. Crawford (1984) 138–49; Alexander (1990) 129–37. As we saw in chapter four, the date of *Pro Cispio* is not certain. As for Cicero's judicial speeches in 55 BCE, Marinone (2004) 127 lists *Pro Caninio Gallo* (and possibly *Pro Ampio Balbo*, p. 275). For the effort these required, see *Fam.* 7.1.4. Cf. David (1992) 237.

43. Some commentators have discerned a similarly critical intent behind Catullus's description of Cicero as *optimus omnium patronus* at Catull. 49.7; Cicero (Catullus implies) will defend *anyone* in court. See, e.g., Schmidt (1914) 273–74; Quinn (1973) 235. Other scholars, however, have forcefully challenged the existence of this double entendre (which relies on an ambiguity in how we construe *omnium*); see, e.g., Laughton (1970) 3; Tatum (1988) 180. For useful bibliography, see Fredericksmeyer (1973); Svavarsson (1999).

44. Indeed, on occasion Cicero can even be glib (in private) about his own rhetorical deceptions. See Quint. *Inst.* 2.17.21 on Cicero's notorious claim that he had shrouded the minds of the jurors in darkness (*se tenebras offudisse iudicibus*) in his defense of Cluentius. Cf. Plut. *Cic.* 25; also Humbert (1938); Powell and Paterson (2004) 19–29.

45. On the hostility that could be provoked among the public by an advocate thought to have gained the acquittal of a guilty defendant, see the remarks of M. Caelius Rufus at *Fam.* 8.2.1 (on Hortensius).

46. Note that Cicero in *Pro Cluentio* shows an awareness of the problem caused by opponents quoting sections of his published orations against him, in an attempt to highlight his hypocrisies (*Clu.* 138): *recitavit ex oratione nescio qua Attius, quam meam esse dicebat cohortationem quandam iudicum* etc.

should be no surprise, however, if the argument that he deploys to support this strained claim creaks a little.

Its basic form is an argument *ex minore ad maiorem*, in which stage-acting constitutes the "lesser" element, and oratorical performance the "greater" one.[47] Often, Antonius claims, we have seen actors blazing with emotion when they play their roles (*De or.* 2.193: *saepe ipse vidi, ut ex persona mihi ardere oculi hominis histrionis viderentur*). And yet acting (and writing plays) are "lesser" activities than oratory because they involve fictional characters and imaginary emotions (*De or.* 2.193: *quid potest esse tam fictum quam versus, quam scaena, quam fabulae?*).[48] Therefore (the argument runs) how much more convincing and authentic must be the performance of an orator, since, when Antonius defended Aquillius, he was not addressing the misfortunes of mythical heroes (*De or.* 2.194: *heroum veteres casus*) or pretending to be a different person (*De or.* 2.194: *neque actor sum alienae personae, sed auctor meae*). His words and actions in the peroration were thus the product of a very profound distress that he felt for Aquillius (*De or.* 2.194: *nolite existimare me ipsum . . . sine magno dolore fecisse*). These theatrics did not derive from any contrived technique (*De or.* 2.195: *non arte de qua quid loquar nescio*) but from the genuine emotion that he felt for the man's predicament (*motu magno animi ac dolore*).

This, then, is the noble ideal that Cicero wants the readers of his treatise to believe. And, as we saw in chapter four, the advocate's close emotional bond with the defendant was something that he stressed in his appeals to jurors as well. He consistently portrays his tears as the dutiful tears of a friend. But Cicero's argument in *De Oratore* fails on at least two grounds. First, it is not really proved that actors do in fact feel genuine emotion. They just *seem* to be moved. Indeed, Cicero's repeated use of *videor* in this step of the argument (*ardere . . . viderentur; furere videretur; lugens dicere videbatur*) is required precisely because the actor's emotional state can only be inferred from his outer appearance.[49] If orators, then, are superior to actors, it may simply be that they are better at faking

---

47. On this form of argument, see Quint. *Inst.* 5.10.87–88; Lausberg (1998) sections 395–96. For discussion of Cicero's comparison here, see Petrone (2004) 36–40; Dugan (2005) 143–45.

48. Cicero also claims that poets likewise must be similarly moved when they write their plays (*De or.* 2.194). See also the similar argument at Quint. *Inst.* 6.2.35.

49. Cicero implicitly acknowledges the contrived nature of the actor's emotions by pointing to the daily repetition of his performances (*De or.* 2.193: *quae si ille histrio, cotidie cum ageret*). But Cicero's own repeated appearances in the courts remain open to the same line of criticism; he too, in a sense, is performing to a schedule. See also Sen. *De Ira* 2.17.1, where it is asserted that orators, like actors, only feign displays of anger.

emotions. Second, the greater "reality" of the orator's situation—the fact that he deals with actual court cases, not mythological fables—in no way guarantees the genuine nature of his emotions. Although Cicero and the other participants in a trial actually exist, this fact does not mean that anything that they say is true. There is a rhetorical sleight of hand in the implied correlation between the two.[50]

Cicero's depiction of the orator's art thus contains an element of guile. These assertions of emotional authenticity serve to disguise the calculating nature of his judicial theatrics. For a more candid assessment of the advocate's practical showmanship, we need to turn instead to Quintilian.

## QUINTILIAN AND JUDICIAL THEATER

As the studies of Crook and Bablitz have shown, the law courts in the time of Quintilian were busy, bustling places.[51] Nevertheless, the experiences of the young advocate during this period differed in various respects from those in Cicero's day. Several different venues were now used for legal business, with lawsuits being conducted not just in the Forum Romanum, but in the fora of Julius Caesar and Augustus as well.[52] On occasions, too, enclosed venues, such as the Basilica Iulia, were used.[53] Moreover, prosecutions of prominent figures were now either conducted before the emperor alone or before the senate.[54] As a speaker in Tacitus's *Dialogus De Oratoribus* points out, grand trials in the forum involving the massed supporters of prestigious aristocrats were a thing of the

---

50. Cicero asserts this distinction between orators and actors again in the third book of the treatise (*De or.* 3.214): *oratores, qui sunt veritatis ipsius actores . . . imitatores autem veritatis histriones.*

51. See Crook (1995) 135–46; Bablitz (2007) 13–50. Bablitz (2007) 52–55 refers to many of the incidents discussed in this chapter but treats them primarily as a source of information regarding the physical arrangement of the courts. For good introductions to the life and writings of Quintilian, see Kennedy (1969); Fernández López (2007). On his discussion of emotional appeals, see Katula (2003).

52. See Mart. *Ep.* 3.38.3–4; Sen. *De Ira* 2.9.4; Bablitz (2007) 44.

53. Plin. *Ep.* 2.14.1; Lintott (2004) 64; Bablitz (2007) 62. Tacitus (*Dial.* 39.1) also refers disparagingly to *auditoria et tabularia* as venues for oratorical activity. Cf. Frier (2010) 71–74. Quintilian even mentions pleading before an arbitrator (*apud disceptatorem*) while sitting down (*Inst.* 11.1.44).

54. On the former, see Plin. *Ep.* 6.22; Sherwin-White (1966) 382; Crook (1955) 106–14 and (1995) 124; 135; Bablitz (2007) 35. On the latter, Jones (1972) 91–118; Talbert (1984) 460–87; Clarke (1996) 101; Rutledge (2001) 16–18.

past.[55] Likewise, orators rarely experienced the rowdy public assemblies (*contiones*) that were typical of Late Republican politics.[56]

Despite these changes, however, the imperial courts still offered considerable scope for judicial theatrics (as we shall see).[57] Various Roman writers may bewail the supposed "decline of oratory" during this period, but this *topos* served primarily as an intellectual construct from which to expatiate on broader themes associated with morality, education, and politics.[58] The fact is that orators still engaged in lively and creative performances.

Quintilian is our first extant writer on rhetoric to discuss directly the role that props and theatrics can play in the persuasive process (*Inst.* 6.1.30): *non solum autem dicendo, sed etiam faciendo quaedam lacrimas movemus.* ("But we stir up tears not just through our words but also through certain actions.") This observation appears in his discussion in Book 6 of the role played by the emotions in oratory, although in Book 11 he acknowledges that the topic could have been included no less appropriately in his analysis of oratorical delivery (*Inst.* 11.3.174). His decision to analyze theatrics in connection with the emotions confirms the topic's close connection in his mind with the peroration (as too does the phrase *lacrimas movemus* above). Quintilian does not, however, analyze each device in detail or attempt to construct a taxonomy of techniques. His focus is pedagogical rather than theoretical. He is writing not for fellow rhetoricians but as a teacher passing on a collection of insights derived primarily from personal experience.[59]

---

55. See Tac. *Dial.* 37; also 39.4: *cum tot pariter ac tam nobiles forum coartarent, cum clientelae quoque ac tribus et municipiorum etiam legationes ac pars Italiae periclitantibus adsisteret.*

56. See Tac. *Dial.* 40, with reference to *contiones adsiduae et datum ius potentissimum quemque vexandi atque ipsa inimicitiarum gloria.* Cf. section 34.

57. See Crook (1995) 27; 138; 184–86; Bablitz (2007) 148. The claim is made at Tac. *Dial.* 38 that Pompey's judicial law of 52 BCE significantly curtailed the pleader's style (*haec . . . adstrinxit imposuitque veluti frenos eloquentiae*) But, as noted above, there were in fact tears aplenty at Milo's trial, and emotive elements too at the trial of Ligarius. The assertion in Tacitus (*Dial.* 39) that the judges of the day often (*saepe*) interjected in the course of an advocate's speech may reflect a significant development; but, as we shall see, there was still plenty of opportunity for innovative theatrics. See discussion in Frier (2010), especially 77: "At any rate, if we may judge from Quintilian, the ideal of the passive judge continued to resonate strongly in the courts of the late first century CE." Indeed Quintilian acknowledges that his own reputation as a pleader was largely founded upon powerfully emotive performances (*Inst.* 6.2.36).

58. See, e.g., Mayer (2001) 12–16; also Kennedy (1972) 446–64; Clarke (1996) 100–108.

59. For Quintilian's work as a practical guide for the orator-in-training, as well as a treatise for professional rhetoricians, see Fantham (1982) 244: "When [Quintilian] opens Book 11 he is still aiming for the double readership, not only of professionals, but of those still learning the trade."

Quintilian begins by listing some of the theatrical devices that may prove useful in court (*Inst.* 6.1.30):

> *unde et producere ipsos qui periclitentur squalidos atque deformes et liberos eorum ac parentis institutum, et ab accusatoribus cruentum gladium ostendi et lecta e vulneribus ossa et vestes sanguine perfusas videmus, et vulnera resolvi, verberata corpora nudari.*

[Hence the established practice of bringing forward defendants themselves in a dirty and unkempt state, and their children and parents as well. We also see prosecutors displaying a bloody sword, bones extracted from wounds, and blood-drenched clothes. We see too wounds being unbandaged and beaten bodies stripped bare.]

These remarks suggest a strong continuity with Republican practice: *sordes* and appeals from family members evidently still played a significant part in judicial pleading.[60] Several of the inanimate props that he mentions here likewise have precedents from Cicero's time. The unwrapping of wounds (*vulnera resolvi*) finds a parallel in the actions of Erucius in his prosecution of Varenus; the display of bruises on a body (*verberata corpora*) reminds us both of the revelation of M'. Aquillius's scars and Fulvia's performance over the body of Clodius; and the bloodstained garments (*vestes sanguine perfusas*) recall the robes at Caesar's funeral (an example that Quintilian himself goes on to adduce at *Inst.* 6.1.31).

Less familiar is the presentation in court of a bloodstained sword (*cruentum gladium*). Nevertheless, although no close parallel from the Late Republic exists, such exploitation of props was presumably not beyond the inventiveness of Cicero and his contemporaries. M. Caelius Rufus, for example, speaking in his own defense in 56 BCE, showed a certain creativity in this regard when he brought into court a small box (*pyxis*) to use as a prop in some obscene byplay at Clodia's expense.[61] Other such props, then, are likely to have found their way into the courts, even though documented instances are difficult to find.[62]

It is rather less certain how we should interpret in this passage Quintilian's phrase *lecta e vulneribus ossa* ("bones extracted from wounds"). The most straightforward view is that it refers to splinters of bone being

---

60. Quintilian reiterates the importance of these elements later in his discussion. See *Inst.* 6.1.33, with reference to *sordes, squalor, propinqui, preces, liberi, coniux, parentes.*
61. See Quint. *Inst.* 6.3.25: *ut in illa pyxide Caeliana, quod neque oratori neque ulli viro gravi conveniat.* For discussion, see Wiseman (1974); Skinner (1982); Moretti (2006) 139–46.
62. On orators and props in general, see Aldrete (1999) 27–28.

brought before the court and presented as evidence of some wound having been inflicted. Modern editors of Quintilian's text, however, seem to have found the detail unbelievable. Burman in 1720 CE proposed emending *vulneribus* to *funeribus*, to give a sense of "bones collected from funeral pyres."[63] More recently, Winterbottom has declared himself dissatisfied with both textual options ("*neutrum placet*").[64] Yet the whole point of this kind of stunt was its luridness. Moreover, Quintilian refers elsewhere to a famous speaker (*clarum actorem*) bringing into court pieces of bone from a head-wound (*lecta in capite cuiusdam ossa*).[65] This event, he notes, took place when he was himself a young man (*iuvenis*); perhaps then this kind of device had become more frequent in recent years, as young advocates followed the lead of the star pleader. (Or perhaps Quintilian in Book 6 is simply generalizing from a single event.)

Another innovation seems to have been the use of paintings as props to enhance the impact of the orator's words (*Inst.* 6.1.32: *depictam in tabula sipariove imaginem rei cuius atrocitate iudex erat commovendus*). Evidently these illustrations sometimes presented a crude visual narrative of the alleged events. Quintilian refers to one example that depicted the accused languishing naked in jail in one scene and being rescued from his gambling debts in another.[66] Certain precedents for this kind of prop can be found in contional oratory of the Late Republic. In 63 BCE, for example, the enemies of C. Rabirius paraded a bust of Saturninus in the forum in an attempt to stir up opprobrium against him prior to his appearance at a *iudicium populi*.[67] And a few years earlier, Aulus Gabinius as tribune of the people had displayed a painting of L. Lucullus's grand villa in order to provoke the mob's indignation at his opulence and extravagance.[68]

This second example brings us close to the practice that Quintilian

---

63. See Winterbottom (1970) 324; on Burman's edition, see Winterbottom (1970) xvi.

64. Winterbottom (1970) 324. Russell (2001) 32 prints *vulneribus*.

65. According to Quintilian, the orator then went on to make a bad pun on the phrase *ossa legere* (usually applied to collecting bones from a funeral pyre) (*Inst.* 8.5.21): "*infelicissima femina, nondum extulisti filium et iam ossa legisti.*" Cf. Russell (2001) 418, n. 35.

66. Quint. *Inst.* 6.3.72: *nam cum eius accusator in sipario omnibus locis aut nudum eum in nervo aut ab amicis redemptum ex alea pinxisset, "ergo ego" inquit "numquam vici?"* Cf. Bablitz (2007) 82; 193.

67. See *Rab. Perd.* 25: *itaque mihi mirum videtur, unde hanc tu, Labiene, imaginem quam habes inveneris;* and *numquam profecto istam imaginem . . . in rostra atque in contionem attulisses.* Cf. Caesar's exploitation of images of Marius in 69 BCE (Plut. *Caes.* 5.1).

68. See *Sest.* 93: *illa villa, quam ipse tribunus plebis pictam olim in contionibus explicabat, quo fortissimum ac summum civem in invidiam . . . vocaret.* Cf. Pina Polo (1996) 53; Aldrete (1999) 27; Kaster (2006) 313. It is possible that Sex. Cloelius as tribune exploited a *librarium* as an oratorical prop, as he tried to push through a suite of controversial laws. See *Mil.* 33; cf. Tatum (1999) 237.

describes: Gabinius's painting, like those of the imperial advocates, was presumably commissioned specifically for that particular oratorical event (unlike, for instance, the bust of Saturninus in the first example). Nevertheless, we have no decisive proof that such techniques were introduced into *judicial* proceedings in Cicero's time, and Quintilian's disdain for their use amongst his own contemporaries may suggest that they were a relatively recent innovation. Indeed, he claims that the well trained orator has no need for such artificial visual aids; he should be able to create the same effect through words alone (*Inst.* 6.1.32).

With advocates striving to contrive elaborate props, much of Quintilian's advice focuses on avoiding the catastrophes that can arise from their use. Generally, these stunts seem to have been deployed toward the conclusion of a speech; hence Quintilian's reference at *Inst.* 6.1.41 to what he calls the "perils of perorations" (*pericula epilogorum*). At one trial (he reports) there were plans to display an image of the accused woman's husband at the very end of the speech (*Inst.* 6.1.40). Things went badly wrong, however, because the advocate's assistants—who were unfamiliar with the term "peroration" (*epilogus*)—held out the image every time he looked at them. This farce was compounded by the fact that the image itself was a disturbing one—a creepy death mask of the deceased.[69]

This kind of disaster reminds us of Caepasius's blundering at the trial of Fabricius, an example that Quintilian himself mentions (*Inst.* 6.1.41). Indeed, he stresses the general point that any defendant who is incorporated into such theatrics needs to be able to play their role competently (*Inst.* 6.1.37): *ingens in epilogis meo iudicio verti discrimen quo modo se dicenti qui excitatur accommodet.* ("In my view in perorations it makes a crucial difference how the defendant who is brought forward adapts himself to the advocate.") The orator's intended effect can be scuppered by a defendant who does not look appropriately sorrowful (*nihil vultu commotos*) or who grins at the wrong moment (*Inst.* 6.1.38: *intempestive renidentis*).[70] We might expect here perhaps a recommendation that the advocate should rehearse these theatrics beforehand with the defendant

---

69. See *Inst.* 6.1.40: *nam senis cadaveri <cera erat> infusa.* The text of Russell (2001) 36 includes an emendation by Halm.

70. Winterbottom (1970) 326 prints the manuscript reading *residentis* ("sitting down"). Russell (2001) 36 adopts the emendation of Spalding (*renidentis*), which matches more closely the surrounding references to the defendant's facial expression (note the repetition of *vultus*). Either action (grinning or sitting down inappropriately) would of course ruin the orator's intended effect. On Spalding as editor, see Winterbottom (1970) xvi.

(together with anyone else who might be involved); but Quintilian does not go this far. He restricts his advice to what is required at the moment of performance.

Quintilian also refers to gaffes in delivery that are, in his view, directly attributable to the influence of the schools of declamation that had grown in popularity during the decades after Cicero's death (*Inst.* 6.1.43: *ex scholis haec vitia*). Students' intensive training in declamation (he claims) often leads them to become detached from the practical realities of pleading in court. Since they have little experience in departing from their planned text, they can end up describing theatrics that are not actually taking place (*Inst.* 6.1.42):

> *at qui a stilo non recedunt aut conticescunt ad hos casus aut frequentissime falsa dicunt. inde est enim "tendit ad genua vestra supplices manus" et "haeret in complexu liberorum miser" et "revocat ecce me" etiam si nihil horum is de quo dicitur faciat.*

> [But those who cannot depart from their written text either fall dumb when confronted with these mishaps, or very often say what is not the case. It is from this kind of situation that we get, "He stretches out his hands to your knees in supplication" and "The poor wretch clings to the embrace of his children" and "Look, he is calling me back"—even if the person he is talking about is doing none of these things.]

These remarks confirm that Cicero's theatrical tropes continued to flourish. The first device (*tendit . . . manus*) finds a close parallel in *Pro Fonteio*, where we saw Fonteia stretching out her arms in supplication to the jurors (see chapter three). The second (*haeret . . . miser*) likewise has a parallel in *Pro Fonteio* with its family tableau and embrace. The third, however, is less familiar. Presumably the phrase *revocat ecce me* required the defendant, at the apparent conclusion of his advocate's speech, to call the man back to continue his pleading. By doing so, the defendant implied that he was in such danger that he required more than the usual emotional appeal. But such an attempt at heightened pathos required precise timing. The orator had to feign surprise (note the interjection *ecce*), and this reaction in turn had to be closely coordinated with a remark or gesture by the defendant.[71] An experienced advocate could negotiate his way through any unexpected departure from this sequence;

---

71. The closest parallel from Cicero's speeches perhaps is the claim that the defendant (or the defendant's relative) is looking at him imploringly (see chapter three).

but the cosseted declaimer tended to push on regardless—with disastrous results.

Appeals, supplication, and tears also seem to have continued to be a part of the imperial advocate's arsenal (*Inst.* 6.1.34):

> *et deorum etiam invocatio velut ex bona conscientia profecta videri solet, stratum denique iacere et genua complecti, nisi si tamen persona nos et anteacta vita et rei condicio prohibebit.*

> [An invocation of the gods too is usually believed to derive from a good conscience, likewise prostration on the ground and embracing the jurors' knees, unless the accused's character, past life and status makes such actions difficult for us.]

The phrases *stratum iacere* and *genua complecti* suggest literal rather than figurative supplication.[72] It is possible, then, that the courtroom dynamics had changed somewhat in the intervening century or so. As we saw in chapter three, many of Cicero's grand defendants appear to have eschewed throwing themselves at the jurors' feet. Perhaps the more compact physical layout in some of these imperial trials made literal supplication easier; or perhaps such prostration was for some reason more palatable (especially among those lacking aristocratic arrogance).[73] It is in this respect that our lack of extant speeches from the imperial period is especially frustrating. Without texts like those that we possess from the Republic, it is difficult to reconstruct how advocates set up their appeals and integrated any elements of supplication into them.

Child props—a staple of oratorical theatrics since the time of Sulpicius Galba—continued to be deployed in Quintilian's courts as well. Again there are signs of creative attempts to enliven the tradition. Quintilian describes one trial in which the relationship between a supposed brother and sister was in dispute (he himself was speaking for the defense).[74] In a bold attempt at emotional theatrics, the opposing advocate led the young girl across the court with the intention of placing her in the lap of her alleged brother. The aim was shrewd enough: by placing the boy and girl next to each other, the advocate could represent in

---

72. See also Sen. *Controv.* 9.6.12 where a declaimer assumes that a defendant is in a position to stretch out hands in supplication to the jurors (*manus ad genua dimitte*), although full prostration is not necessarily implied here.

73. Cf. Bablitz (2007) 53 and 87 on supplication in imperial courts.

74. See Quint. *Inst.* 6.1.39: *puellam, quae soror esse adversarii dicebatur. nam de hoc lis erat.*

visual terms the intimate relationship between them that his argument was trying to prove. Quintilian, however, somehow heard about the trick in advance and arranged for the boy to slip away from his seat. The opposing advocate thus found himself among the defense benches unable to complete his ploy as planned. The awkward walk back to his own side of the court drained the moment of all pathos (*infantem suam frigidissime reportavit*).

Such anecdotes vividly convey the sharp contests of wit that these trials often involved. The astute advocate tried his best to anticipate and foil the theatrics of his opponent, deploying whatever tricks he could. Quintilian tells of one leading speaker using knucklebones (items typically used in children's games) to distract the children his opponent was preparing to exploit as props (*Inst.* 6.1.47). (He threw the knucklebones on the ground, thus causing the children to gather them up excitedly.) This trick (Quintilian observes) certainly succeeded in ruining the mood of the peroration; but it could easily have backfired. The sight (he suggests) of children scrambling around with wide-eyed eagerness at a time of danger to their family could have produced its own form of pathos that would have worked to the opponent's advantage (6.1.47: *haec ipsa discriminis sui ignorantia potuit esse miserabilis*). Moreover, its methods were not especially dignified. The sensible orator should steer clear of anything farcical (*non debent esse mimicra*, 6.1.47).[75] For Quintilian, verbal repartee was a better way of puncturing an opponent's theatrical attempts to generate pity and sympathy (see, e.g., *Inst.* 6.1.46 and 47).

But what about judicial tears? Quintilian in fact postpones his detailed discussion of such appeals until the later sections on ethos and pathos (see *Inst.* 6.2). Here it is refreshing to find that, unlike Cicero, he is not especially interested in trying to convince the reader of his emotional authenticity; instead, he offers practical advice on how best to generate tears when performing. The ingredient necessary for success (he suggests) is a lively and sensitive imagination. If the young orator can form vivid images in his mind of the situation he is speaking about, he will then be able to evoke in himself feelings appropriate to the subject. From these will arise in turn the vocal tones and gestures suited to such emotions.[76] If the orator can then convey these images effectively

---

75. In another case, an advocate undermined his opponent's presentation of a sword during a trial by pretending to take fright and run away (*Inst.* 6.1.48). Quintilian again has reservations about this approach. Although it was effective in practical terms, it risked compromising the advocate's dignity.

76. See Quint. *Inst.* 6.2.29–32; 11.3.61–63.

to the audience, he will succeed in rousing the same powerful emotions in them too.[77]

These precepts derive in part from *De Oratore*, where Cicero asserts that the orator himself must feel emotion if he wants to make the audience feel emotion as well (*De or.* 2.195: *non prius sum conatus misericordiam aliis commovere quam misericordia sum ipse captus*).[78] And yet, as we have seen, there is a self-serving element to Cicero's claims. Quintilian, in contrast, is happy enough to acknowledge that an element of technique may lie behind the advocate's tears.

## CONCLUSIONS

In the course of this survey, we have seen judicial theatrics being used by several of Cicero's fellow advocates, including Erucius, Hortensius, and Caepasius, as well as by witnesses and defendants such as Scaurus, Caelius, Faustus Sulla, and Fonteius. And even if Mark Antony did not arrange for a crane and effigy to be deployed at Caesar's funeral, his exploitation of the dictator's robes demonstrates his shrewd understanding of how to manipulate a crowd with oratorical props. At first glance, this accumulation of examples may seem decisive proof that such showmanship was a regular feature in the courts. And yet, from a methodological perspective, we lack a background sample of significant size against which we can accurately gauge the typicality of these incidents. If, as seems likely, at least ninety per cent of the speeches delivered in the courts during the Late Republic are now lost to us, we have no measuring stick against which to judge whether any particular device was the exception or the norm.[79] Indeed, we know that *some* advocates deliberately eschewed an emotional style of delivery. Best known amongst Cicero's contemporaries perhaps is M. Calidius.[80] But judging the typicality of

---

77. On this topic, see Schryvers (1982); Webb (1997).

78. See also *De or.* 2.189: *non mehercule umquam apud iudices, aut dolorem aut misericordiam aut invidiam aut odium dicendo excitare volui, quin ipse in commovendis iudicibus his ipsis sensibus, ad quos illos adducere vellem, permoverer.*

79. The statistical analysis by Alexander (1993) illustrates some of the methodological problems posed by the nature of our extant evidence. Despite the diligent compendia of modern scholars, the speeches that have been preserved must represent only a tiny fraction of the entire oratorical activity in the courts of Cicero's time. For surveys of the extant fragments, see Malcovati (1976) and David (1992). Useful material also in Crawford (1984), Alexander (1990) and Crawford (1994).

80. See *Brut.* 277 on Calidius's prosecution of Q. Gallius. Cf. Alexander (1990) 107 (no. 214), who suggests a date of 64 BCE, followed by Marinone (2004) 81; Malcovati

this contrasting approach to performance is likewise hampered by our minute sample size.

Nevertheless, Quintilian's typically sensible advice helps us to set the use of judicial theatrics within a general context (*Inst.* 6.1.44):

> *illud praecipue monendum, ne qui nisi summis ingenii viribus ad movendas lacrimas adgredi audeat; nam ut est longe vehementissimus hic cum invaluit adfectus, ita si nil efficit tepet; quem melius infirmus actor tacitis iudicum cogitationibus reliquisset.*

[In particular, I must warn against a speaker boldly trying to stir up tears if he does not possess a really strong natural talent. For just as this emotional mood is far and away the most powerful when it is successfully aroused, so it creates a correspondingly lukewarm response when it fails. The weak performer is better off leaving the matter to the silent reflections of the jurors.]

In other words, these were high-risk, high-reward strategies that did not suit every orator.[81] In this respect, our reliance on the Ciceronian evidence may distort our overall impression. Since generating high emotion was his particular forte, there is a self-serving design behind presenting the charismatic, elegantly theatrical performer as the oratorical ideal. Many contemporaries probably did not subscribe to this model. They were realistic enough to recognize that their talents did not equip them for such ambitious efforts.

At the same time, we have seen that there was consistent exploitation of theatrics across several centuries of judicial activity in Rome. We find elements of showmanship in the trials that took place during Cicero's youth; in those in which he himself participated as advocate; and in those observed by Quintilian. This simple fact points to the existence of a deeply rooted cultural tradition whose existence did not rely on the special talents of just one or two outstanding speakers. As the previous chapters have demonstrated, Roman grandees inhabited a world in which energetic showmanship and public posturing formed a crucial

---

(1976) 435 gives a date of 66. For scholarship on the issue, see Alexander (1990) 107 (no. 214), n. 1. The main charge was related to electoral bribery, but Calidius evidently also claimed that Gallius had tried to poison him (*Brut.* 277: *dedisset sibi eum venenum paravisse*).

81. Cf. Quint. *Inst.* 6.1.45: *quare metiatur ac diligenter aestimet vires suas actor, et quantum onus subiturus sit intellegat; nihil habet ista res medium, sed aut lacrimas meretur aut risum.* See also Antonius's remarks at *De or.* 2.205: *ne aut inrisione aut odio digni putemur, si aut tragoedias agamus in nugis aut convellere adoriamur ea, quae non possint commoveri.*

part of political life. In many regards, the courts represented an extension of this familiar aristocratic milieu.

The anecdotes in Quintilian's discussion, however, also remind us that such theatrics could go badly wrong. It is significant, then, that we hear of no comparable disasters in any of Cicero's perorations. Our sources record a couple of incidents where his delivery was supposedly not as accomplished as usual;[82] yet we hear of no disasters during the grand appeals of his perorations. This professionalism in execution presumably derived from careful preparation and rehearsal—although, for the most part, this feature of the orator's craft has disappeared from view. We know that Cicero held private interviews with his clients when first planning a defense, with the aim of ascertaining the general strengths and weaknesses of the case.[83] Presumably these would also have been good occasions on which to clarify which friends and relatives were available for use in his concluding appeals and to determine the extent to which the defendant himself was willing to engage in a submissive pose. But other meetings would still have been necessary to ensure that everyone understood what was required of them. The family tableaux and child props that Cicero employed could not be left to chance. (As we have seen, Caepasius managed to botch a relatively simple form of appeal.) And yet of these practical tasks there is not a word in his treatises. These too were matters that lay beyond rhetoric.

---

82. Plutarch (*Cic.* 35.4–5) states that Cicero's performances were substandard at the trials of Murena in 63 BCE and of Milo in 52 BCE; but his assertions are questionable. On the possible distortion in his account of the delivery of *Pro Murena*, see Moles (1988) 183: "elsewhere unattested and irreconcilable. . . . Presumably P. has adjusted the facts to suit his thesis." Cf. Settle (1962) 250–51. Asconius (*Mil.* 41C) confirms that Cicero encountered difficulties in the delivery of his speech on behalf of Milo; but, as modern scholars have noted, the later accounts of Plutarch and Dio Cassius (40.54.2) are exaggerated and inaccurate. See Lintott (1974) 74; Berry (2000) 167; Lewis (2006) 247. Moles (1988) 183–84, however, stresses Plutarch's accuracy rather than his distortions.

83. See *De or.* 2.102. Cf. Quint. *Inst.* 12.8.1–15, with the good comments of Austin (1948) xii–xiii; also Tac. *Dial.* 14.1.

# CONCLUSION

This survey of Cicero's judicial theater has placed us in an unfamiliar world—one where millionaires on occasion dressed in dirtied clothes, engaged in submissive supplication, and wept profusely in public. And yet, as startling as such practices may appear, we have seen that they were underpinned by a certain social logic. The Roman system of patronage, for example, encouraged individuals to display their private grievances to those around them. Various mechanisms thus arose that helped to broadcast distress to the wider community and to express social solidarity with those in difficulty. And given the close connection in Rome between patronage and politics, such devices readily found their way into the political wrangles of the forum as well. Ambitious grandees quickly learned to strike poses calculated to elicit sympathy and indignation from onlookers. It was from this world—and not the intellectualizing principles of the rhetorical handbooks—that Roman orators drew as they planned their performances in the courts.

Nevertheless, despite this Roman cultural affinity for showmanship, we have seen too that many advocates did not exploit such theatrics to the same extent as Cicero. In some cases, the decision not to do so presumably derived from a realistic appraisal of their talents. Not everyone was as well equipped as Cicero to engage in these high-risk strategies. Yet there may have been other reasons too. It is possible that other advocates did not in fact consider such techniques particularly effective. There were other ways, after all, of prevailing in a trial. To what extent, then, does the narrow focus of our study risk distorting the overall importance of these devices?

Certainly, if we judge matters solely in quantitative terms, the part played by judicial theater in most trials was unquestionably rather small. Cicero's orations contain many, many pages of exposition and argument whose impact depended scarcely at all on stage action. From this perspective, a brief embrace (for example) between the advocate and defendant seems a relatively trivial adornment. Indeed, as we saw in chapter three, Cicero recognized that jurors expected a defense to be based primarily on a denial of the accusations at hand and to be supported by reasoned argument. It is clear that he took these aspects of pleading very seriously. Judged on this criterion, then, judicial theater constituted only a minor mode of persuasion, one that was supplementary to Cicero's verbal argument.

Yet we have also seen that Cicero sometimes went to considerable lengths to incorporate emotional theatrics into his speeches, even when he faced significant obstacles in deploying them. In *Pro Caelio* and *Pro Milone*, for example, he managed to integrate tears into his arguments despite the defendants' unwillingness to participate in any pleas for sympathy. He also wept when defending Cispius and Rabirius Postumus, even though (we may suspect) he was not especially intimate with them. Such examples attest to the importance that he attached to this aspect of his craft. Indeed, this use of judicial theater is closely linked to Cicero's belief in the effectiveness of emotional oratory more generally (an aspect of his pleading that he attempts to justify in *Brutus* and *Orator.*)

Moreover, the impact of judicial theatrics cannot be assessed solely in quantitative terms. Both Cicero and Quintilian assign an especially strong persuasive power to the peroration and the *miseratio* often included within it.[1] At first glance, we may wonder whether this view derived ultimately from the Greek tradition. In the Athenian courts, it seems that jurors did indeed cast their votes shortly after the final speech from the defense; in such a context, the proximity of an emotional appeal to the jurors' verdict might be crucial.[2] In many Roman trials, by contrast, Cicero's peroration would have been followed by hours of testimony from numerous witnesses. The persuasive dynamic was not the same.

And yet, it is clear that Cicero himself believed that the peroration could exert a significant and powerful effect on the jurors. In cases where the pleading duties were shared between several advocates, he himself was regularly assigned the role of speaking last, precisely because this part of the defense was perceived as being so important (see *Brut.* 190). Moreover, since the business of reaching a verdict is an inherently reductive process—one that involves sorting through a myriad of competing arguments and concerns in order to arrive (in most cases) at a binary yes or no conclusion—it is not impossible that Cicero's concluding theatrics did in fact prove to be the decisive factor for many jurors.

These elements of practical performance, then, could be important

---

1. See *Brut.* 190: *perorandi locum, ubi plurimum pollet oratio*; Quint. *Inst.* 6.1.23: *plurimum tamen valet miseratio.*

2. See Bonner (1927) 55; Boegehold et al. (1995) 27–28; Carey (1997) 13–17.

weapons in the orator's arsenal, and the foregoing chapters have tried to identify some of the ways in which Cicero exploited them. Nevertheless, the gap between text and performance remains difficult to bridge. Practical advocacy is inevitably a transitory, evanescent business, whose subtle dynamics are difficult to recapture once a speech has concluded. This difficulty has manifested itself most notably perhaps on the various occasions where we have encountered the fallacy of conventionalization. As we have seen, from a purely logical perspective, any advocate in Quintilian's time using young children as props should have been laughed out of court. As any educated Roman knew, this was a well-worn device that had been used in judicial pleadings for at least two hundred years since the time of Sulpicius Galba. Yet the practice continued.

The best solution to this conundrum is to suppose that the urgency and tension of an actual trial often diverted jurors away from a rigorously rational evaluation of the scene in front of them. The emotions of the moment, stirred up in part by the advocate and in part by the very real consequences that flowed from the jurors' verdict, helped to sweep away pedantic concerns with oratorical trope and technique. It was the unfortunate drama unfolding in front of their very eyes that compelled the audience's attention, and it was the emotion of this moment that the skilled orator's theatrics sought to augment. As we have seen, the surviving texts of Cicero's speeches allow us to appreciate how he set up and manipulated these scenes; but to understand their full impact during performance still requires from the modern reader a considerable effort of the historical imagination.

We have seen too that Cicero almost certainly excelled in the business of performance. This is an important point. Cicero's towering literary achievement has long been recognized: his published speeches demonstrate a remarkable mastery of language, and we can discern in his rhetorical and philosophical treatises a profound interest in theoretical constructs and intellectual systematization. Yet in the bear pit of the Roman courts, it was practical know-how that carried the day. The men he defended cared about acquittal not literary style. And for this they needed an advocate who would deliver the best possible performance on the day, in front of an audience that could be difficult and unpredictable. As our numerous examples have shown, this was a role that Cicero embarked upon with energy and imagination—and, in most instances, with great success. His reputation in this regard suffers only from the lack of contemporary accounts describing in detail how he achieved his various effects.

To conclude my discussion, I would like to consider two further examples of theatrics, one ancient, the other modern, both of which illustrate in interesting ways some of the themes examined in the foregoing chapters. The first comes from 43 BCE, in the days immediately following the deaths of the two consuls, Hirtius and Pansa, at Mutina. Cicero tells us that hostile rumors began to circulate in Rome alleging that he was about to seize political control of the city.[3] Such allegations of despotic ambition were standard fare in Roman political invective; and yet Cicero goes on to reveal that his enemies were planning to expose his supposed coup in a highly theatrical fashion: they were arranging to present the *fasces* to him at a public meeting, as if on his request, and then, upon his apparent acceptance of these symbols of authority, a hired gang would attack and kill him in outrage at this tyrannical bid for power.[4]

The plot seems an ambitious one, and we have no independent verification of its existence. Yet the notorious stunt in February 44 BCE, in which Antony publicly offered Caesar a crown at the Lupercalia, suggests that we should not discount Cicero's assertions too quickly.[5] As we have seen throughout our investigations, Roman politicians were sophisticated exponents of this kind of political theater. Indeed, in this case Cicero's opponents seem to have been well aware that it was not enough simply to assassinate him; they needed to manufacture an acceptable—and publicly verifiable—motive for his death that would help them win the ensuing war of words as well. In this environment of inventive political theatrics, it is no surprise to find Roman aristocrats carefully stage managing their appearances in the courts as well.

My second example comes from a setting two millennia and half a world away from the Roman forum: modern-day New Zealand. A report from the *Otago Daily Times*, dated February 23, 2008, describes the pretrial hearing of a fifty-year-old man from a suburb in Auckland charged with killing a fifteen-year-old youth, who had allegedly been defacing some property near his house. (The two individuals had become engaged in an altercation, which ended with the teenager dying after being stabbed with a knife.) The accompanying photo in the newspaper shows one of the dead boy's relatives attending court in a specially made t-shirt that featured on the front a photo of the young vandal as a smiling,

3. Reported at *Phil.* 14.15: *ad me concursum futurum civitatis putabant. quod ut cum invidia mea fieret et cum vitae etiam periculo, famam istam fascium dissipaverunt.*

4. See *Phil.* 14.15: *fasces ipsi ad me delaturi fuerunt. quod cum esset quasi mea voluntate factum, tum in me impetus conductorum hominum quasi in tyrannum parabatur.*

5. See *Phil.* 2.84–87; Suet. *Caes.* 79; Plut. *Caes.* 61; *Ant.* 12; Dio Cass. 44.11; App. *B Civ.* 2.109; Nic. Dam. 71–75. Cf. Weinstock (1971) 331–40; Pelling (1988) 144–45.

well-groomed lad—in other words, one that depicted him in a way as far removed as possible from the delinquent thug that the initial press reports had first suggested. The overall effect was thus carefully contrived. The presence of several family members in court wearing these shirts conveyed the impression of a decent boy located within a strong, caring social network. He was not (apparently) some neglected runaway roaming wild on the streets.

This example helps perhaps to make Roman practices appear a little less alien. Although Cicero's use of judicial theater derives in many respects from the idiosyncratic practices of ancient Rome, some of its elements can be found in other societies as well. In our New Zealand case, we see a family mobilizing its members (as in Rome) in a display of solidarity when one of the group encounters a perceived injustice. This family from Auckland also shows a degree of creativity in its attempts to broadcast this grievance to the wider community. Indeed, the printed t-shirt serves much the same function as *sordes* in ancient Rome. The grief and outrage of the moment produce a calculated and assertive form of protest.

Yet it is significant that the judge of the court took immediate and decisive action. He banned the wearing of these t-shirts at future hearings, commenting: "I would not like it to be thought that any messages that you wore in here . . . were seen as unduly influencing the judicial process. . . . You're perfectly welcome to be here, but I think you should dress appropriately." In doing so, he ensured that this kind of performance did not become a familiar convention in the courts of New Zealand. As we have seen, the Romans approached such matters very differently.

# Bibliography

Achard, G. 1981. *Pratique rhétorique et idéologie politique dans les discours "optimates"
de Cicéron.* Leiden.

Aldrete, G. S. 1999. *Gestures and Acclamations in Ancient Rome.* Baltimore and London.

Alexander, M. C. 1976. "Hortensius' Speech in Defense of Verres." *Phoenix* 30:46–53.

Alexander, M. C. 1990. *Trials in the Late Roman Republic, 149BC—50BC.* Toronto.

Alexander, M. C. 1993. "How Many Roman Senators Were Ever Prosecuted? The Evidence from the Late Republic." *Phoenix* 47:238–55.

Alexander, M. C. 2002. *The Case for the Prosecution in the Ciceronian Era.* Ann Arbor, MI.

Alston, R. 1998. "Arms and the Man: Soldiers, Masculinity and Power in Republican and Imperial Rome." In L. Foxhall and J. Salmon, eds., *When Men Were Men: Masculinity, Power and Identity in Classical Antiquity,* 205–23. London.

Arnould, D. 1990. *Le Rire et Les Larmes dans la Littérature Grecque d'Homère à Platon.* Paris.

Astin, A. E. 1967. *Scipio Aemilianus.* Oxford.

Astin, A. E. 1978. *Cato the Censor.* Oxford.

Atkinson, M. 2004. *Lend Me Your Ears: All You Need to Know about Making Speeches and Presentations.* London.

Austin, R. G. 1933. *M. Tulli Ciceronis Pro M. Caelio Oratio.* 1st ed. Oxford.

Austin, R. G. 1948. *Quintiliani Institutionis Oratoriae Liber XII.* Oxford.

Austin, R. G. 1952. *M. Tulli Ciceronis Pro M. Caelio Oratio.* 2nd ed. Oxford.

Austin, R. G. 1960. *M. Tulli Ciceronis Pro M. Caelio Oratio.* 3rd ed. Oxford.

Axer, J. 1989. "Tribunal-Stage-Arena: Modelling of the Communication Situation in M. Tullius Cicero's Judicial Speeches." *Rhetorica* 7:299–311.

Bablitz, L. 2007. *Actors and Audience in the Roman Courtroom.* London and New York.

Bablitz, L. 2008. "The Platform in Roman Art, 30 BC–AD 180: Forms and Functions." In C. Deroux, ed., *Studies in Latin Literature and Roman History: Volume 14,* 235–82. Brussels.

Badian, E. 1957. "Caepio and Norbanus: Notes on the Decade 100–90 B.C." *Historia* 6:318–46.

Badian, E. 1958a. "Appian and Asinius Pollio." *Classical Review* n.s. 8:159–62.

Badian, E. 1958b. *Foreign Clientelae (264–70 B.C.)*. Oxford.

Badian, E. 1964. *Studies in Greek and Roman History*. Oxford.

Balsdon, J. P. V. D. 1938. "The History of the Extortion Court at Rome, 123–70 B.C." *Papers of the British School at Rome* 14:98–114.

Barwick, K. 1964. *Flavii Sosipatri Charisii Artis Grammaticae Libri V*. Leipzig.

Bell, A. 2004. *Spectacular Power in the Greek and Roman City*. Oxford.

Beness, J. L., and Hillard, T. W. 2001. "The Theatricality of the Deaths of C. Gracchus and Friends." *Classical Quarterly* 51:135–40.

Bernstein, A. H. 1978. *Tiberius Sempronius Gracchus: Tradition and Apostasy*. Ithaca and London.

Berry, D. H. 1996. *Cicero: Pro P. Sulla Oratio, Edited with Introduction and Commentary*. Cambridge.

Berry, D. H. 2000. *Cicero: Defence Speeches*. Oxford.

Berry, D. H. 2003. "*Equester Ordo Tuus Est*: Did Cicero Win His Cases because of His Support for the *Equites*?" *Classical Quarterly* 53:222–34.

Bers, V. 1985. "Dikastic *Thorubos*." In P. Cartledge and F. Harvey, eds., *Crux: Essays in Greek History Presented to G. E. M. de Ste. Croix*, 1–15. London.

Bers, V. 2009. *Genos Dikanikon: Amateur and Professional Speech in the Courtrooms of Classical Athens*. Cambridge, MA.

Birkett, N. 1961. *Six Great Advocates*. Harmondsworth.

Blänsdorf, J. 2001. "Cicero auf dem Forum und im Senat: Zur Mündlichkeit der Reden Ciceros." In L. Benz, ed., *ScriptOralia Romana: Die römische Literatur zwischen Mündlichkeit und Schriftlichkeit*, 205–28. Tübingen.

Blanshard, A. 2004. "The Birth of the Law-Court: Putting Ancient and Modern Forensic Rhetoric in Its Place." In M. Edwards and C. Reid, eds., *Oratory in Action*, 11–32. Manchester and New York.

Blonski, M. 2008. "Les 'sordes' dans la vie politique romaine: la saleté comme tenue de travail?" *Métis* n.s. 6:41–56.

Bodel, J. 1999. "Death on Display: Looking at Roman Funerals." In B. Bergmann and C. Kondoleon, eds., *The Art of Ancient Spectacle*, 258–81. Washington, DC.

Boegehold, A. L. et al. 1995. *The Lawcourts at Athens: Sites, Buildings, Equipment, Procedure, and Testimonia. Athenian Agora Volume 28*. Princeton, NJ.

Boegehold, A. L. 1999. *When a Gesture Was Expected: A Selection of Examples from Archaic and Classical Greek Literature*. Princeton, NJ.

Bonner, R. J. 1927. *Lawyers and Litigants in Ancient Athens: The Genesis of the Legal Profession*. New York and London.

Boyancé, P. 1953. *Cicéron Discours. Volume 8: Pour Cluentius*. Paris.

Braund, D. 1998. "*Cohors*: The Governor and His Entourage in the Self-Image of the Roman Republic." In R. Laurence and J. Berry, eds., *Cultural Identity in the Roman Empire*, 10–24. London and New York.

Brennan, T. C. 2000a. *The Praetorship in the Roman Republic: Volume 1*. Oxford and New York.

Brennan, T. C. 2000b. *The Praetorship in the Roman Republic: Volume 2.* Oxford and New York.

Bringmann, K. 1986. "Der Diktator Caesar als Richter? Zu Ciceros Reden 'Pro Ligario' und 'Pro rege Deiotaro'." *Hermes* 114:72–88.

Briscoe, J. 2012. *A Commentary on Livy Books 41–45.* Oxford.

Broughton, T. R. S. 1951. *The Magistrates of the Roman Republic: Volume 1.* New York.

Broughton, T. R. S. 1952. *The Magistrates of the Roman Republic: Volume 2.* New York.

Brunt, P. A. 1980. "Patronage and Politics in the Verrines." *Chiron* 10:273–89.

Bucher, G. S. 2000. "The Origins, Program, and Composition of Appian's *Roman History*." *Transactions of the American Philological Association* 130:411–58.

Bucher, G. S. 2005. "Fictive Elements in Appian's Pharsalus Narrative." *Phoenix* 59:50–76.

Butler, H. E. 1921. *The Institutio Oratoria of Quintilian: Volume 2.* Cambridge, MA.

Butler, S. 2002. *The Hand of Cicero.* London and New York.

Calboli, G. 1983. "Oratore senza microfono." In C. Gastaldo, ed., *Ars Rhetorica antica e nuova*, 23–56. Genoa.

Calboli, G. 1997. "The Asiatic Style of Antony: Some Considerations." In B. Czapla, T. Lehmann, and S. Liell, eds., *Vir bonus dicendi peritus: Festschrift für A. Weische*, 13–26. Wiesbaden.

Campbell, S. G. 1926. *Livy Book XXVII.* Cambridge.

Carey, C. 1997. *Trials from Classical Athens.* London and New York.

Carey, C. 2007. *Lysiae Orationes Cum Fragmentis.* Oxford.

Carney, T. F. 1970. *A Biography of C. Marius.* Chicago.

Carotta, F., and Eickenberg, A. 2011. "*Liberalia Tu Accusas!* Restituting the Ancient Date of Caesar's *Funus*." *Revue des Études Anciennes* 113:447–67.

Carter, J. 1996. *Appian: The Civil Wars.* London.

Casamento, A. 2004. "'Parlare e lagrimar vedrai insieme.' Le lacrime dell'oratore." In G. Petrone, ed., *Le Passioni della Retorica*, 41–62. Palermo.

Casamento, A. 2006. "Spettacolo della giustizia, spettacolo della parola: il caso della *Pro Milone*." In G. Petrone and A. Casamento, eds., *Lo Spettacolo della Giustizia: Le Orazioni di Cicerone*, 181–98. Palermo.

Cavarzere, A. 2004. "La voce delle emozioni. 'Sincerità' e 'simulazione' nella teoria retorica dei Romani." In G. Petrone, ed., *Le Passioni della Retorica*, 11–28. Palermo.

Cavarzere, A. 2011. *Gli Arcani dell'oratore: alcuni appunti sull'actio dei Romani.* Rome and Padua.

Cichorius, C. 1908. *Untersuchungen zu Lucilius.* Berlin. (1964 reprint used.)

Claassen, J.-M. 1996. "Dio's Cicero and the Consolatory Tradition." *Papers of the Leeds International Latin Seminar* 9:29–45.

Clark, A. C. 1907. *Q. Asconii Pediani orationum Ciceronis quinque enarratio.* Oxford.

Clark, A. C. 1909. *M. Tulli Ciceronis Orationes. Volume IV.* Oxford.

Clark, A. C. 1911. *M. Tulli Ciceronis Orationes. Volume VI.* Oxford.

Clark, A. C. 1918. *M. Tulli Ciceronis Orationes. Volume II.* 2nd ed. *Oxford.*

Clark, M. E., and Ruebel, J. S. 1985. "Philosophy and Rhetoric in Cicero's *Pro Milone.*" *Rheinisches Museum für Philologie* 128:57–72.

Clarke, M. L. 1996. *Rhetoric at Rome: A Historical Survey.* 3rd ed. Revised by D. H. Berry. London and New York.

Classen, C. J. 1985. *Recht—Rhetorik—Politik: Untersuchungen zu Ciceros Rhetorischer Strategie.* Darmstadt.

Cloud, D. 1994. "The Constitution and Public Criminal Law." In J. A. Crook, A. Lintott, and E. Rawson, eds., *The Cambridge Ancient History (Second Edition) Volume IX: The Last Age of the Roman Republic, 146–43 B.C.,* 491–530. Cambridge.

Coarelli, F. 1985. *Il Foro Romano: Periodo Repubblicano e Augusteo.* Rome.

Coarelli, F. 2009. "I luoghi del processo." In B. Santalucia, ed., *La Repressione Criminale nella Roma repubblicana fra norma e persuasione,* 3–13. Pavia.

Connolly, J. 2007. "Virile Tongues: Rhetoric and Masculinity." In W. Dominik and J. Hall, eds., *A Companion to Roman Rhetoric,* 83–97. Oxford.

Corbeill, A. 1996. *Controlling Laughter: Political Humor in the Late Roman Republic.* Princeton, NJ.

Corbeill, A. 2002. "Political Movement: Walking and Ideology in Republican Rome." In D. Fredrick, ed., *The Roman Gaze: Vision, Power, and the Body,* 182–215. Baltimore and London.

Corbeill, A. 2004. *Nature Embodied: Gesture in Ancient Rome.* Princeton and Oxford.

Cotton, H. M. 1985. "*Mirificum genus commendationis*: Cicero and the Latin Letter of Recommendation." *American Journal of Philology* 106:328–34.

Cotton, H. M. 1986. "The Role of Cicero's Letters of Recommendation: *iustitia* versus *gratia?*" *Hermes* 114:443–60.

Courtney, E. 1961. "The Prosecution of Scaurus in 54 B.C." *Philologus* 105:151–56.

Cowan, E. Forthcoming. "Deceit in Appian." In K. Welch, ed., *Appian's Rhomaika, Empire and Civil War.* Swansea.

Craig, C. P. 1984. "The Central Argument of Cicero's Speech for Ligarius." *Classical Journal* 79:193–99.

Craig, C. P. 2010. "Means and Ends of *indignatio* in Cicero's *Pro Roscio Amerino.*" In D. H. Berry and A. Erskine, eds., *Form and Function in Roman Oratory,* 75–91. Cambridge.

Crawford, J. W. 1984. *M. Tullius Cicero: The Lost and Unpublished Orations.* Göttingen.

Crawford, J. W. 1994. *M. Tullius Cicero, The Fragmentary Speeches: An Edition with Commentary.* 2nd ed. Atlanta.

Crawford, M. H. 1983. *Roman Republican Coinage: Volume 2.* (Corrected reprint of 1974 edition.) Cambridge.

Crawford, M. H., ed. 1996. *Roman Statutes: Volume 1.* Bulletin of the Institute of Classical Studies Supplement 64. London.

Criniti, N. 1981. *Grani Liciniani Reliquiae*. Leipzig.

Cronin, J. F. 1939. "The Athenian Juror and Emotional Pleas." *Classical Journal* 34:471–79.

Crook, J. A. 1955. *Consilium Principis*. Cambridge.

Crook, J. A. 1967. *Law and Life of Rome, 90 B.C.–A.D. 212*. London.

Crook, J. A. 1995. *Legal Advocacy in the Roman World*. Ithaca, NY.

David, J.-M. 1980. "'Eloquentia popularis' et conduites symboliques des orateurs de la fin de la République: Problèmes d'efficacité." *Quaderni di Storia* 6:171–211.

David, J.-M. 1992. *Le Patronat judiciaire au dernier Siècle de la République romaine*. Rome.

De Libero, L. 2009. "*Precibus ac lacrimis*: Tears in Roman Historiographers." In T. Fögen, ed., *Tears in the Graeco-Roman World*, 209–34. Berlin and New York.

Deniaux, E. 1993. *Clientèles et Pouvoir à l'époque de Cicéron*. Rome.

Desmouliez, A. 1976. *Cicéron et son goût: Essai sur une définition d'une esthétique romaine à la fin de la République*. Brussels.

Dessau, H. 1954. *Inscriptiones Latinae Selectae: Volume 1*. Berlin.

Dessau, H. 1955. *Inscriptiones Latinae Selectae: Volume 2, Pars II*. Berlin.

Deutsch, M. E. 1928. "Antony's Funeral Speech." *University of California Publications in Classical Philology* 9:127–48.

Diels, H., and Kranz, W. 1952. *Die Fragmente der Vorsokratiker (Bd. 2)*. 6th ed. Berlin.

Dixon, S. 1991. "The Sentimental Ideal of the Roman Family." In B. Rawson, ed., *Marriage, Divorce, and Children in Ancient Rome*, 99–113. Canberra and Oxford.

Dolansky, F. 2008. "*Togam virilem sumere*: Coming of Age in the Roman World." In J. Edmondson and A. Keith, eds., *Roman Dress and the Fabrics of Roman Culture*, 47–70. Toronto.

Douglas, A. E. 1966. *M. Tulli Ciceronis Brutus*. Oxford.

Dover, K. J. 1974. *Greek Popular Morality in the Time of Plato and Aristotle*. Berkeley, CA.

Drumann, W., and Groebe, P. 1899. *Geschichte Roms, Erster Band: Aemilii-Antonii*. Berlin. (1964 reprint used.)

Dugan, J. 2005. *Making a New Man: Ciceronian Self-Fashioning in the Rhetorical Works*. Oxford.

Dugan, J. 2013. "Cicero and the Politics of Ambiguity: Interpreting the *Pro Marcello*." In C. Steel and H. van der Blom, eds., *Community and Communication: Oratory and Politics in Republican Rome*, 211–25. Oxford.

Dumont, J. C. 2004. "Roscius et Labérius." In C. Hugoniot, F. Hurlet, and S. Milanezi, eds., *Le Statut de L'Acteur dans L'Antiquité Grecque et Romaine*, 241–50. Tours.

Dyck, A. R. 1998. "Narrative Obfuscation, Philosophical Topoi, and Tragic Patterning in Cicero's *Pro Milone*." *Harvard Studies in Classical Philology* 98:219–41.

Dyck, A. R. 2001. "Dressing to Kill: Attire as a Proof and Means of Characterization in Cicero's Speeches." *Arethusa* 34:119–30.

Dyck, A. R. 2003. "Evidence and Rhetoric in Cicero's *Pro Roscio Amerino*: The Case Against Sex. Roscius." *Classical Quarterly* 53:235–46.

Dyck, A. R. 2008. "Rivals into Partners: Hortensius and Cicero." *Historia* 57:142–73.

Dyck, A. R. 2010. *Cicero: Pro Sexto Roscio*. Cambridge.

Dyck, A. R. 2012. *Marcus Tullius Cicero: Speeches on Behalf of Marcus Fonteius and Marcus Aemilius Scaurus*. Oxford.

Dyer, R. R. 1990. "Rhetoric and Intention in Cicero's *Pro Marcello*." *Journal of Roman Studies* 80:17–30.

Earl, D. 1967. *The Moral and Political Tradition of Rome*. London.

Edmondson, J. 2008. "Public Dress and Social Control in Late Republican and Early Imperial Rome." In J. Edmondson and A. Keith, eds., *Roman Dress and the Fabrics of Roman Culture*, 21–46. Toronto.

Edwards, C. 1997. "Unspeakable Professions: Public Performance and Prostitution in Ancient Rome." In J. Hallett and M. Skinner, eds., *Roman Sexualities*, 66–95. Princeton, NJ.

Enders, J. 1997. "Delivering Delivery: Theatricality and the Emasculation of Eloquence." *Rhetorica* 15:253–78.

Epstein, D. F. 1987. *Personal Enmity in Roman Politics, 218–43 B.C.* London.

Erskine, A. 1997. "Cicero and the Expression of Grief." In S. M. Braund and C. Gill, eds., *The Passions in Roman Thought and Literature*, 36–47. Cambridge.

Fairweather, J. 1981. *Seneca the Elder*. Cambridge.

Fantham, E. 1975. "The Trials of Gabinius in 54 B.C." *Historia* 24:425–43.

Fantham, E. 1982. "Quintilian on Performance: Traditional and Personal Elements in *Institutio* 11.3." *Phoenix* 36:243–63.

Fantham, E. 1997. "The Contexts and Occasions of Roman Public Rhetoric." In W. J. Dominik, ed., *Roman Eloquence: Rhetoric in Society and Literature*, 111–28. London and New York.

Fantham, E. 2002. "Orator and/et actor." In P. Easterling and E. Hall, eds., *Greek and Roman Actors: Aspects of an Ancient Profession*, 362–76. Cambridge.

Fantham, E. 2004. *The Roman World of Cicero's De Oratore*. Oxford.

Ferguson, W. S. 1921. "The Lex Calpurnia of 149 B.C." *Journal of Roman Studies* 11:86–100.

Fernández López, J. 2007. "Quintilian as Rhetorician and Teacher." In W. Dominik and J. Hall, eds., *A Companion to Roman Rhetoric*, 307–22. Oxford.

Flaig, E. 2003. *Ritualisierte Politik. Zeichen, Gesten und Herrschaft im Alten Rom*. Göttingen.

Flower, H. I. 1996. *Ancestor Masks and Aristocratic Power in Roman Culture*. Oxford.

Flower, H. I. 2004. "Spectacle and Political Culture in the Roman Republic." In H. Flower, ed., *The Cambridge Companion to the Roman Republic*, 322–43. Cambridge.

Flower, H. I. 2013. "Beyond the *Contio*: Political Communication in the Tribunate of Tiberius Gracchus." In C. Steel and H. van der Blom, eds., *Community and Communication: Oratory and Politics in Republican Rome*, 85–100. Oxford.

Fögen, T., ed. 2009. *Tears in the Graeco-Roman World.* Berlin and New York.

Forsythe, G. 1988. "The Political Background of the Lex Calpurnia of 149 B.C." *Ancient World* 17:109–19.

Fortenbaugh, W. W. 1985. "Theophrastus on Delivery." In W. Fortenbaugh, P. Huby, and A. A. Long, eds., *Theophrastus of Eresus: On His Life and Work*, 269–88. New Brunswick, NJ.

Frazel, T. D. 2004. "The Composition and Circulation of Cicero's *In Verrem.*" *Classical Quarterly* 54:128–42.

Fredericksmeyer, E. A. 1973. "Catullus 49, Cicero and Caesar." *Classical Philology* 68:268–78.

Freeman, K. 1946. *The Pre-Socratic Philosophers: A Companion to Diels, Fragmente der Vorsokratiker.* Oxford.

Freyburger, G. 1988. "Supplication grecque et supplication romaine." *Latomus* 47:501–25.

Freyburger-Galland, M.-L. 1993. "Le rôle politique des vêtements dans l'*Histoire romaine* de Dion Cassius." *Latomus* 52:117–28.

Frier, B. W. 1985. *The Rise of the Roman Jurists: Studies in Cicero's Pro Caecina.* Princeton, NJ.

Frier, B. W. 2010. "Finding a Place for Law in the High Empire: Tacitus *Dialogus* 39.1–4." In F. de Angelis, ed., *Spaces of Justice in the Roman World*, 67–87. Leiden.

Gabba, E. 1956. *Appiano e la Storia delle Guerre Civili.* Florence.

Gabelmann, H. 1984. *Antike Audienz- und Tribunalszenen.* Darmstadt.

Garcea, A. 2005. *Cicerone in esilio: L'Epistolario e le Passioni.* Hildesheim.

Gardner, J. F., and Wiedemann, T. 1991. *The Roman Household: A Sourcebook.* London.

Gardner, R. 1958. *Cicero the Speeches: Pro Sestio and In Vatinium.* Cambridge, MA.

Geffcken, K. A. 1973. *Comedy in the Pro Caelio: With an Appendix on the In Clodium et Curionem.* Leiden.

Gelzer, M. 1969. *Cicero, Ein Biographischer Versuch.* Wiesbaden.

Gildenhard, I. 2011. *Creative Eloquence: The Construction of Reality in Cicero's Speeches.* Oxford.

Gleason, M. W. 1995. *Making Men: Sophists and Self-Presentation in Ancient Rome.* Princeton, NJ.

Goldbeck, F. 2010. *Salutationes: Die Morgenbegrüssungen in Rom in der Republik und der frühen Kaiserzeit.* Berlin.

Gotoff, H. C. 1993a. *Cicero's Caesarian Speeches: A Stylistic Commentary.* Chapel Hill, NC.

Gotoff, H. C. 1993b. "Oratory: The Art of Illusion." *Harvard Studies in Classical Philology* 95:289–313.

Gould, J. 1973. "Hiketeia." *Journal of Hellenic Studies* 93:74–103.

Gowing, A. M. 1990. "Appian and Cassius' Speech before Philippi (*Bella Civilia* 4.90–100)." *Phoenix* 44:158–81.

Gowing, A. M. 1992. *The Triumviral Narratives of Appian and Cassius Dio.* Ann Arbor, MI.

Graf, F. 1991. "Gestures and Conventions: The Gestures of Roman Actors and Orators." In J. Bremmer and H. Roodenburg, eds., *A Cultural History of Gesture: From Antiquity to the Present Day*, 36–58. London.

Greenidge, A. H. J. 1901. *The Legal Procedure of Cicero's Time*. New York. (1971 reprint used.)

Greenwood, L. H. G. 1928. *Cicero: The Verrine Orations. Volume 1*. Cambridge, MA.

Gregory, A. P. 1994. "'Powerful Images': Responses to Portraits and the Political Uses of Images in Rome." *Journal of Roman Archaeology* 7:80–99.

Griffin, M. T. 2003. "*Clementia* after Caesar: From Politics to Philosophy." In F. Cairns and E. Fantham, eds., *Caesar against Liberty? Perspectives on His Autocracy*, 157–82. Cambridge.

Gruen, E. S. 1966. "Political Prosecutions in the 90's BC." *Historia* 15:32–64.

Gruen, E. S. 1967. "Cicero and Licinius Calvus." *Harvard Studies in Classical Philology* 71:215–33.

Gruen, E. S. 1968. *Roman Politics and the Criminal Courts, 149–78 B.C.* Cambridge, MA.

Gruen, E.S. 1971. "Pompey, Metellus Pius, and the Trials of 70–69 B.C.: The Perils of Schematism." *American Journal of Philology* 92:1–16.

Gruen, E. S. 1974. *The Last Generation of the Roman Republic*. Berkeley, CA.

Gunderson, E. 2000. *Staging Masculinity: The Rhetoric of Performance in the Roman World*. Ann Arbor, MI.

Hall, E. 1995. "Lawcourt Dramas: The Power of Performance in Greek Forensic Oratory." *Bulletin of the Institute for Classical Studies* 40:39–58.

Hall, J. 2004. "Cicero and Quintilian on the Oratorical Use of Hand Gestures." *Classical Quarterly* 54:143–60.

Hall, J. 2007. "Oratorical Delivery and the Emotions: Theory and Practice." In W. Dominik and J. Hall, eds., *A Companion to Roman Rhetoric*, 218–34. Oxford.

Hall, J. 2009a. *Politeness and Politics in Cicero's Letters*. Oxford.

Hall, J. 2009b. "Serving the Times: Cicero and Caesar the Dictator." In W. Dominik, J. Garthwaite, and P. Roche, eds., *Writing Politics in Imperial Rome*, 89–110. Leiden.

Harries, J. 2007. *Law and Crime in the Roman World*. Cambridge.

Hatfield, E. et al. 1994. *Emotional Contagion*. Cambridge.

Heckenkamp, M. 2010. "Cicero's Tears." In L. Calboli Montefusco, ed., *Papers on Rhetoric: Volume 10*, 173–82. Bologna.

Herzog-Hauser, G. 1937. "Trauerkleidung." *RE* VI A.2:2225–31.

Heskel, J. 1994. "Cicero as Evidence for Attitudes to Dress in the Late Republic." In J. L. Sebesta and L. Bonfante, eds., *The World of Roman Costume*, 133–45. Madison, WI.

Higginbotham, J. 1997. *Piscinae: Artificial Fishponds in Roman Italy*. Chapel Hill, NC.

Holden, H.A. 1881. *M. Tulli Ciceronis Pro Gnaeo Plancio Oratio ad Iudices*. Cambridge.

Hölkeskamp, K.-J. 1995. "*Oratoris maxima scaena*: Reden vor dem Volk in der politischen Kultur der Republik." In M. Jehne, ed., *Demokratie in Rom? Die Rolle des Volkes in der Politik der römischen Republik*, 11–49. Stuttgart.

Hopwood, K. 2007. "Smear and Spin: Ciceronian Tactics in *De Lege Agraria* II." In J. Booth, ed., *Cicero on the Attack: Invective and Subversion in the Orations and Beyond*, 71–103. Swansea.

Hubbell, H. M. (with G. L. Hendrickson). 1939. *Cicero: Brutus, Orator*. Cambridge, MA.

Humbert, J. 1925. *Les Plaidoyers écrits et les Plaidoiries réelles de Cicéron*. Paris.

Humbert, J. 1938. "Comment Cicéron mystifia les juges de Cluentius." *Revue des Études Latines* 16:275–96.

Hutchinson, G. O. 1998. *Cicero's Correspondence: A Literary Study*. Oxford.

Iodice di Martino, M. G. 1987. "Il rapporto oratore-pubblico nel Brutus di Cicerone." *Atene e Roma* 32:147–51.

Johnson, J. P. 2004. "The Dilemma of Cicero's Speech for Ligarius." In J. Powell and J. Paterson, eds., *Cicero the Advocate*, 371–99. Oxford.

Johnstone, S. 1999. *Disputes and Democracy: The Consequences of Litigation in Ancient Athens*. Austin, TX.

Jones, A. H. M. 1972. *The Criminal Courts of the Roman Republic and Principate*. Oxford.

Kallet-Marx, R. M. 1990. "The Trial of Rutilius Rufus." *Phoenix* 44:122–39.

Kaster, R. A. 1995. *Suetonius: De Grammaticis et Rhetoribus*. Oxford.

Kaster, R. A. 2006. *Cicero: Speech on Behalf of Publius Sestius*. Oxford.

Kaster, R. A. 2009. "Some Passionate Performances in Late Republican Rome." In R. K. Balot, ed., *Companion to Greek and Roman Political Thought*, 308–20. Chichester and Malden, MA.

Katula, R. A. 2003. "Quintilian on the Art of Emotional Appeal." *Rhetoric Review* 22:5–15.

Keil, H. 1855. *Grammatici Latini: Volume 2*. Leipzig.

Kellogg, G. D. 1907. "Study of a Proverb Attributed to the Rhetor Apollonius." *American Journal of Philology* 28:301–10.

Kelly, G. P. 2006. *A History of Exile in the Roman Republic*. Cambridge.

Kendon, A. 1981. "Geography of Gesture." *Semiotica* 37:129–63.

Kennedy, G. 1968a. "Antony's Speech at Caesar's Funeral." *Quarterly Journal of Speech* 54:99–106.

Kennedy, G. 1968b. "The Rhetoric of Advocacy in Greece and Rome." *American Journal of Philology* 89:419–36.

Kennedy, G. 1969. *Quintilian*. New York.

Kennedy, G. 1972. *The Art of Rhetoric in the Roman World 300 BC–AD 300*. Princeton, NJ.

Kinsey, T. E. 1971. *M. Tulli Ciceronis Pro P. Quinctio Oratio*. Sydney.

Kinsey, T. E. 1980. "Cicero's Case Against Magnus, Capito and Chrysogonus in the Pro Sex. Roscio Amerino and Its Use for the Historian." *L'Antiquité Classique* 49:173–90.

Kinsey, T. E. 1985. "The Case Against Sextus Roscius of Ameria." *L'Antiquité Classique* 54:188–96.

Kondratieff, E. 2010. "The Urban Praetor's Tribunal in the Roman Republic." In F. de Angelis, ed., *Spaces of Justice in the Roman World*, 89–126. Leiden.

Konstan, D. 2001. *Pity Transformed*. London.

Konstan, D. 2010. *Before Forgiveness: The Origins of a Moral Idea*. Cambridge.

Kroll, W. 1913. *M. Tullii Ciceronis Orator*. Berlin. (1958 reprint used.)

Kroll, W. 1933. *Die Kultur der Ciceronischen Zeit*. Leipzig.

Krostenko, B. A. 2001. *Cicero, Catullus, and the Language of Social Performance*. Chicago, IL.

Kübler, B. 1927. "Luctus." *RE* XIII.2:1697–1705.

Kumaniecki, K. 1967. "Der Prozess des Ligarius." *Hermes* 95:434–57.

Lachenaud, G., and Coudry, M. 2011. *Dion Cassius: Histoire Romaine. Livres 38, 39 & 40*. Paris.

Laidlaw, W. A. 1960. "Cicero and the Stage." *Hermathena* 94:56–66.

Laughton, E. 1970. "Disertissime Romuli Nepotum." *Classical Philology* 65:1–7.

Laurand, L. 1938. *Études sur le style des Discours de Cicéron*. 4th ed. Paris.

Lausberg, H. 1998. *Handbook of Literary Rhetoric: A Foundation for Literary Study*. Ed. D. E. Orton and R. D. Anderson. Trans. M. T. Bliss, A. Jansen, and D. E. Orton. Leiden.

Laws, J. 2004. "Epilogue: Cicero and the Modern Advocate." In J. Powell and J. Paterson, eds., *Cicero the Advocate*, 401–16. Oxford.

Leach, E. W. 2000. "The *Spectacula* of Cicero's *Pro Sestio*: Patronage, Production and Performance." In S. K. Dickison and J. P. Hallett, eds., *Rome and Her Monuments: Essays on the City and Literature of Rome in Honor of Katherine A. Geffcken*, 369–97. Wauconda, IL.

Lebek, W. D. 1970. *Verba Prisca: Die Anfänge des Archaisierens in der lateinischen Beredsamkeit und Geschichtsschreibung*. Göttingen.

Leeman, A. D., and Pinkster, H. 1981. *M. Tullius Cicero De Oratore Libri III Kommentar: Buch I, 1–165*. Heidelberg.

Leigh, M. 1995. "Wounding and Popular Rhetoric at Rome." *Bulletin of the Institute for Classical Studies* 40:195–215.

Lewis, R. G. 2006. *Asconius: Commentaries on Speeches of Cicero*. Oxford.

Linderski, J. 1971. "Three Trials in 54 B.C.: Sufenas, Cato, Procilius and Cicero, 'Ad Atticum', 4.15.4." In *Studi in onore di Edoardo Volterra: Volume 2*, 281–302. Milan.

Linderski, J. 1995. *Roman Questions: Selected Papers 1958–1993*. Stuttgart.

Lintott, A. W. 1974. "Cicero and Milo." *Journal of Roman Studies* 64:62–78.

Lintott, A. W. 1992. *Judicial Reform and Land Reform in the Roman Republic: A New Edition, with Translation and Commentary, of the Laws from Urbino*. Cambridge.

Lintott, A. W. 1999. *Violence in Republican Rome*. 2nd ed. Oxford.

Lintott, A. W. 2004. "Legal Procedure in Cicero's Time." In J. Powell and J. Paterson, eds., *Cicero the Advocate*, 61–78. Oxford.

Lintott, A. W. 2008. *Cicero as Evidence: A Historian's Companion*. Oxford.

Liva, S. 2009. "Sulla funzione del quaesitor. Testi e ipotesi." In B. Santalucia, ed., *La Repressione Criminale nella Roma repubblicana fra norma e persuasione*, 115–25. Pavia.

Lussky, A. 1928. *The Appeal to the Emotions in the Judicial Speeches of Cicero as Compared with the Theories Set Forth on the Subject in the De Oratore*. Diss. Minnesota.

Lutz, T. 2001. *Crying: The Natural and Cultural History of Tears*. New York and London.

MacDowell, D. M. 1971. *Aristophanes: Wasps*. Oxford.

MacDowell, D. M. 1995. *Aristophanes and Athens: An Introduction to the Plays*. Oxford.

MacMullen, R. 1980. "Romans in Tears." *Classical Philology* 75:254–55.

Mahy, T. 2013. "Antonius, Triumvir and Orator: Career, Style, and Effectiveness." In C. Steel and H. van der Blom, eds., *Community and Communication: Oratory and Politics in Republican Rome*, 329–44. Oxford.

Maier-Eichhorn, U. 1989. *Die Gestikulation in Quintilians Rhetorik*. Frankfurt am Main.

Makhlayuk, A. V. 2008. "The Roman General in Times of Mutiny: Gestures and Expression of Emotions." *Vestnik drevnej istorii* 4:114–31.

Malcovati, H. 1976. *Oratorum Romanorum Fragmenta*. 4th ed. Turin.

Manuwald, G. 2007. *Cicero, Philippics 3–9. Volume 1: Introduction, Text and Translation, References and Indexes*. Berlin and New York.

Marinone, N. 2004. *Cronologia Ciceroniana*. 2nd ed. Rome and Bologna.

Marshall, A. J. 1984. "Symbols and Showmanship in Roman Public Life: The Fasces." *Phoenix* 38:120–41.

Marshall, B. A. 1985. *A Historical Commentary on Asconius*. Columbia, MO.

Marx, F. 1904. *C. Lucilii Carminum Reliquiae: Volume 1*. Leipzig. (1963 reprint used.)

Marx, F. 1905. *C. Lucilii Carminum Reliquiae: Volume 2*. Leipzig. (1963 reprint used.)

May, J. M. 1981. "The Rhetoric of Advocacy and Patron-Client Identification: Variation on a Theme." *American Journal of Philology* 102:308–15.

May, J. M. 1988. *Trials of Character: The Eloquence of Ciceronian Ethos*. Chapel Hill, NC.

May, J. M. 1994. "Persuasion, Ciceronian Style." *Classical Outlook* 71:37–41.

May, J. M. 1995. "Patron and Client, Father and Son in Cicero's 'Pro Caelio'." *Classical Journal* 90:433–41.

May, J. M. 2001. "Cicero's *Pro Milone*: An Ideal Speech of an Ideal Orator." In C. W. Wooten, ed., *The Orator in Action and Theory in Greece and Rome*, 123–34. Leiden.

Mayer, R. 2001. *Tacitus: Dialogus De Oratoribus*. Cambridge.

McDermott, W. C. 1977. "The Verrine Jury." *Rheinisches Museum für Philologie* 120:64–75.

McGushin, P. 1992. *Sallust: The Histories Volume I, Books i–ii.* Oxford.

Mendelssohn, L. 1881. *Appiani Historia Romana: Volume 2.* Leipzig.

Millar, F. 1964. *A Study of Cassius Dio.* Oxford.

Mitchell, T. N. 1986. *Cicero: Verrines II.1.* Warminster.

Moles, J. 1988. *Plutarch: The Life of Cicero.* Warminster.

Montague, H. W. 1992. "Advocacy and Politics: The Paradox of Cicero's *Pro Ligario.*" *American Journal of Philology* 113:559–74.

Moretti, G. 2004. "Mezzi visuali per le Passioni Retoriche: Le Scenografie dell'oratoria." In G. Petrone, ed., *Le Passioni della Retorica,* 63–96. Palermo.

Moretti, G. 2006. "Lo Spettacolo della *Pro Caelio*: Oggetti di Scena, Teatro e Personaggi allegorici nel Processo contro Marco Celio." In G. Petrone and A. Casamento, eds., *Lo Spettacolo della Giustizia: Le Orazioni di Cicerone,* 139–64. Palermo.

Morstein-Marx, R. 1998. "Publicity, Popularity and Patronage in the *Commentariolum Petitionis.*" *Classical Antiquity* 17:259–88.

Morstein-Marx, R. 2004. *Mass Oratory and Political Power in the Late Roman Republic.* Cambridge.

Mortimer, J. 1983. *The First Rumpole Omnibus.* London.

Münzer, F. 1899. "Cispius no. 4." *RE* III.2:2589.

Münzer, F. 1927. "Livius no. 33." *RE* XIII.2:891–99.

Münzer, F. 1929. "Stenius." *RE* IIIA.2:2335–36.

Naiden, F. S. 2006. *Ancient Supplication.* New York and Oxford.

Narducci, E. 1997. *Cicerone e l'eloquenza romana: Retorica e progetto culturale.* Rome and Bari.

Narducci, E. 2002. "Brutus: The History of Roman Eloquence." In J. M. May, ed., *Brill's Companion to Cicero: Oratory and Rhetoric,* 401–25. Leiden.

Nisbet, R. G. M. 1961. *M. Tulli Ciceronis In L. Calpurnium Pisonem Oratio.* Oxford.

North, H. F. 2000. "Lacrimae Virginis Vestalis." In S. K. Dickison and J. P. Hallett, eds., *Rome and Her Monuments: Essays on the City and Literature of Rome in Honor of Katherine A. Geffcken,* 357–67. Wauconda, IL.

Oakley, S. P. 1997. *A Commentary on Livy Books VI–X, Volume I: Introduction and Book VI.* Oxford.

Ogilvie, R. M. 1965. *A Commentary on Livy Books 1–5.* Oxford.

Olson, K. 2007 (2004–5). "*Insignia lugentium*: Female Mourning Garments in Roman Antiquity." *American Journal of Ancient History* 3–4:89–130.

Osgood, J. 2006. *Caesar's Legacy: Civil War and the Emergence of the Roman Empire.* Cambridge.

O'Sullivan, T. M. 2011. *Walking in Roman Culture.* Cambridge.

Paterson, J. 2004. "Self-Reference in Cicero's Forensic Speeches." In J. Powell and J. Paterson, eds., *Cicero the Advocate,* 79–95. Oxford.

Pelling, C. B. R. 1979. "Plutarch's Method of Work in the Roman Lives." *Journal of Hellenic Studies* 99:74–96.

Pelling, C. B. R. 1988. *Plutarch: Life of Antony.* Cambridge.

Peter, H. 1914. *Historicorum Romanorum Reliquiae. Volume II.* Leipzig. (1967 reprint used.)

Peterson, W. 1917. *M. Tulli Ciceronis Orationes. Volume III.* 2nd ed. Oxford.

Petrone, G. 2004. *La parola agitata: teatralità della retorica latina.* Palermo.

Petrone, G., and Casamento, A., eds. 2006. *Lo Spettacolo della Giustizia: Le Orazioni di Cicerone.* Palermo.

Pierini, R. D.' I. 2006. "Scenografie per un ritorno: la (ri)costruzione del personaggio Cicerone nelle orazioni *post reditum.*" In G. Petrone and A. Casamento, eds., *Lo Spettacolo della Giustizia: Le Orazioni di Cicerone,* 119–37. Palermo.

Pina Polo, F. 1996. *Contra arma verbis: Der Redner vor dem Volk in der späten römischen Republik.* Stuttgart.

Pina Polo, F. 2013. "Foreign Eloquence in the Roman Senate." In C. Steel and H. van der Blom, eds., *Community and Communication: Oratory and Politics in Republican Rome,* 247–66. Oxford.

Pocock, L. G. 1926. *A Commentary on Cicero In Vatinium.* London.

Pöschl, V. 1975. "Zur Einbeziehung Anwesender Personen und Sichtbarer Objekte in Ciceros Reden." In A. Michel and R. Verdière, eds., *Ciceroniana: Hommages à Kazimierz Kumaniecki,* 206–26. Leiden.

Powell, J. G. F. 2010. "Court Procedure and Rhetorical Strategy in Cicero." In D. H. Berry and A. Erskine, eds., *Form and Function in Roman Oratory,* 21–36. Cambridge.

Powell, J., and Paterson, J. 2004. "Introduction." In J. Powell and J. Paterson, eds., *Cicero the Advocate,* 1–57. Oxford.

Prag, J. R. W. 2013. "Provincials, Patrons, and the Rhetoric of *repetundae.*" In C. Steel and H. van der Blom, eds., *Community and Communication: Oratory and Politics in Republican Rome,* 267–83. Oxford.

Quinn, K. 1973. *Catullus: The Poems.* 2nd ed. Basingstoke and London.

Ramage, E. S. 2006. "Funeral Eulogy and Propaganda in the Roman Republic." *Athenaeum* 94:39–64.

Ramsey, J. T. 2003. *Cicero Philippics I–II.* Cambridge.

Ramsey, J. T. 2010. "Debate at a Distance: A Unique Rhetorical Strategy in Cicero's Thirteenth Philippic." In D. H. Berry and A. Erskine, eds., *Form and Function in Roman Oratory,* 155–74. Cambridge.

Rathofer, C. 1986. *Ciceros "Brutus" als literarisches Paradigma eines Auctoritas-Verhältnisses.* Frankfurt am Main.

Rawson, E. 1985. *Intellectual Life in the Late Roman Republic.* London.

Richardson, J. S. 1987. "The Purpose of the *Lex Calpurnia de Repetundis.*" *Journal of Roman Studies* 77:1–12.

Richlin, A. 1997. "Gender and Rhetoric: Producing Manhood in the Schools." In W. J. Dominik, ed., *Roman Eloquence: Rhetoric in Society and Literature,* 90–110. London and New York.

Ridgway Jones, M. 2001. "The Performer's Curious Power: Theater and Anxiety in Ancient Rome." In E. Tylawsky and C. Weiss, eds., *Essays in Honor of Gordon Williams: Twenty-Five Years at Yale*, 129–45. New Haven, CT.

Riggsby, A. 1997. "Did the Romans Believe in Their Verdicts?" *Rhetorica* 15:235–51.

Riggsby, A. 1999. *Crime and Community in Ciceronian Rome*. Austin, TX.

Risselada, R. 1993. *Imperatives and Other Directive Expressions in Latin: A Study in the Pragmatics of a Dead Language*. Amsterdam.

Rohde, F. J. A. 1903. *Cicero, Quae De Inventione Praecepit, Quatenus Secutus Sit In Orationibus Generis Iudicialis*. Diss. Könisberg.

Roisman, J. 2005. *The Rhetoric of Manhood: Masculinity in the Attic Orators*. Berkeley, CA.

Rolfe, J. C. 1998. *Suetonius Volume 1*. Cambridge, MA.

Rosenstein, N. 2006. "Aristocratic Values." In N. Rosenstein and R. Morstein-Marx, eds., *A Companion to the Roman Republic*, 365–82. Oxford.

Rossi, A. 2000. "The Tears of Marcellus: History of a Literary Motif in Livy." *Greece and Rome* 47:56–66.

Ruebel, J. S. 1979. "The Trial of Milo in 52 B.C.: A Chronological Study." *Transactions of the American Philological Association* 109:231–49.

Russell, D. A. 2001. *Quintilian: The Orator's Education, Books 6–8*. Cambridge, MA.

Rutledge, S. H. 2001. *Imperial Inquisitions: Prosecutors and Informants from Tiberius to Domitian*. London.

Saglio, E. 1877. "*Bulla*." In C. Daremberg and E. Saglio, eds., *Dictionnaire des antiquités grecques et romains*, 754–55. Paris.

Saller, R. P. 1982. *Personal Patronage under the Early Empire*. Cambridge.

Sandys, J. E. 1885. *M. Tulli Ciceronis ad M. Brutum Orator*. Cambridge.

Scalais, R. 1951. "Cicéron Avocat." *Études Classiques* 19:190–208.

Schenkeveld, D. M. 1988. "*Iudicia vulgi*: Cicero, *De Oratore* 3.195ff. and *Brutus* 183ff." *Rhetorica* 6:291–301.

Schmidt, B. 1914. "Die Lebenszeit Catulls und die Herausgabe seiner Gedichte." *Rheinisches Museum für Philologie* 69:267–83.

Schöggl, J. 2002. *Misericordia: Bedeutung und Umfeld dieses Wortes und der Wortfamilie in der antiken lateinischen Literatur*. Graz.

Scholz, U. W. 1962. *Der Redner M. Antonius*. Diss. Erlangen.

Schottländer, R. 1967. "Der römische Redner und sein Publikum." *Wiener Studien* n.s. 1: 125–46.

Schryvers, P. H. 1982. "Invention, Imagination et Théorie des Émotions chez Cicéron et Quintilien." In B. Vickers, ed., *Rhetoric Revalued: Papers from the International Society for the History of Rhetoric*, 47–57. Binghamton, NY.

Seager, R. 1972. "Cicero and the Word *popularis*." *Classical Quarterly* n.s. 22:328–38.

Seager, R. 2007. "The Guilt or Innocence of Sex. Roscius." *Athenaeum* 95: 895–910.

Settle, J. N. 1962. *The Publication of Cicero's Orations*. Diss. Chapel Hill, NC.

Shackleton Bailey, D. R. 1965. *Cicero's Letters to Atticus: Volume 2*. Cambridge.

Shackleton Bailey, D. R. 1977. *Cicero Epistulae Ad Familiares, Volume 1: 62–47 B.C.* Cambridge.

Shackleton Bailey, D. R. 1999. *Cicero: Letters to Atticus. Volumes I–IV.* Cambridge, MA.

Shackleton Bailey, D. R. 2000. *Valerius Maximus: Memorable Doings and Sayings Books VI–IX.* Cambridge, MA.

Shackleton Bailey, D. R. 2001. *Cicero: Letters to Friends. Volumes I–III.* Cambridge, MA.

Shackleton Bailey, D. R. 2002. *Letters to Quintus and Brutus, Letter Fragments, Letter to Octavian, Invectives, Handbook of Electioneering.* Cambridge, MA.

Shackleton Bailey, D. R. 2009. *Cicero Orations: Philippics 7–14.* Revised by J. T. Ramsey and G. Manuwald. Cambridge, MA.

Sherwin-White, A. N. 1966. *The Letters of Pliny: A Historical and Social Commentary.* Oxford.

Shields, S. A. 2002. *Speaking from the Heart: Gender and the Social Meaning of Emotion.* Cambridge.

Siani-Davies, M. 2001. *Cicero's Speech Pro Rabirio Postumo.* Oxford.

Skinner, M. 1982. "The Contents of Caelius' Pyxis." *Classical World* 75:243–45.

Stangl, T. 1912. *Ciceronis orationum scholiastae.* Vienna. (1964 reprint used.)

Steel, C. E. W. 2002–3. "Cicero's *Brutus*: The End of Oratory and the Beginning of History?" *Bulletin of the Institute for Classical Studies* 46:195–211.

Steel, C. E. W. 2010. "Tribunician Sacrosanctity and Oratorical Performance in the Late Republic." In D. H. Berry and A. Erskine, eds., *Form and Function in Roman Oratory*, 37–50. Cambridge.

Stevenson, T. 2008. "Tyrants, Kings and Fathers in the Philippics." In T. Stevenson and M. Wilson, eds., *Cicero's Philippics: History, Rhetoric, Ideology*, 95–113. Auckland.

Stockton, D. 1979. *The Gracchi.* Oxford.

Stone, A. M. 1980. "Pro Milone: Cicero's Second Thoughts." *Antichthon* 14:88–111.

Stroh, W. 1975. *Taxis Und Taktik: Die Advokatische Dispositionskunst in Ciceros Gerichtsreden.* Stuttgart.

Sumi, G. S. 1997. "Power and Ritual: The Crowd at Clodius' Funeral." *Historia* 46:80–102.

Sumi, G. S. 2002a. "Impersonating the Dead: Mimes at Roman Funerals." *American Journal of Philology* 123:559–85.

Sumi, G. S. 2002b. "Spectacles and Sulla's Public Image." *Historia* 51:414–32.

Sumi, G. S. 2005. *Ceremony and Power: Performing Politics in Rome between Republic and Empire.* Ann Arbor, MI.

Svavarsson, S. H. 1999. "On Catullus 49." *Classical Journal* 95:131–38.

Syme, R. 1939. *The Roman Revolution.* Oxford.

Talbert, R. J. A. 1984. *The Senate of Imperial Rome.* Princeton, NJ.

Tatum, W. J. 1988. "Catullus' Criticism of Cicero in Poem 49." *Transactions of the American Philological Association* 118:179–84.

Tatum, W. J. 1999. *The Patrician Tribune: Publius Clodius Pulcher.* Chapel Hill, NC.

Tatum, W. J. 2007. "*Alterum est tamen boni viri, alterum boni petitoris*: The Good Man Canvasses." *Phoenix* 61:109–35.

Tatum, W. J. 2011. "Invective Identities in *Pro Caelio*." In C. Smith and R. Covino, eds., *Praise and Blame in Roman Republican Rhetoric*, 165–79. Swansea.

Thierfelder, A. 1965. "Über den Wert der Bemerkungen zur eigenen Person in Ciceros Prozessreden." *Gymnasium* 72:385–414.

Todd, S. 1990. "Lady Chatterley's Lover and the Attic Orators: The Social Composition of the Athenian Jury." *Journal of Hellenic Studies* 110:146–73.

Toner, J. P. 2009. *Popular Culture in Ancient Rome*. Cambridge.

Tzounakas, S. 2009. "The Peroration of Cicero's *Pro Milone*." *Classical World* 102:129–41.

Unceta Gómez, L. 2009. *La Petición Verbal en Latín: Estudio Léxico, Semántico y Pragmático*. Madrid.

Usher, S. 2008. *Cicero's Speeches: The Critic in Action*. Oxford.

van den Hout, M. P. J. 1988. *M. Cornelii Frontonis Epistulae*. Leipzig.

van der Blom, H. 2010. *Cicero's Role Models: The Political Strategy of a Newcomer*. Oxford.

van Wees, H. 1998. "A Brief History of Tears: Gender Differentiation in Archaic Greece." In L. Foxhall and J. Salmon, eds., *When Men Were Men: Masculinity, Power and Identity in Classical Antiquity*, 10–53. London.

Vasaly, A. 1985. "The Masks of Rhetoric: Cicero's *Pro Roscio Amerino*." *Rhetorica* 3:1–20.

Vasaly, A. 1993. *Representations: Images of the World in Ciceronian Oratory*. Berkeley, CA.

Vasaly, A. 2000. "The Quality of Mercy in Cicero's *Pro Murena*." In S. K. Dickison and J. P. Hallett, eds., *Rome and Her Monuments: Essays on the City and Literature of Rome in Honor of Katherine A. Geffcken*, 447–63. Wauconda, IL.

Vasaly, A. 2009. "Cicero, Domestic Politics, and the First Action of the Verrines." *Classical Antiquity* 28:101–37.

Verboven, K. 2002. *The Economy of Friends: Economic Aspects of Amicitia and Patronage in the Late Republic*. Brussels.

Vickers, B. 1988. *In Defence of Rhetoric*. Oxford.

Walker, J. 2011. *The Genuine Teachers of This Art: Rhetorical Education in Antiquity*. Columbia, SC.

Wallace-Hadrill, A. 1989. "Patronage in Roman Society: from Republic to Empire." In A. Wallace-Hadrill, ed., *Patronage in Ancient Society*, 63–87. London and New York.

Walsh, P. G. 1973. *T. Livi Ab Urbe Condita Liber XXI*. London.

Warmington, E. H. 1967. *Remains of Old Latin Volume 3: Lucilius, The Twelve Tables*. Rev. ed. Cambridge, MA.

Webb, R. 1997. "Imagination and the Arousal of the Emotions in Greco-Roman Rhetoric." In S. M. Braund and C. Gill, eds., *The Passions in Roman Thought and Literature*, 112–27. Cambridge.

Webster, T. B. L. 1931. *M. Tulli Ciceronis Pro L. Flacco Oratio*. Oxford.

Weinstock, S. 1971. *Divus Julius*. Oxford.

Welch, K. E. 1995. "Antony, Fulvia and the Ghost of Clodius in 47 B.C." *Greece and Rome* 42:182–201.

Williams, C. A. 1999. *Roman Homosexuality: Ideologies of Masculinity in Classical Antiquity*. New York and Oxford.

Wills, G. 2011. *Rome and Rhetoric: Shakespeare's Julius Caesar*. New Haven and London.

Wilson, M. 1997. "The Subjugation of Grief in Seneca's *Epistles*." In S. M. Braund and C. Gill, eds., *The Passions in Roman Thought and Literature*, 48–67. Cambridge.

Winniczuk, L. 1961. "Cicero on Actors and the Stage." *Atti del I Congresso internazionale di Studi Ciceroniani* 1:213–22. Rome.

Winterbottom, M. 1970. *M. Fabi Quintiliani Institutionis Oratoriae Libri Duodecim. Volume I*. Oxford.

Winterbottom, M. 1994. *M. Tulli Ciceronis De Officiis*. Oxford.

Winterbottom, M. 2002. "Believing the *Pro Marcello*." In J. F. Miller, C. Damon, and K. S. Myers, eds., *Vertis in usum. Studies in Honor of Edward Courtney*, 24–38. Leipzig.

Winterbottom, M. 2004. "Perorations." In J. Powell and J. Paterson, eds., *Cicero the Advocate*, 215–30. Oxford.

Wiseman, T. P. 1974. *Cinna the Poet and Other Roman Essays*. Leicester.

Wiseman, T. P. 1982. "*Pete nobiles amicos*: Poets and Patrons in Late Republican Rome." In B. K. Gold, ed., *Literary and Artistic Patronage in Ancient Rome*, 28–49. Austin, TX.

Wiseman, T. P. 1985. *Catullus and His World: A Reappraisal*. Cambridge.

Wiseman, T. P. 1998. *Roman Drama and Roman History*. Exeter.

Wisse, J. 1989. *Ethos and Pathos from Aristotle to Cicero*. Amsterdam.

Wisse, J. 1995. "Greeks, Romans and the Rise of Atticism." In J. G. J. Abbenes, S. R. Slings, and I. Sluiter, eds., *Greek Literary Theory after Aristotle: A Collection of Papers in Honour of D. M. Schenkeveld*, 65–82. Amsterdam.

Wisse, J. 2013. "The Bad Orator: Between Clumsy Delivery and Political Danger." In C. Steel and H. van der Blom, eds., *Community and Communication: Oratory and Politics in Republican Rome*, 163–94. Oxford.

Wistrand, M. 1992. *Entertainment and Violence in Ancient Rome: The Attitudes of Roman Writers of the First Century A.D.* Gothenburg.

Wöhrle, G. 1990. "*Actio*: Das fünfte officium des antiken Redners." *Gymnasium* 97:31–46.

Wray, D. 2001. *Catullus and the Poetics of Roman Manhood*. Cambridge.

Wright, F. W. 1931. *Cicero and the Theater*. Northampton, MA.

Wülfing, P. 1994. "Antike und moderne Redegestik: Quintilians Theorie der Körpersprache." *Der altsprachliche Unterricht* 37:45–63.

Yavetz, Z. 1969. *Plebs and Princeps*. Oxford.

Yavetz, Z. 1983. *Julius Caesar and His Public Image*. London.
Ziegler, K. 1994. *Plutarchi Vitae Parallelae. Vol. 1, Fasc. 2.* 4th ed. Leipzig.
Ziegler, K. 1996. *Plutarchi Vitae Parallelae. Vol. 3, Fasc. 1.* 3rd ed. Leipzig.
Ziegler, K. 2000. *Plutarchi Vitae Parallelae. Vol. 1, Fasc. 1.* 5th ed. Leipzig.

# Index Locorum

Appian
  B Civ.      2.144: 138
              2.145: 138
              2.146: 138, 139
              2.147: 134, 135, 139
              3.35: 140
Aristotle
  Rh.         3.1: 11
Asconius
  Mil.        32C: 133
              33C: 60, 134
              40C: 61
  Scaur.      20C: 133
              28C: 71–72, 133

Cicero
  Ad Brut.    1.13.1: 74
  Arch.       31: 73
  Att.        1.14.5: 68
              3.15.5: 47
              3.22.2: 107
              3.23: 107
              4.2.4: 69
              6.1.8: 104
              10.14.1: 103
              10.14.3: 103
              15.27.2: 104
  Balb.       64: 74
              65: 74
  Brut.       190: 156
              192: 24–25
              200: 22
              203: 28–29
              224: 30–31
              239: 33
              290: 25, 29–30, 123
              313: 26
              314–16: 26

  Cael.       58–60: 119
              59: 120
              60: 120–21
              78: 79
              79: 78, 79
              80: 79
  Clu.        58: 131–32
              196: 87
              197: 87
              197–98: 87
              199–200: 89
              200: 87
              201: 88, 97
  De or.      1.18: 27
              1.128: 28
              1.228: 9
              1.229: 32
              1.230: 32
              2.190: 109
              2.191: 141–42
              2.193: 143
              2.194: 143
              2.195: 143, 152
              2.196: 19, 107
              2.211: 108
              2.214: 108–9
              3.220: 27
  Fam.        4.4.3: 93
              6.14.2: 94
              10.35.2: 74
              14.1.5: 101–2
              14.4.1: 101
  Flac.       103: 84
              106: 84, 85
  Font.       33: 56
              46: 75, 76
              47: 77
              48: 76

179

# Index Nominum

Acilius Glabrio, M'. (cos. 67), 20
Acilius Glabrio, M'. (pr. 56), 71
Aelius Tubero, Q. (sen. by 31), 94–95
Aemilius Buca, L. (monetal. 44), 71
Aemilius Lepidus, M. (triumvir), 74
Aemilius Paullus, L. (cos. 182), 5, 6, 50
Aemilius Paullus, L. (cos. 50), 71
Aemilius Scaurus, M. (cos. 115), 58
Aemilius Scaurus, M. (pr. 56), 58, 71–72,
    98, 132–33, 152
Albius, Statius Oppianicus, 88
Albius, Statius Oppianicus (son of preced-
    ing), 97
Alfius Flavus, C. (tr. pl. 59), 124–25
Annius Milo, T. (pr. 55), 52, 60–61, 72, 83,
    89–93, 97, 119, 130, 133–34, 142
Antonius, M. (cos. 99), 18–20, 24, 29,
    31–32, 64, 76, 107, 126–27, 130, 131, 140,
    141–44
Antonius, M. (triumvir), 134–40, 152, 158
Appian, 134–35, 137–40
Appuleius Saturninus, L. (tr. pl. 103),
    30–31, 147–48
Aquillius Gallus, C. (pr. 66), 74
Aquillius, M'. (cos. 101), 18–20, 24, 64, 70,
    76, 77, 79, 107, 126, 130, 131, 140, 143,
    146
Aristophanes, 12
Aristotle, 11
Asconius, 60, 72, 133
Asicius, P., 142
Asinius Pollio, C. (cos. 40), 135
Atilius Serranus Gavianus, Sex. (tr. pl.
    57), 69
Atticus. See Pomponius
Augustus. See Julius

Bestia. See Calpurnius

Caecilia Metella, 34, 88
Caecilius Metellus, L. (cos. 68), 53
Caecilius Metellus Celer, Q. (cos. 60), 44,
    119–20, 126
Caecilius Metellus Nepos, Q. (cos. 57), 44,
    46, 106–7
Caecilius Metellus Numidicus, Q. (cos.
    109), 106
Caelius Rufus, M. (father of M. Caelius
    below), 78–80, 87
Caelius Rufus, M. (pr. 48), 38, 78–80, 81,
    82, 87, 97, 119–21, 142, 146, 152
Caepasius, C. (the elder), 131–32, 148,
    152, 154
Caesar. See Julius
Calidius, M. (pr. 57), 152–53
Calpurnius Bestia, L. (aed. by 57), 111, 142
Calpurnius Piso, C. (cos. 67), 33
Calpurnius Piso Caesoninus, L. (cos. 112),
    70–71, 72, 98
Calpurnius Piso Caesoninus, L. (cos. 58),
    48–49, 93, 108
Cassius Dio. See Dio
Cassius, L. (tr. pl. 44), 111, 112
Catiline. See Sergius
Cato. See Porcius
Catulus. See Lutatius
Charisius, 130
Chrysogonus. See Cornelius
Cicero. See General Index
Cispius, M. (tr. pl. 57), 109–10, 112–13, 116,
    142, 156
Claudia (Vestal Virgin), 77
Claudius Asellus, Tib. (tr. pl. 140), 50
Claudius Marcellus, C. (cos. 50), 93–94
Claudius Marcellus, M. (cos. 222), 105
Claudius Marcellus, M. (cos. 51), 93, 94,
    96

# General Index

acting, actors: and oratorical performance, 2, 27–30, 85, 143–44
appeals, 1, 9–10, 11–13, 19, 57, 70–98, 115, 117, 131–32, 146, 149–51, 156
  absence of, 31–32, 89, 121
  criticism of, 10, 12, 33, 109–12, 142–43
  and military commanders, 108
  and political life, 17, 47–48, 50, 53, 64, 67–70, 98
  planning of, 77–78, 148–49, 154
  poor performance of, 131–32
  and *sordes*, 41–42, 47–48, 53, 57–61
  and tears, 104, 109–11, 113, 116, 119, 124, 126–27, 133, 142
  terminology of, 65–66
  *See also* entreaties; supplication
Arginusae, 62
aristocrats in Rome
  comportment of, 7, 29, 31, 65, 108
  funerals of, 14, 18, 134–40
  and self–fashioning, 14–15, 48
  and socialization, 18
Athenian courts, 6, 12–13, 62, 74, 99, 156
Atina, 55
Atticist/Asianist controversy, 24, 141
attire. *See* clothes; *sordes*
audience: at trials, 11, 23–25, 28–30, 49, 82, 83, 106, 110, 123–24, 127, 152, 157
  *See also* corona; jurors

bandages: oratorical exploitation of, 129–30, 146
bodyguards: oratorical exploitation of, 33–35, 55
breastplate: oratorical exploitation of, 35, 140
*bulla*: oratorical exploitation of, 37

Catilinarian conspiracy, 80, 84, 122
children: used as oratorical props, 1, 3, 8–10, 12–13, 17, 36–37, 80–86, 96, 121, 123, 146, 149, 150–51, 154, 157
  absence of, 34
Cicero
  bases pleas around his own suffering, 83–85, 89–93, 97
  disguises manipulative element of judicial theater, 143–44
  exploits his exile as source of emotion, 114–16, 118–19, 120, 126–27
  pre–trial planning of judicial theater, 77–78, 148–49, 154
  skill in oratorical performance, 26–30, 154, 157
  training in Asia, 26
*clementia*, 95–96
clothes: used in oratorical theatrics, 5, 12, 30–31, 37, 50, 59–60, 69, 108, 146, 155
  Gallic dress, 56–57
  military cloak, 51
  *toga praetexta*, 36, 37, 46, 136
  *toga pulla*, 41–42, 44, 51
  tunic, 5–6, 19, 24, 42, 108
  *See also sordes*
comportment in court, 7–8, 25, 64–65, 155
*contiones*: and oratorical theatrics, 9, 15–18, 33, 52, 108, 134, 145, 147
corruption: judicial, 21, 125
*corona*, 23–25, 128
  *See also* audience
criticisms: of judicial theater, 10, 12, 33, 36, 99, 109–12, 141–44
crying. *See* tears

dagger: oratorical exploitation of, 16, 35
declamation, 149–50

Printed and bound by CPI Group (UK) Ltd, Croydon, CR0 4YY

09/06/2025

14685644-0002